THROUGH THE TURNSTILES

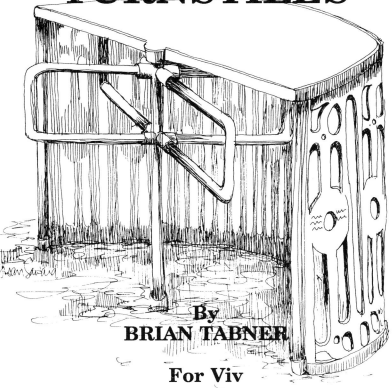

By
BRIAN TABNER

For Viv

Brian Tabner was born in Wolverhampton in 1939, and inherited his father's love for football. In 1958 he moved to Cardiff, where he studied Chemistry, before moving to live near Lancaster in 1966. He is now a senior lecturer in Environmental Chemistry at Lancaster University.

A member of the "Association of Football Statisticians", Brian has written for "The Footballer" and has helped in the preparation of the official history of Walsall F.C. due to be published in Autumn 1992. He has followed the fortunes of the Saddlers since 1953 and has always been interested in the historical side of the game. His wife, Viv, is a keen Bolton Wanderers supporter.

Published by:
Yore Publications,
12 The Furrows,
Harefield
Middx.
UB9 6AT

British Library Cataloguing–in–Publication Data
A catalogue record for this book is
available from the British Library.

ISBN 1 874427 05 4

Printed by:
The Bath Press
Lower Bristol Road,
Bath. BA2 3BL.

The photograph on the cover shows large crowds waiting for the gates to open at Burnden Park, Bolton, in 1947 (Bolton Evening News). Cover design by Dave Twydell. 'Turnstile' on title page drawn by Susan Saward.

In respect of photographs and illustrations, every effort has been made to ensure that copyright has not been infringed.

Yore Publications specialise in the production of Football books – that are generally of an historic nature – and is led by Dave Twydell, a football writer himself. Former titles include: *Rejected F.C.* – Histories of the ex–Football League Clubs (reprinted), *Rejected F.C.* – *The Video* – based on the books and *Football League Grounds For A Change* – a comprehensive study of all the former grounds upon which the Football League clubs once played. For full details of these books, and others, please send a S.A.E. for the latest copy of the free newsletter, which is issued every four months.

CONTENTS

The origins of football; the origins of the clubs; the pre–League friendly; the formation of the Football League; the early League seasons; the formation of a second Division; new teams arrive as the League expands; the inter–war years – the League expands to 4 Divisions;
1946 onwards;
The game;
Football grounds;
The supporters;
General overview of attendances from 1888 to 1992; 1888–1898 the early seasons – Everton dominate at home; 1898–1904 Aston Villa take over; 1904–1915 Chelsea and Spurs impress; 1919–1929 Huddersfield Town's remarkable years; 1929–1939 Arsenal dominate; 1946–1956 Matthews, Carter, and Lawton; 1956–1968 Manchester United emerge; 1968–1974 Leeds United's golden years; 1974–1992 Manchester United and Liverpool well ahead;

Average attendances at home games 1888–1992;
Season–by–season statistics;
Home attendances 1888–1992 divisional averages;
The top supported clubs at home;
The most attractive visiting clubs;
Season tickets;

Aberdare Athletic to York City
The all–time attendance table 1921–1992

"To say that these men paid their shillings to watch twenty–two hirelings kick a ball is merely to say that a violin is wood and cat–gut, that Hamlet is so much paper and ink. For a shilling the Bruddersford United A.F.C. offered you Conflict and Art; it turned you into a critic, happy in your judgment of fine points, ready in a second to estimate the worth of a well–judged pass, a run down the touch line, a lightning shot, a clearance kick by back or goalkeeper; it turned you into a partisan, holding your breath when the ball came sailing into your own goalmouth, ecstatic when your forwards raced away towards the opposite goal, elated, downcast, bitter, triumphant by turns at the fortunes of your side, watching a ball shape Iliads and Odysseys for you; and what is more, it turned you into a member of a new community, all brothers together for an hour and a half, for not only had you escaped from the clanking machinery of this lesser life, from work, wages, rent, doles, sick pay, insurance cards, nagging wives, ailing children, bad bosses, idle workmen, but you had escaped with most of your mates and your neighbours, with half the town, and there you were, cheering together, thumping one another on the shoulders, swopping judgements like lords of the earth, having pushed your way through a turnstile into another and altogether more splendid kind of life, hurtling with Conflict and yet passionate and beautiful in its Art."

(J.B.Priestley, *The Good Companions*, 1929)

Acknowledgements

I am grateful to all of those people associated with football whose enthusiasm for the game has encouraged me with the preparation of this book. Among those to whom special thanks are due are the dozens of football historians and statisticians up and down the country who have so carefully recorded details of their clubs. Without their enthusiasm the idea for this book might not have materialised.

Special thanks must go to the Football League for allowing me access to their attendance ledgers without which the statistics in this book, from 1925 onwards, would have been much more difficult to assemble and would have been far less accurate. In particular I must thank Liz Ashforth and Lorna Parnell for their never failing courtesy and willing help despite the large number of visits made to St. Anne's.

Thanks to the many librarians who have been so helpful over the last few years. The staff of the Archives and Local Studies Service at Bolton Library deserve special thanks for first pointing out to me the vast amount of football information, including pre–1925 attendances, to be found in the "Football Field". Thanks to them also for so cheerfully coping with the innumerable subsequent visits. The facilities at the Central Library, Manchester, have also been regularly used and again thanks are due to the staff there. Other libraries who have always so courteously handled enquiries and visits include those at Blackpool, Bury, Crewe, Lincoln, Northwich, Walsall, and Wolverhampton.

Thanks must also be made to Dave Twydell (Yore Publications) for taking this project on board and for his obvious love and enthusiasm for the game.

Finally, but certainly not least, I must thank my wife, Viv, for all of the help she has given me with the preparation of this book. Without her unfailing help and support the project would have taken at least twice as long and, indeed, might well have not reached fruition. It would be impossible to understate her overwhelming contribution to every phase of the research and preparation of its contents. My thanks are also due to her for encouraging me during some of the more difficult problems encountered. No doubt she will give a huge sigh of relief now that domestic life can return to normality.

Introduction

My interest in football was undoubtedly generated by my father and his tales of games he had been to during the 1930s. His stories of the huge crowds at some of the games he had watched helped to create my interest in attendances. This interest was further aroused in the mid 1950s when I came across an issue of the *"News Chronicle"* which gave the average attendance for each club in all four Divisions of the Football League. (These were based largely on newspaper estimated attendances). From then onwards I did my best to log these average attendances each season until they became readily available in the annual issues of *"Rothmans Football Yearbook"*. But what were attendances really like in the 1930s (and earlier) and was there a realistic chance of ever discovering such information?

The idea of this book began to form in the mid–1980s when I discovered that the Football League kept attendance figures back to 1925. These figures have proved invaluable as they provide the accurate information required to calculate the average attendance for the home League games of each club each season. The main problem, however, was how to cover the period from 1888 to 1925.

I had an enormous stoke of luck when I discovered that a Bolton Saturday evening sports paper *"The Football Field"* gave a complete match report of every Saturday Division 1 game between 1888 and 1925. These reports invariably contained an estimated attendance figure. Reports on Division 2 matches were less extensive but still provided an invaluable source. Division 3 North was also well covered from 1921. All unattributed quotes are taken from this sportspaper.

The next stage was to search for missing data in the *"Athletic News"* and the *"Sunday Chronicle"*. The Monday edition of the *"Daily Herald"* also proved valuable particularly as it covered Division 3 South fairly thoroughly. Other data, particularly for the smaller clubs, has been obtained from local newspaper reports.

The book itself is divided into three parts; a narrative history; a statistical season–by–season survey; and a section with information on each individual League club.

The bulk of the historical section is detailed in chronological sequence. This section looks at the origins of the clubs as well as of the Football League and its development from 1888 to date. The development of the game and of football grounds is also described along with a brief look at football supporters over the years. The final part of this section takes a general look at the way in which attendances have changed over the last 100 years or so.

Readers can follow the fortunes of their favourite teams throughout the statistical section. This section monitors the average attendance at home games season–by–season so that the fortunes of clubs can be seen through good years and bad.

Naturally some clubs have always attracted greater support than others but now, for the first time, this support can be followed back to 1888. The top supported clubs clearly emerge – only 9 different clubs have ever finished top of these average home attendance tables. A brief survey of the most 'attractive' visiting clubs is also given.

The final section concentrates on information for each individual club. This includes details of attendance records at home League games together with some brief historical notes and a guide to their attendances over the years. Readers will, hopefully, find the information on others clubs as interesting as that on their own favourites.

As with all statistical books some errors are possible despite the fact that each number has been checked many times. Unfortunately, the very nature of the game is such that it is easier to find data on some clubs more than on others. In particular I have found it more difficult to discover attendance data in the early seasons on some of the smaller Division 2 clubs than on the more glamorous clubs. I would be delighted to hear from any historian or statistician who has data on these smaller clubs covering the period between 1892 and about 1908.

The aim of this book is to trace the popularity of football over the last one hundred years or so and to record the support for each individual club during their lifetime as members of the Football League. However, before examining these statistics in detail it is worthwhile describing the development of the game during its formative years.

Some features of the game during this early period would seem curious to today's football fan and player alike. Although the game would be recognisable as football many of the laws were different as was the style of play. The Football League itself, when formed in 1888, also had a very different format and the reasons for its formation are worth exploring.

The majority of the clubs currently making up the English Football League were formed between 1870 and 1900. But why were so many of our famous clubs formed during this period and what were their origins? The answer to these questions is related to the nature of our society during the latter part of the nineteenth century. Surprisingly, we find that many of our football clubs have fairly similar origins and exploring these origins makes an interesting study of its own.

* * * * * * * * * * * * * *

Historical Background

The Origins of Football:

There is no doubt that football is a very ancient game and has always had an enormous popular following. This popularity is due, at least in part, to its simplicity. Before the late 1800s football was played in a variety of ways with the rules (if there were any at all) varying from one locality to another. The number of players in each team, the size of the playing area, of the goals, and of the ball all varied as did the duration of the game. These early games usually took place on the day of a public holiday or local festival and contemporary accounts indicate that they were often extremely rough.

From the villages and towns the game spread to some public schools and hence to the "upper" classes. Slowly it became a slightly more organised game played by the sons of gentlemen at school on afternoons when they were free from schoolwork. The church too played a formative role. Playing team games was considered to develop the correct qualities in a young man and so it is not surprising to find that many clubs were originally affiliated to a church or chapel. More on that later, however. It became obvious during the later years of the nineteenth century that if teams from different parts of the country were to play one another then a common set of rules had to be agreed. It was not unusual for visiting teams to refuse to play because, for example, they did not agree with the size of the playing area or of the ball. This situation must have been extremely frustrating not only for those taking part but also for those who turned up to watch.

In 1863 a small number of clubs (mainly from the South of England) agreed to form the Football Association and to play against one another under a common set of rules. As other local associations formed they affiliated to the Football Association and so, by about 1882, a common set of rules had spread throughout the country. However, it is important to remember that whilst there were a common set of rules the style of play still varied from one locality to another and that these differences in style were still evident when the Football League was formed.

By the early 1880s the structure of the modern game had taken shape. Leading clubs agreed to play each other in "friendly" games throughout the winter months (early September until late April). In between these friendlies were FA Cup, local county cup and various charity cup ties. Cup ties were the games that attracted the largest crowds and the winners of these local cups gained considerable prestige at the expense of their neighbours. Most of these local rivalries are still evident today.

It was also during the latter part of the nineteenth century that the working man first had some free time to spend as he liked. Many trades had a half-day holiday on Saturday afternoons and as the number of people with a free Saturday afternoon grew so did their interest in taking part in, and watching, sporting events. Saturday afternoons became the accepted time to play and watch both cricket and football.

The Origins of the Clubs:

Action at Deepdale, Preston in 1889

As the working man began to take an interest in football there was a move away from public schools towards the "working classes". However, public schools played an important part in the formation of many clubs. Boys who had played soccer at school wanted to continue enjoying the game. Several clubs owe their existence to the enthusiasm of such people. Blackburn Rovers were formed by former pupils of Blackburn Grammar School, boys from Wiggleston School formed Leicester Fosse (now Leicester City) and the fact that Sunderland were originally The Sunderland and District Teachers Association Football Club clearly reveals their origin.

It may surprise many of today's supporters to find that their favourite team was originally affiliated to a church or chapel. Yet a significant number of our clubs started in exactly this way. Two of the oldest and more famous clubs have a remarkably similar beginning. Aston Villa were formed in 1874 when members of the Villa Cross Wesleyan Chapel cricket team decided that they would like a sport to play during the winter months. Exactly the same motives led to members of St. Domingo's Church cricket team forming Everton in 1878. Members of Christ Church Sunday School formed Christ Church (now Bolton Wanderers), and Fulham were originally Fulham St. Andrew's. We find that boys from the local YMCA formed Burnley

Rovers (now Burnley) and that a keen football playing clergyman formed Swindon Town.

There are many other clubs that could be listed; those mentioned only provide some typical examples.

Another institution playing a part in the life of the working man was, of course, his place of work. It is not surprising, therefore, to find several of today's major clubs started life as works' football teams. Many readers will know that Arsenal were formed by a group of munitions workers from the Royal Arsenal at Woolwich but there are many other examples scattered throughout the country. In the Midlands the George Salter Springs works cricket team formed a football section then known as West Bromwich Strollers (now West Bromwich Albion) and Singers of Coventry (the cycle manufacturers) later became Coventry City. Returning to the London area Thames Ironworks FC was formed by a works' foreman (the club later becoming West Ham United) and Millwall Rovers (now Millwall) was formed by workers at Morton's jam factory. Three different railway companies were involved in the formation of present day League clubs. Crewe Alexandra was formed by employees of the LNWR (who used to meet at the Alexandra Hotel), Stoke City by employees of the Staffordshire Railway, and Manchester

9

United (then Newton Heath) by workers from the engine sheds of the L&YR. Not all clubs were formed in an informal and haphazard way. In some cases public meetings were arranged with an open invitation to anyone interested in forming a team in that locality to attend. Norwich City, Bradford City, and Portsmouth were formed by this rather more systematic approach.

Some examples of clubs who started life when a cricket club formed a football section have already been described. Two other famous clubs who started life in this way are Sheffield Wednesday (formed by members of the Wednesday cricket club) and Tottenham Hotspur (formed from the Hotspur cricket club).

The Olive Grove, Sheffield Wednesday in 1892. Note the changing tent.

When I first started researching information on early club histories I expected to come across examples of clubs that had started life as pub teams. After all, the public house plays a major role as a meeting place and a glance at almost any present day local newspaper reveals teams associated with pubs playing in local leagues. Although I did not come across any genuine examples in the case of League clubs it is quite possible that some club historians have been able to trace their club's origins back to a public house team. There can be no doubt that the public house played an important role in the early life of many clubs.

In the early days of the Football League players often had to change in a pub before making their way to the ground. Both team and result sheets were available there together, presumably, with notices of forthcoming fixtures.

Like other local people publicans often dug deep into their pockets to keep their local team going during hard times.

These examples give an insight into the early history of the English professional football club. Once formed, however, staying in existence has never been easy except for a privileged few. Even during the so-called golden eras of English football most clubs have struggled financially. The simple reason is that the income through the turnstiles has been insufficient to meet the running expenses (including, of course, players wages). Hence, we find teams of some repute during the 1870s and 1880s disappearing from the scene although there has never been any shortage of those wishing to take their place. In many cases there were simply too many teams in the locality compared to the size of the local population. In some towns the only sensible way to survive was to amalgamate and to try and form one successful team from two moderate ones. Examples are Wolverhampton Wanderers formed by the amalgamation of St. Luke's (Blakenhall) with the football section of the Wanderers cricket club; Walsall Town and Walsall Swifts amalgamated to form Walsall Town Swifts (now Walsall) and the East End and West End teams of Newcastle combined to form Newcastle United.

The Pre–League Friendly:

Of the ninety–two clubs that were members of the Football League during the 1990/91 season, fifty one were already in existence when the League was formed in 1888. These fifty one clubs were supplemented by many others who were successful in these early years, but have never quite achieved League status, and by some that may have had their early moments but have since become defunct. How, then, did these clubs arrange their fixtures before 1888?

— A Goalmouth Scrimmage in the 1880's —

With only Saturday afternoons available to play and watch football the number of fixtures in a season was limited to about thirty. This number was supplemented by additional fixtures over the Christmas and Easter periods but other midweek fixtures were only possible at the very beginning and end of the season when there was sufficient light to complete a game before dusk. In any case attendances were generally poor at these midweek fixtures. A number of the available fixture dates were reserved for the FA Cup and local cup ties with friendlies arranged to fill in the vacant Saturdays. In compiling a list of fixtures each club would try to ensure a good scattering of local Derbys, augmented by games against 'crack' sides from other parts of the country. Thus in the Midlands teams from Scotland, Lancashire, and the South would be invited, whilst in Lancashire a good range of Scottish teams as well as Midland teams would be included. This might sound a very casual and haphazard way of doing things – and, indeed, it was! Friendlies were often cancelled at short notice for almost any reason. Sometimes because a 'star' player was not available or because the pitch was considered unfit for play. Here the close association between a football club and the cricket club from which it had been formed was a source of amusement by present day standards. Such teams often considered football to be a 'fair weather' game. The players would leave the field if it started to rain heavily!

In some instances the visiting team would be late arriving having perhaps missed a connection on their rail journey. In any case starting times were considered approximate.

There were several occasions when the visiting team arrived so late that the spectators had long since gone home. In other cases they would fail to arrive at all. To add to the confusion friendlies were often cancelled in order to give preference to cup replays which were always financially more lucrative. Although this may give the impression that the organisation of the game was fairly chaotic the majority of friendly games were completed as arranged.

The playing strengths of these early clubs varied significantly from those of today and the results of these friendly games often bore little resemblance to the result that might be anticipated between the same two sides today. These were the days when a Merseyside Derby referred to a game between Bootle and Everton. The meeting between these two teams in a local cup tie in 1881 was perhaps the most remarkable of the games between these two old rivals. Bootle had only managed to assemble eight players but succeeded in persuading three spectators to play for them and then went on to win 1-0! In another game involving Everton in 1884 the Merseysiders lost heavily to the amateurs of Crewe Alexandra but a local reporter simply noted that: *Crewe Alexandra naturally proved too strong for Everton.* Games between amateur and professional sides were common enough but it was the amateurs who were considered to be the true sportsmen. Referees do not appear to have been entirely impartial in such encounters. When Bolton Wanderers met the then amateur Sheffield Wednesday in 1885 the referee *conceived it to be part of his duty to encourage and excite the lamb-like Wednesdayites to deeds of slaughter. As innocent amateurs they need have no qualms at disabling a nauseous professional or two.*

The first representative game between amateurs (Gentlemen) and professionals (Players) took place at Preston in January 1886. As if almost to typify their 'purity' the amateurs were provided with clean white shirts (or costumes as they were then referred to) while the professionals had to play in any coloured shirts they were able to lay their

hands on. The Players line up gives a rough guide to the stronger teams of the era consisting of two players from both Aston Villa and Blackburn Rovers and one each from Preston North End, Stafford Road (Wolverhampton), Darwen, Stoke, Accrington, Bolton Wanderers, and Blackburn Olympic. (The Gentlemen won 1-0). The annual match between the North and the South a few days later featured a North line-up similar to that of the Players [but included also representatives from Nottingham (County) and Nottingham Forest]. The South line-up, however, was typical of the amateur game south of the Midlands featuring four from the Old Carthusians, two each from the Old Westminsters, and the Swifts, and one each from the Pilgrims, the Old Forresters, and the Corinthians.

Long before the idea of forming a football league was put forward there was considerable interest in establishing which were the strongest teams in each locality. The results of friendlies and cup-ties, together with players selected for representative matches, give some guidance to the top clubs of the era.

In the early 1880s professional football was mainly restricted to Lancashire and the Midlands. Towards the end of season 1884-5 a Lancashire sportspaper, the Football Field, published a merit table of the top Lancashire clubs. The list is interesting not only because of the names of the clubs included but also because the list was sequenced in terms of goal average rather than on the proportion of matches won. The first eight Lancashire clubs listed were Preston North End, Bolton Wanderers, Great Lever, Blackburn Olympic, Accrington, Blackburn Rovers, Church, and Burnley.

Towards the end of the 1885-6 season the same paper published another merit table this time covering the entire country. Altogether 33 clubs were listed with 8 each from Scotland, Lancashire, and the South of England, and 9 from the Midlands. The only change in the Lancashire listing was that Darwen was included in place of Church.

The top Midland clubs were Walsall Swifts, Staveley, Notts County, West Bromwich Albion, Wednesbury Old Athletic, Derby County, Aston Villa, Nottingham Forest, and Wolverhampton Wanderers.

Again goal average seems to have been considered rather more important than the proportion of games won. No doubt the list is not truly representative of relative playing strengths as a few high scoring friendlies could make a tremendous difference. However, it gives an interesting guide.

There can be little doubt that by the end of 1885-6 Preston North End were considered the top Lancashire side. Not only do contemporary match reports continually praise the neatness, style and skill of their play but by the end of that season their playing record was quite remarkable:-

P.64   W.59   D.3   L.2   F.318   A.60

No wonder they were already known as the Invincibles!

At the beginning of the 1886-7 season Lancashire played Staffordshire at Pike's Lane, Bolton. The Lancashire team was dominated by players drawn from Preston North End and Bolton Wanderers and the Staffordshire team by players drawn from West Bromwich Albion, Stoke, and Wolverhampton Wanderers. Not surprisingly the Football Field's correspondent found the fact that both

teams played in red rather confusing. When Lancashire played Nottinghamshire players from Nottingham Forest and Notts Rangers dominated the Nottinghamshire team. Preston North End, however, continued to be accepted as the top English professional team although it was noted that the top Merseyside teams, Bootle and Everton, were beginning to hold their own against the other Lancashire sides; West Bromwich Albion appear to have been accepted as the top Midlands team.

By the end of the 1887-88 season Preston had undoubtedly established themselves as one of the greatest English football sides. They started their season with a Scottish tour losing their first game 1-2 to Edinburgh Hibernians. However, this was quickly remedied in their second game against Dundee Strathmore on August 18 when they won 16-2. This match was the first of 42 consecutive wins in friendlies and cup ties which was terminated when Crewe Alexandra held them to a 1-1 draw.

This most remarkable of records is unlikely ever to be approached again:-

P.42   W.42   D.0   L.0   F.241   A.45

Of the 42 games only 18 were at home and on January 2 1888 they won an additional game, against Hearts, substituting their reserve team when the first team were in training for an important FA Cup tie!

The Formation of the Football League

It took the foresight of William McGregor to see that some progress was needed to make the game more attractive to the spectator. He was concerned about the short notice by which friendlies were cancelled and the fact that many games started well after the advertised kick-off time. Some games were also becoming one sided high scoring affairs which generated little public interest.

In March 1888 he wrote to five of the leading professional clubs in the Midlands and the

North suggesting that: *Ten or twelve of the most prominent clubs in England combine to arrange home and away fixtures each season.* As several Saturdays were already committed to cup ties McGregor reasoned that just over twenty fixtures a season would be possible and hence the suggestion that ten or twelve clubs would be sufficient to form such a League. There would also be a limitation of one club from any one town or city. Strangely, the response was not over enthusiastic.

Although West Bromwich Albion, Stoke, Wolverhampton Wanderers, Derby County, and McGregor's own club Aston Villa were keen others were not. Sheffield Wednesday, for example, saw problems with the idea being particularly concerned about the costs of such a scheme. As there were no professional clubs very much south of Birmingham, McGregor sought the support of some of the top Lancashire sides, particularly Blackburn Rovers, Preston North End, Burnley, and Bolton Wanderers. Notts County also readily agreed to join in. Eventually, following a meeting on 22 March 1888, the names of the original twelve clubs to form the Football League were finalised:- Accrington, Blackburn Rovers, Bolton Wanderers, Burnley, Everton, Preston North End representing Lancashire and Aston Villa, Derby County, Notts County, Stoke, West Bromwich Albion, and Wolverhampton Wanderers representing the Midlands. The same meeting agreed that each club must always play its strongest side and it was provisionally agreed that points should be awarded based on the number of games won rather than on the number of goals scored.

In order that different clubs could take part in the League the bottom four clubs each season would retire but could seek re-election.

It was also agreed that a player could only play for one club in any particular season (i.e., transfers were not to be allowed) and that the League should be run for the mutual benefit of all its members clubs.

Although the points scoring system had been a provisional part of McGregor's original plan it seems odd in retrospect that the method of awarding points was not finalised until 21 November 1888. By this time the first League season was well under way. Should points be awarded for goals scored or for games won and drawn? Eventually the latter proposal won the day, but should points be awarded for a drawn game? Eventually the two points for a win and one for a draw system was approved by a majority of 6 to 4. This system was to remain in operation until revised in 1981. The same meeting also agreed to form a Second Division, also of twelve clubs, with "test" matches to decide issues of promotion and relegation.

The Early League Seasons

The first Football League season began on Saturday 8 September 1888 with the following results:

Bolton Wanderers	3	Derby County	6
Everton	2	Accrington	1
Preston North End	5	Burnley	2
Stoke	0	West Brom. A.	2
Wolverhampton W.	1	Aston Villa	1

Notts County and Blackburn Rovers did not open their League programmes until 15 Sept.

Accurate attendance figures are not available for League games until 1925, but about 25,000 spectators appear to have watched these first 5 games. These first set of results show the fickle and exciting nature of the game. Within the first five minutes of their first ever League game Bolton led Derby 2-0 and soon added a third to lead 3-0 after 15 minutes.

It seemed as though Derby were going to be overwhelmed and yet by half-time they had recovered to lead 4-3 and eventually won 6-3. Blackburn Rovers' first game, at home to Accrington, was also an exciting high scoring affair ending as a 5-5 draw. These events, though, were only ripples on the majestic progress made by Preston North End who were unbeaten by the end of the season dropping only four points:-

P.22 W.18 D.4 L.0 F.74 A.15 Pts.40
The runners up, Aston Villa, finished eleven points behind.

McGregor's fears that football was becoming too one sided looked as though they were to be confirmed. He need not have worried, however, as these remarkable statistics have never been, nor are likely to be, repeated in the League Championship.

Horton is tripped by Goodall

Action from Sheffield in 1889 (Preston North End versus West Bromwich Albion)

The first Football League season proved a success and immediately led to the formation of other Leagues in time for the 1889–90 season. Three of these, the Northern League, the Midland League, and the Birmingham League were all regional. The Football Alliance, however, reflected the Football League with teams drawn from the Midlands and the North and was to play a significant role in the next development of the Football League 3 seasons later.

The League was faced with two new problems during season 1890–91. First, both Accrington and Blackburn Rovers indicated that they were likely to leave the League at the end of the season. Presumably the League was not judged by all to have been an immediate success when two of its founder members thought that they might be better off elsewhere. In the event both clubs remained within the League.

Secondly, the annual re–election procedure caused a problem when Aston Villa and Bolton Wanderers tied on 19 points for the last re–election place. On goal average Bolton Wanderers finished below Aston Villa and yet, incredibly by today's standards, there was some uncertainty about the result of their game against Notts County on October 26. The referee reported that Notts County had won 4–0 but Bolton protested that the score was, in fact, only 3–0. (This latter scoreline is reported in contemporary newspapers). If the latter was the correct score then Aston Villa would have to apply for re–election on goal average rather than Bolton! In the event the League Management Committee felt unable to decide on the precise score in the game and exempted both teams from applying for re–election.

The end of the same season saw the first change in League membership. Sunderland had ambitions of becoming one of the country's top clubs but the long distances that all of their opponents would have to travel to play there was a factor against their election. Eventually they agreed to pay a proportion of their visitors travelling expenses and were elected in place of Stoke. Stoke, however, regained their League status the following season when the League was extended to 14 clubs the other newly elected team being Darwen.

December 12 1891 saw several unusual games as blizzards swept Northern England on a bitterly cold day. Play in the Accrington v Aston Villa game lasted only 7 minutes before *"the players held a short council of war, invaded the stand, and finally broke away in a concerted run the whole length of the ground to the pavilion. It was a grand movement and the wisest of the day."*

Play at least progressed as far as the second half at Burnley where Blackburn Rovers were the visitors. *"Before the game there was a real old fashioned snow storm, the ground being quickly covered with snow – correct play, however, was impossible owing to the slippery state of the ground."* At half-time Burnley led 2–0. *"Soon after the restart, however, a proper fracas took place. Lofthouse (Blackburn Rovers) kicked Stewart and the latter retaliated. The game was at once stopped and the referee ordered both players off the field. The Rovers' team with the exception of the goalkeeper quit the field amid loud hooting. The referee at once threw the ball up and it was put thro' the Rovers goal but Arthur (Rovers goalkeeper) appealed for offside and gained his point. After waiting a time the Burnley players left the field winners by 3–0. What will result from the above it is impossible to say."*

The weather at Deepdale was little better. *"Snow and sleet began to fall about noon with the result that Deepdale had a white covering, and as far as spectators – you had to look for 'em. At half past two there were not 300. The ball would not travel a yard or two in the snow, and passing was almost impossible. After playing half an hour [Preston leading 1–0] there was a collision between Oswald [Notts County] and Drummond and blows were struck. The Notts men walked off the pitch after being spoken to by the referee, and another squabble occurred near the tent. The spectators rushed across the field, players and referee went into the dressing tent, but in a minute all returned, Oswald being the only absentee. He had the option to come back but declined as he was hurt."* [Preston led 3–0 at half time.] *"The light by this time was very bad and both teams played as if they meant business. Drummond scored a fourth goal after which five of the Notts men left the pitch saying it was too cold to continue play. They refused to return and play was continued against five Notts men. The difficulty now was that the home team were often offside, but two more goals were scored."*

The Formation of a Second Division

Sunderland's "team of all talents" quickly replaced Preston as the dominant team finishing League Champions in 1891–2 and again in 1892–3. There were some significant changes at the end of the first of these two seasons. First, the League was expanded again this time to 16 clubs. The bottom four were Darwen, Stoke, West Bromwich Albion and Accrington. However, West Bromwich Albion, who had won the FA Cup, were exempted from applying for re-election. Both Accrington and Stoke were re-elected and the remaining 3 places were all taken by clubs from the Football Alliance (Sheffield Wednesday, Nottingham Forest, and Newton Heath). Secondly, McGregor's original plan had been for a two Division League structure and the new Second Division (of 12 clubs) was created at the same time. It was formulated from the remaining Football Alliance teams (Ardwick, Bootle, Burton Swifts, Crewe Alexandra, Grimsby Town, Lincoln City, Small Heath, and Walsall Town Swifts) plus Burslem Port Vale (from the Midland League), Northwich Victoria (from the Combination), Sheffield United (from the Northern League), and ex-Division 1 Darwen. The unlucky Football Alliance team not to gain League status was Birmingham St. George's who were in financial difficulties and were shortly to disband.

In the second of their Championship seasons Sunderland became the first League side to score 100 goals in a League programme. Altogether, during 1892–3, they played 30 League games, 3 FA Cup ties, and 26 friendlies with the following record:

P.59 W.45 D.5 L.9 F.199 A.68

It is interesting that many clubs did not consider a total of 60 games in season excessive. There are stories, in the pre-League era, of some clubs being prepared to play two games on the same day with more or less the same line-ups.

Action from the Bury versus Liverpool Test Match in 1895 (Played at Blackburn Rovers ground)

The new problem facing the Football League at the end of the 1892–93 season was promotion and relegation between Division 1 and Division 2. Test matches were introduced in order to decide these issues. In these the top 3 clubs from Division 2 met the bottom three clubs from Division 1. Darwen and Sheffield United duly won their games against Notts County and Accrington respectively and were promoted, but Division 2 Champions Small Heath lost (in a replay after a drawn game) to Newton Heath. Hence, the first Champions of Division 2 failed to gain promotion while the bottom team in Division 1 retained their status. However, the two relegated clubs, Notts County and Accrington, indicated that they: *could not give a definite reply to joining the Second Division.* To add to this complication it was decided to strengthen Division 2 by increasing it to 16 clubs. In the absence of Notts County and Accrington there were 6 places to be filled. Newcastle United and Rotherham Town were immediately elected and, in the meantime, Notts County and Accrington decided to continue and were elected along with Woolwich Arsenal (the first Southern professional club to gain entry to the League) and Liverpool.

Ironically, however, Accrington were concerned about the expense of continuing as a Second Division club and resigned to join the Lancashire League. Middlesbrough Ironopolis were asked to replace them but then, just before the commencement of the new season, Bootle also resigned because of financial difficulties leaving one unfilled vacancy.

Liverpool's first season in Division 2 was almost as spectacular as Preston's first Championship season five years earlier. For the second, and so far last, time a League club went through an entire season unbeaten:–

P.28 W.22 D.6 L.0 F.77 A.18 Pts.50

The test match system continued to decide issues of promotion and relegation for the next few seasons, taking the form of a mini–league from 1895–6. However, things reached a head at the end of the 1897–8 season when (with the system now reduced to four participating teams) Stoke (who had finished bottom of Division 1) and Burnley (who had finished as Champions of Division 2) found themselves both with 4 points from their first two games and due to meet each other in their last game. In the meantime Newcastle United and Blackburn Rovers, both with 2 points from their two games, were due to play each other in the other game. Clearly, if Stoke and Burnley could manage a draw with one another both would gain promotion. The resulting game, on 30 April 1898, was a farce. Despite the pitch being in a shocking condition after torrential rain the game went ahead. It is impossible to establish whether or not both teams had arranged a draw before the game started. Nevertheless neither side seemed anxious to score and when half-time arrived both sides were booed off the pitch having failed to achieve a single shot on goal between them. The second half was even worse and the crowd, who by now had had enough, entertained themselves by keeping the ball when ever they could. By the end of the game five different balls had been used but still neither team had managed a shot on goal.

The League decided enough was enough. As a way out of the dilemma an enlargement of both Divisions to 18 clubs was suggested with all 4 clubs involved in the test matches being placed in Division 1. Eventually it was agreed that the election of Newcastle United and Blackburn Rovers to Division 1 would have to go to the vote along with any other Division 2 teams who thought that they had a claim to Division 1 status. Thus Manchester City, Newton Heath, Woolwich Arsenal, and Small Heath also contested the vote but Newcastle United and Blackburn Rovers were the clear victors. The newly elected clubs to Division 2 were Barnsley, New Brighton Tower, Glossop North End, and Burslem Port Vale. Needless to say test matches were thereafter abandoned and replaced with automatic promotion and relegation.

Although two "small town" teams (Darwen and Loughborough) lost their League status during the next few seasons other "small town" teams such as Glossop, Burton United (an amalgamation of the Burtons Swifts and Wanderers), and Gainsborough Trinity were still League members. Gainsborough, though, must have been quite pleased to see the 1901–02 season draw to a close.

With only two games remaining they were well and truly bottom of Division 2 with only three wins to their credit. April 19 saw Blackpool as the visitors and spirits must have lifted a little when the visitors arrived with only 10 men, one of their number having missed his train. By the kick off only a small crowd had gathered. During the second half a large fire broke out at a timber yard on the far side of the town and most of the spectators left to witness this counter attraction. At the final whistle only a handful of spectators remained to witness a rare Gainsborough victory.

New Teams Arrive as the League Expands

No further changes in the size of the two Divisions occurred until after the end of season 1904–05 when they were both increased to 20 clubs. Division 1 was increased by simply promoting the top 2 teams in Division 2 (Preston North End and Woolwich Arsenal) with the bottom two teams in Division 1 (Liverpool and West Bromwich Albion) retaining their status. With Doncaster Rovers failing to gain re-election there were five vacant places in Division 2 to be filled. Four of them were taken by Clapton Orient, Hull City, Leeds City and Stockport County, and the fifth by Chelsea.

The story behind the election of Chelsea to the Football League is remarkable. The club was not formed until 8 May 1905 and yet shortly afterwards they were elected to the Second Division. The club owes its origins to the Mears brothers who set about creating, at Stamford Bridge, what they hoped would be the most modern football stadium in London. They (incorrectly) assumed that, once the stadium was ready, Fulham would be happy to move there. When Fulham declined the offer Frederick Parker set about organising the formation of a new club to play at the Bridge. The aim was for the new club to join the Southern League but when Fulham petitioned against this they turned their attention to the Football League. Hence Chelsea were born and, within a few months, elected to the Football League without ever having played a game!

The election of Clapton Orient and Chelsea brought the number of Southern based clubs in the League to four. The growing number of Southern based clubs applying to join the League reflects, to some extent, the growing strength of the Southern League. The original suggestion leading to the formation of a "Southern League" appears to have come from Royal Arsenal in 1892–93. However, their enthusiasm naturally diminished with their election to the Football League one year later. The Southern League was eventually formed in 1894–5 (but Arsenal's audacious suggestion that they should be allowed to enter their reserve team was rejected). The performances of some of the Southern League clubs in the FA Cup suggested that they were at least as good if not better than most Division 2 clubs and equal to some Division 1 clubs. However, there was a growing awareness by some of the strongest clubs in the Southern League that they could be in danger of not maintaining their successes if they stayed outside the Football League much longer.

If 12 December 1891 had been one of the coldest days on which a League programme had been played then 1 September 1906 may well have been the hottest. A crowd of around 17,000 saw an eventful game at Hyde Road, Manchester, where Woolwich Arsenal were the visitors. *"The opening of this eventful season was heralded by weather of record conditions. In the recollection of the writer Manchester has never experienced a higher register of the sun's heat in the shade."* At half–time Woolwich Arsenal led the City by 2–0. *"City were slow to re–appear and then only 6 men came out. Referee Barber went in to interview the others, and Steele came out followed shortly by Kelso. It was evident that Kelso was disinclined to play after the interval, and the game resolved itself into an exhibition of the possibilities of offside play. Conlin at length appeared with his white cloth headgear, but the contest was not worthy of serious chronicling as a League game. Dorsett collapsed, the Linesman and trainer attending to him for 10 minutes, and the referee, Barber, had consultations with the captains and linesmen. 'No postponement' was eventually decided upon.*

Kelso succumbed at last and required a cold douche with the sponge to get him to his feet. He walked wearily too and I am strongly of the opinion he risked sunstroke." Woolwich Arsenal eventually won the game 4–1 against depleted opposition.

The re–election process at the end of the 1907–08 season produced another unusual situation involving a London club. When Tottenham Hotspur applied for election the Southern League, perhaps not unreasonably, insisted that they should resign their Southern League membership. There was, therefore, an obvious danger that should they not gain election to the Football League they would be without a place in either league and hence would find themselves doomed to oblivion. This is, in fact, exactly what happened. Grimsby Town and Chesterfield Town were both re–elected with Watford gaining Lincoln City's place. However, just when the London club looked doomed Stoke, worried about lack of support, resigned. A special meeting was called in June to elect a club to this new vacancy. Lincoln City, who had finished above Spurs in the original vote, and Spurs contested the election along with Stoke who were having second thoughts about the wisdom of their decision. The ballot ended in a tie between Lincoln and Tottenham. The clubs who had voted for Stoke (who had finished well behind in the vote) were instructed to recast their votes in favour of either Lincoln or Tottenham. The final result was still a tie (20 votes each) and the League Management Committee were left the awkward task of deciding which club should be favoured. Finally Spurs were elected, possibly because of sympathy with their position, but only by the narrowest of margins.

There was an unusual end to the 1908–09 season when Nottingham Forest found themselves in serious danger of relegation from Division 1. Two games remained, both at home, the first saw Leicester Fosse as the visitors. The Fosse had had a poor season and were already relegated but very few of the 7,000 spectators present could have predicted that the Nottingham club would run out victors by 12 goals to nil.

The extraordinary scoreline in such a critical game raised more than a few eyebrows and there was a suspicion that the result of the game had been "fixed" beforehand. However, an enquiry found that on the previous day the Leicester players had attended a colleagues wedding and as a result of the evening's celebrations were in no fit state to play a serious game of football the following day. The result was allowed to stand much to the dismay of Manchester City who were relegated along with Leicester.

Possibly as a consequence of the problems relating to Spurs' election but also because of pressure from the Southern League talks took place early in 1909 with a view to an amalgamation of the two Leagues. After several meetings between the two Management Committees a scheme was eventually devised, in which 20 Southern League clubs would form Division 2 South with the Division 2 of the Football League forming Division 2 North. However, the clubs of both Leagues strongly opposed the scheme with the outcome that the project was shelved.

Yet another London club was in the news in 1913 when Woolwich Arsenal, who were in financial difficulties, decided to move their ground from Plumstead to North London. The scheme did not please Tottenham Hotspur, Chelsea, and Clapton Orient, however, who saw a danger to their interests if there was to be another successful League club in their vicinity. The Management Committee were not impressed by these objections. They pointed out that several clubs had moved grounds over the years but, in any case, they believed that there was a sufficient population to maintain another club in that part of the city.

The outbreak of hostilities brought League football to a close at the end of the 1914–15 season. This season was also the last for little Glossop who, after 17 seasons of League membership, received only one vote in the re-election ballot with Stoke being elected in their place. The decision to continue with League fixtures during 1914–15 season after virtually all other sporting activities had been cancelled undoubtedly affected the future of the game.

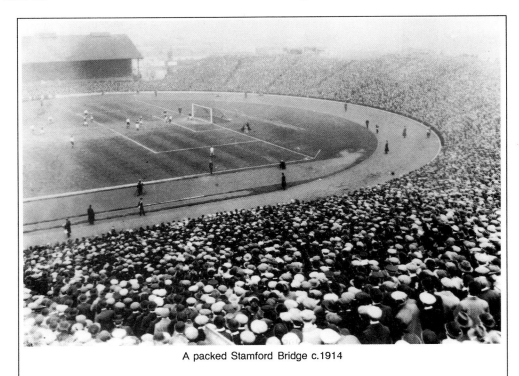

A packed Stamford Bridge c.1914

The Times was forced to comment *"British sports and British games have done our race a service......except, however, in this one solitary instance of professional football"*. There was a considerable public feeling that those who played the game were not 'patriotic' particularly when compared with rugby. This myth was maintained and the Times again commented in 1919 that *"there is much talk of making rugby the game in all our public schools"*. There was, of course, another aspect to all of this. Rugby Union was still an amateur sport and the increasing professionalism of football was disliked by the true amateurs of the period who saw rugby as the 'purer' sport. These changes in attitude towards the sports played at school had a vital impact on the future development of football.

The Inter-war Years
The League expands to 4 Divisions

The return of League football in season 1919-20 started in controversy when it was decided to increase the size of both Divisions to 22 clubs. Derby County and Preston North End were both promoted and Chelsea, who had finished last but one in Division 1, were elected to Division 1 without going to the vote. The remaining place being contested between Tottenham Hotspur (who had finished bottom of Division 1) and six Division 2 clubs Barnsley, Birmingham, Arsenal, Hull City, Nottingham Forest, and Wolverhampton Wanderers. Arsenal won the vote impressively thus leap-frogging over Barnsley, Wolves, and Birmingham all of whom had finished above them. The four new clubs elected to Division 2 were Coventry City, Rotherham County, South Shields, and West Ham United. However, the season had barely got under way before a further controversy, this time surrounding Leeds City, arose. The Leeds club were expelled from the League for a scandal involving alleged illegal payments to players during the war. Their fixtures for the remainder of the season were completed by Port Vale.

At the end of this first post war season the League was extended by forming a Third

Division from the Southern League (the new clubs becoming associate members). At the same time it was agreed that if the new Division was a success a Northern Section would be created in time for the 1921-22 season. Newly formed Leeds United and Southern League Cardiff City were elected to Division 2 in place of Grimsby Town and Lincoln City. Lincoln City moved down to the Midland League but Grimsby Town found a home in the new Third Division together with the remaining Southern League clubs. The new clubs included several who have since gained Division 1 status (Brentford, Brighton & Hove Albion, Crystal Palace, Luton Town, Millwall, Northampton Town, Norwich City, Portsmouth, Queens Park Rangers, Southampton, Swansea Town, and Watford), two who are no longer League members (Merthyr Town and Newport County), along with Bristol Rovers, Exeter City, Gillingham, Plymouth Argyle, Reading, Southend United, and Swindon Town.

The formation of Division 3 South had been straight forward in as much that there was a regional league of obvious status. This was not the case in the North, however, where no apparently dominant league existed. All Northern clubs who believed that they had ability to compete at this level, and who could prove their financial stability were invited to apply for admission to the new Northern Section. In the event 28 clubs applied for the 18 vacancies. Grimsby Town, who were transferred from Division 3 South, and the bottom club in Division 2 (Stockport County) filled the remaining two places. Thus Crewe Alexandra, Nelson, Rochdale, and Tranmere Rovers of the Central League, Ashington, Darlington, Durham City, and Hartlepools United of the North Eastern League, Accrington Stanley and Barrow of the Lancashire Combination, Chesterfield and Lincoln City of the Midland League, and Walsall and Wrexham of the Birmingham League were all elected on the recommendation of the Management Committee. The remaining 14 applicants went to the vote for the remaining four places. This resulted in the election of Southport and Stalybridge Celtic both of the Central League,

Wigan Borough of the Lancashire Combination, and Halifax Town of the Midland League. The Northern Section clubs have been significantly less successful than their Southern Section counterparts. Only one of them (Grimsby Town) has achieved Division 1 status and 8 are no longer League members.

The noticeable difference between the success of the original Northern and Southern Section clubs is not quite as surprising as it may at first appear. The Southern Section contained four London based clubs plus several others from large population centres such as Bristol, Plymouth, Portsmouth, and Southampton. In contrast the original Northern Section clubs originated from much smaller towns and, in many cases, had to contend with severe competition from local, well established, Rugby League clubs. Many of the Northern Section clubs were almost immediately faced with a financial struggle to survive. The danger signs were obvious fairly quickly when Stalybridge Celtic, despite finishing 11th, decided to resign at the end of the 1922–23 season after only two years of League membership. At the end of the same season the Northern Section was brought up to its full strength of 22 clubs with the election of Doncaster Rovers and New Brighton with Bournemouth & Boscombe Athletic gaining a place in the Southern Section.

One of the closest ever promotion finishes occurred at the end of the 1926–27 season. When the last day of the season arrived Middlesbrough were already promoted but Portsmouth and Manchester City were level on 52 points in 2nd and 3rd place. Portsmouth had a slightly superior goal average but there wasn't much in it. Manchester City beat Bradford City 8–0 and must have thought that they had done enough. Portsmouth, however, ran out 5–1 winners against Preston North End and in the days before calculators, pencil and paper were required to work out their respective goal averages. One London evening newspaper announced that Manchester City had done it but they were wrong. Portsmouth had a slightly superior goal average (1.776 to 1.771) but one goal either way on that final day would have reversed the placings.

On the basis of goal difference (as used today) Manchester City would have been promoted. They did not have to wait too long, however, as they were to finish Champions of Division 2 the following season.

The industrial recession soon placed several small clubs in financial difficulties leading almost inevitably to poorer playing performances and the period between seasons 1919–20 and 1938–39 saw several such clubs failing to maintain League status. The casualties included teams such as Merthyr Town, Aberdare Athletic, Thames, Nelson, Ashington, Durham City, and Wigan Borough. South Shields also found themselves in some difficulty and investigated the possibilities of moving to Newcastle. However, the club eventually decided on a move to Gateshead in the hope that greater support would be forthcoming there.

Only a handful of the larger clubs actually made a working profit during this period. Most clubs anxiously awaited a successful run in the FA Cup to boost income or, in the case of many others, only the sale of their better players to the top clubs enabled them to survive.

By the mid–thirties only two of the original 12 League members, Aston Villa and Blackburn Rovers, had never lost their Division 1 status. Curiously, they were to be relegated together at the end of the 1935–36 season. Fate had paired them together in Villa's last game of the season (at Villa Park) which Villa had to win to stand a chance of retaining their status. However, Rovers, bottom of the table but with a game in hand, won the encounter 4–2 thus relegating Villa. After the game Rovers found that they too were relegated following the results of the other fixtures involving clubs in danger of relegation.

When war broke out in 1939 the new season had just started with most clubs having completed their first three fixtures. The League, mindful of the way the game had been criticised when the 1914–15 season was allowed to continue, immediately cancelled the remaining fixtures and so League football ceased until the start of the 1946–47 season.

1946 Onwards

Queues of fans at Burnden Park in 1947 – before the gates were open! (Bolton Evening News)

The immediate post–war years saw a boom with tremendous crowds watching football at all levels. The structure of the Football League itself, however, remained virtually unchanged with a modest increase in size at the beginning of the 1950–51 season when the two Division 3 sections were increased to 24 clubs. The successful applicants were Colchester United, Gillingham, Scunthorpe United, and Shrewsbury Town. However, two innovations were to have a significant impact during this period; the arrival of floodlights and the introduction of European competitions.

There was nothing particularly novel in the use of floodlights to illuminate football matches. As long ago as 1878 two Sheffield teams had met in a friendly match before 20,000 spectators. However, the 1950s saw floodlight football arrive as a permanent feature in English football. September 1951 saw the first serious floodlit post–war friendly when Arsenal met Hapoel–Tel–Aviv. Most of the contemporary newspapers were more concerned with the unusual kick off time and with the floodlights themselves than with the game, but the Daily Mail commented that the game was an *"extraordinarily attractive spectacle. Perhaps floodlit League football is not so very far off."* Two further floodlit friendlies at Highbury during 1952–53 (Arsenal v Hibernian and London v Berlin)

attracted over 100,000 spectators between them and it was clear that floodlit football had arrived. By the end of the season 14 League clubs had installed floodlights although, surprisingly, only 4 of these were in Division 1. Clearly the smaller clubs were quick to see the improved income from such games was one way in which they could survive.

Although some of the smaller clubs were enthusiastic some of the larger clubs had their doubts. They argued that it would not be fair to use floodlights in League or Cup games and saw them as only being practical for friendlies and for training purposes. Another initial deterrent was the cost of installation (between £3,000 and £8,000) which was beyond the financial resources of many clubs. However, the advantages were very apparent. Midweek League games and Cup Replays, which could only be played in the afternoon during most of the winter, could then be played in the evening when spectators were not at work and so could attend hence increasing match receipts.

Floodlit friendly games against European sides rapidly captured the spectators imagination. Although the English National team had suffered spectacular defeats at the hands of Hungary there was still a belief that our club sides could match the best in Europe.

In the late 1940's and early 1950's there were few cars.....
(Above) Villa fans arriving in fleets of trams.
(Below) Bolton pedestrian supporters fill Manchester Road.
(Photo: Bolton Evening News)

Wolverhampton Wanderers were quick to prove the point in two major floodlit encounters. First they beat the crack Russian side, Spartak, 4–0 and then, in a dramatic game, they beat the top Hungarian side, Honved, 3–2 (capacity 54,998 crowd). The proud claim by manager Stan Cullis after the latter game that Wolves were now "the Champions of the World" played its part in the introduction of European competitions. The first floodlit League game was now almost inevitable. This took place at Portsmouth on 22 February 1956 when the home side lost 0–2 to visitors Newcastle Utd.

League football is full of great moments and sensational games. As in the FA Cup the fancied team is never guaranteed victory. One of the most remarkable of all games, however, must be that played at the Valley on 21 December 1957 when Huddersfield Town were the visitors in a Division 2 fixture.

Charlton Athletic lost their captain and centre–half (Derek Ufton) through injury after only 15 minutes and, in the days before substitutes, played out the remainder of the game with only 10 men. Two goals behind at half–time the scoreline continued to decline until after 62 minutes they trailed 1–5. The remaining 28 minutes, however, were sensational. A magnificent fight back saw the scores level at 5 goals each with 12 minutes still remaining. Further drama was to follow as the scoreline reached 6–6 before a final goal in the dying seconds made the final result Charlton 7 Huddersfield 6.

The start of the following season, 1958–59, saw a major re–structuring of the Football League when Divisions 3 South and North were finally abandoned with the top 12 clubs in each section forming the new Division 3 and the bottom 12 clubs in each section forming Division 4. With four teams being promoted and relegated between the two Divisions rapid changes in status became possible for the first time. Under the old system only the top side in each section was promoted to Division 2 leaving most Third Division sides without any real chance of promotion comparatively early in the season.

Although only two Division 3 sides were promoted to Division 2 the new system opened up a real opportunity for the smaller clubs to move up in status for the first time.

Not all clubs were to benefit with declining attendances making it hard for some to survive. The first casualty was Accrington Stanley who, in 1961–62, became only the second club to withdraw from the League during the playing season. (The other team was Wigan Borough who withdrew during 1931–32 after completing 12 games). Accrington's departure was not without controversy. Early in 1962 the club were in significant debt but Bob Lord, Chairman of near neighbours Burnley, offered to save the club. However, he quickly judged that the club's financial debts were too great and withdrew his offer. The club then sent a letter to the League indicating that they wished to resign but it appears that this hasty decision was taken without consulting all of the directors. Three days later a second letter correcting the first, was sent but the League decided the first letter must stand. No doubt the full story never emerged but nevertheless the Stanley was doomed.

The 1960s and 1970s saw some minor changes which did not effect the structure of the League but which were nevertheless significant. First, at the beginning of the 1965–66 season a single substitute was allowed but only to replace an injured player (this latter point was soon changed to allow any player to be substituted). Secondly, as from the 1973–74 season a three–up three–down promotion–relegation system was introduced between Divisions 1 and 2 and between Divisions 2 and 3. Thirdly, as from the 1976–77 season goal difference replaced goal average as the means of sequencing clubs with the same number of points. The greater movement possible between Divisions as the result of the changes in the number of teams promoted and relegated has led to some very sharp changes in fortune. For example Swansea City and Wimbledon have achieved promotion from Division 4 to Division 1 in only 5 seasons.

In the reverse direction both Bristol City and Wolverhampton Wanderers have 'achieved' successive relegations from Division 1 to Division 4, and Northampton Town, Huddersfield Town, and Swansea City have all taken only 5 seasons. Northampton Town and Swansea City share a record in moving from Division 4 to Division 1 and back again in only 10 seasons.

Although there have been many changes to the original Football League as conceived by William McGregor in 1888 the fundamental way in which points had been awarded had remained the same. One of the original alternatives, the idea of awarding points only for a win, had been rejected in 1888 but a move towards this system was undertaken in time for the beginning of the 1981–82 season when three points were awarded for a win with only one point for a draw. The motivation behind this change was to try and introduce more attacking football. Whether or not brighter football has resulted is, of course, debatable as the protection of a single goal lead becomes even more vital under this system. Nevertheless the system seems set to remain, at least for the time being.

Two other changes concern the re–structuring of the League to change the number of clubs in the various Divisions between 1986–87 and 1988–89 and the introduction of automatic promotion and relegation between Division 4 and the Vauxhall Conference.

The re–structuring of the League has followed a strange pattern. During the mid 1980s it was felt that Division 1 clubs undertook too many fixtures. Not only were there 42 League games to be completed but there were also FA Cup, League Cup, and European Cup fixtures. In addition it was felt that the preparation of the National side was being inhibited by such heavy demands. It was, therefore, agreed to decrease the size of Division 1 to 20 clubs and increase the size of Division 2 to 24 clubs over a two year period. Starting at the end of the 1986–87 season automatic promotion and relegation continued but the final place in each Division was to be decided by a play–off involving the 3rd from bottom club in Division 1 and the three highest placed teams in Division 2 not gaining automatic promotion. Similar arrangements were also introduced between Divisions 2 and 3 and between Divisions 3 and 4. Games were played on a home and away basis with a two–leg final. Having achieved the reduction in the size of Division 1 the play off system was retained, but altered so that the final promotion place was decided between the four highest placed clubs not achieving automatic promotion. This arrangement keeps a larger number of clubs involved in promotion issues until the last game of the season. However, it also has the consequence that the highest placed of the play off teams does not necessarily gain promotion. (This apparent unfairness was one of the factors which led to the demise of the old Test Match system).

The second change has been the introduction of automatic promotion and relegation of one club between Division 4 and the Vauxhall Conference. The Vauxhall Conference (then known as the Alliance Premier League) was formed in time for the 1979–80 season from 8 Northern Premier League and 12 Southern League (Premier Division) clubs. The motive behind its formation was to form a single strong League for the best non–League teams. The champions of this new league would then be forwarded as the sole representative of non–League football at the annual re–election vote in the hope that they would stand a better chance of election.

The hopes that the formation of the Alliance Premier league would lead to more non–League teams entering the League, thus introducing a few fresh clubs, failed. However, during the summer of 1986 the League clubs took a bold step forward when they agreed that the top Vauxhall Conference side would replace the bottom club in Division 4 commencing from the end of the 1986–87 season. The first automatic promotion–relegation season, however, was not without its own drama.

With one game remaining any one of Lincoln City (48 points), Tranmere Rovers and Torquay United (both 47 points), or Burnley (46 points) could be relegated. Burnley's position was desperate. They were one of the founder members of the League and had been in Division 1 as recently as 1975-76. Tranmere Rovers eased their worries with a victory on Friday night but the remaining three sides had their last fixtures to play on the afternoon of Saturday 9 May. Burnley slowly eased their way to safety as Lincoln City fell behind at Swansea. Torquay, however, were trailing 0-2 at home to Crewe Alexandra and looked doomed to take bottom place. They reduced the arrears in the 48th minute and during the resulting celebrations the goalscorer, Jim McNichol, was bitten by an equally excited police dog. He needed attention for a full four minutes before he could resume which meant, of course, that the games at Burnley and Swansea were completed before that at Torquay. Hundreds of portable radios on the terraces at Torquay reported the results of these other games to their supporters. Torquay, by the grace of a police dog, had 4 minutes to score again and so avoid non-League football. A spell of frenzied play led to an equalising goal in the dying seconds leaving Lincoln City to be the first League club to be automatically relegated to non-League football.

Lincoln's sojourn in non-League football was short and relatively sweet when they regained their status one year later by winning the Conference Championship. Darlington repeated the feat two years later but this contrasts starkly with the fate of Newport County sandwiched between. Two successive relegations from Division 3 to the Vauxhall Conference led to increasing financial difficulties and the collapse of the club before the end of their first Conference season. However, the pyramid structure now established in non-League football offers the opportunity for former League clubs to return to League football.

At the moment 2 ex-League clubs (Northwich Victoria and Stalybridge Celtic) are within one promotion of League football and three other former League clubs (Barrow, Gainsborough Trinity and Southport) are within two promotions.

The revised structure of the League achieved at the end of the 1988-89 season was retained for only two seasons before a further re-structuring was agreed to commence at the end of the 1990-91 season this time to return the size of Division 1 to 22 clubs! In the meantime relegation from Division 4 would cease until it returned to a final size of 24 clubs by promotion of the top Vauxhall Conference side for two consecutive seasons. Obviously one motive behind the change was to increase the revenue available to Division 1 clubs by including two extra home fixtures per season. The net result of these bizarre changes was to increase the total number of League clubs from 92 to 94.

These changes led to a conflict between the 1st Division clubs and the Football League with respect to the number of clubs in Division 1; an arrangement that they themselves had voted for.

However, of greater importance in the dispute was the distribution of the income from televised matches between the various Divisions. The Division 1 clubs believed they could obtain a better financial deal with the television companies if they were outside the structure of the Football League and on August 16 1991 all 22 Division 1 clubs resigned their League membership. At the time of writing full details of the arrangements for the new "Super League" and for the remaining 71 clubs forming the Football League have not reached fruition. What is clear, however, is that the end of the 1991-92 season will see the end of an era in English senior league football with the first major changes in the structure of the Football League since 1921-22.

The Game

Football in the 1870s and 1880s was a very different game to that played today. The players would, almost certainly, all be public school educated gentlemen, as indeed, would be most of the spectators. Since many football grounds of the era would have no changing facilities they may well have had to change into their playing 'gear' elsewhere; possibly in a local pub. The game would probably start late and the players would walk on to the pitch, quite possibly with hands in pockets, and kick off without any real attempt at a warm-up. They would be accompanied by two umpires, one appointed by each team, and a referee. The referee, however, would not enter the playing area but would sit or stand near the centre line and would only be required to adjudicate when the two umpires were unable to agree. Play was vigorous and rough with fierce shoulder charges very much a part of the game. The umpires were not often called on, however, but appeals for fouls, offside, and for other infringements would be made as would an appeal that a goal had been scored.

The players themselves would wear a shirt corresponding to the club colours and long trousers. Since socks were not part of the club's colours they would vary from man to man. The goalkeeper would wear the same strip as the rest of his team mates and some of the players might possibly be wearing caps. Since players shirts were not numbered it was quite difficult to distinguish one player from another at least as far as the casual spectator was concerned. Contemporary team-sheets usually gave sock and cap colours to allow identification.

Club colours were often different from those worn by the same teams today. Chocolate and blue was a favourite combination (Grimsby Town and others), maroon and orange quarters were selected by Burton Swifts, pink and white stripes by Burnley, and Stoke wore red and blue stripes rather than their now familiar red and white stripes. Newton Heath (Manchester United) started with green and yellow and Liverpool with blue and white quarters. (The 'Reds' was then the traditional nickname for Accrington). Salmon pink also seems to have been popular (Everton). Pride of place, however, must go to Bolton Wanderers who, in 1884, adopted white shirts with red spots. This was too much for the Bolton correspondent of the Football Field. *"I have seen a great variety of shirts and jerseys as most folks, but must award the palm of uniqueness to the new fangled dress of the Wanderers. It is something like you would expect in a circus ring"*. The nickname of 'The Spots' remained with the Wanderers for many years afterwards. These outfits were usually referred to as costumes and comments such as 'Blackburn Rovers took the field in their smart blue and white costumes' were common enough in press reports of the day.

The teams would line up with a goalkeeper, two full backs, one half back, and seven forwards. In modern terminology this would have to be referred to as 2:1:7. This was a very attack minded line-up but the style of play was very different. The game was played at a very much slower pace than today's high speed game but the forwards, in particular, were capable of great dribbling skills. Once in possession a forward would dribble the ball as far up the field as possible surrounded and supported by the other forwards until he eventually lost possession.

A goal was often scored by several players following a 'scrimmage' near goal following which the ball was eventually forced over the line. These 'rushes' must have looked quite frightening to the opposing goalkeeper who was ill advised to try and catch the ball. He was better advised to try and clear the ball by punching or kicking it clear. If the goalkeeper did catch the ball a goal was likely to result as the following description from the Football Field indicates when the Belfast Distillery goalkeeper having caught the ball fell to the ground the "[Bolton] *Wanderers attempted to roll him through the posts, whilst the visitors manfully strove to prevent them. More than half the players were struggling in the mud, but eventually the Wanderers managed to drag the custodian, backs, and others through the coveted space, and thereby registered their third point* [goal]."

Goalkeepers did have one advantage, however, in as much as they were allowed to handle the ball anywhere on the field of play. This freedom continued until 1912, when the present rule came into force.

The full backs were selected for their ability to clear the danger by kicking the ball well up field. It was a robust game particularly when it is born in mind that a player could be shoulder charged with or without possession of the ball. Virtually all goals were scored from close range and the ball was rarely headed.

The first major change to the English game came with the arrival of Scottish professional players many of whom joined the top Lancashire sides. They brought with them the 'passing' or 'combination' game. The first English team to master this aspect of football were Preston North End whose play during the 1880s was not only much admired but was very effective. The pass was often among fellow forwards aimed at retaining possession when challenged by a defender but this quickly developed to include long crossfield passes. The dribbling game had not disappeared, of course, it simply became an important aspect of the new passing game.

As the passing game developed so did the first major change in playing formation. It now became imperative to find new ways of counteracting the strength of the forwards and in order to achieve this two forwards were brought back as defensive midfield players. The change wasn't instantaneous, but it must have been effective as it was adopted by more and more clubs. The new system required the full backs to mark the inside forwards and the half backs to mark the wingers. The centre half, however, did not mark the opposing centre forward. He had much greater freedom to roam than any of the other players defending when danger threatened but principally supporting his forwards when they

were on the attack. The successful centre half had to be fast and constructive and an extremely skilful player.

By 1891 the referee had replaced the umpires and was in control of the game. The umpires were relegated to linesmen giving their judgement on matters such as offside and direction of throw-ins etc. Another different feature of the game was that the offside rule required three opposing players to be between a forward and the goal line when the ball was played. However, apart from these minor changes the game as a whole remained unchanged until the offside rule was amended in time for the commencement of the 1925-26 season. One comical change to the rules of the game arose in 1904 when the short length of the players shorts was deemed to be causing offence. A rule was passed requiring players to wear 'knickerbockers' long enough to cover their knees!

The new pattern of play which had developed remained unchanged until the 1920s. Play was a little faster than in the 1870s but still slow compared to the modern game. The passing game predominated and it appears from contemporary reports that the passing was extremely accurate. Dribbling had not disappeared completely, however, and was still an extremely popular part of the game. This was now the province of the wing- and inside-forwards. Goals were still scored from close range and were created by the skilful wingers whose centres were forced home or by a through ball which left a forward with a clear sight of goal. Heading was now part-and-parcel of the game, but the tackling was still hard and the heavy shoulder charge was still allowed.

There were critics of the new style of play. In particular it was felt that the new defensive awareness introduced by the half- and full-backs had reduced the technical ball skills of the forwards. There was criticism that the ball was passed too much and that the art of dribbling was not being fully exploited. However, things came to a head in the 1920s when teams began to exploit the offside game.

It appears that full-backs such as McCracken and Hudspeth of Newcastle United, and many others no doubt, had perfected the art of playing the opposing forwards offside. Unfortunately, not only did this tactic lead to fewer goals and less goalmouth action it also restricted play to a narrow zone either side of the halfway line. By 1925 enough appears to have been enough and the offside law was changed in order to restore the balance of the game in favour of the forwards.

The new offside law reduced the number of players necessary to put an opposing player onside from 3 to 2. The effect was immediate and dramatic. During the 1924-25 season 4700 goals had been scored in all League games. In the first season after the change the number rocketed to 6373. From a defensive point of view, however, too many goals were being conceded and it was almost inevitable that there would be a tactical reaction to the new found freedom experienced by the forwards.

The first reaction appears to have come from the Arsenal after a 7-0 defeat by Newcastle United in October 1925. The Arsenal captain, Charlie Buchan, and manager, Herbert Chapman, decided to plug the hole in defence by completely withdrawing the centre half from his roving attacking role and convert him into an out-and-out defender to mark the opposing centre forward.

Charlie Buchan of Arsenal

The centre half no longer needed the same skills. He became a stopper capable of handling the robust play of the centre forward and, almost inevitably, he had to be a good header of the ball. The move, however, needed another player to take over the centre half's midfield role and so at first one and then both inside forwards were withdrawn from the five-in-line forward line. The two full-backs now played either side of the centre-half with the sole task of marking the opposing wingers. In a sense football had now reached a perfect balance with five forwards being marked by five defenders. Herbert Chapman made other alterations, however. The traditional clever wingmen were replaced by fast wingers who could not only create goals but score them as well. In 1932-33 Cliff Bastin scored 33 goals from the left wing; a record which remains unbeaten in Division 1.

By the late 1940s English football had settled down to a standard formation. This was the classic WM formation, perhaps best described in modern terms as 3-2-2-3. It is interesting that most football programmes, well into the mid 1960s, insisted on printing team line-ups in a 2-3-5 formation. It is also somewhat amusing that players were still deemed to be wearing 'knickers' rather than shorts.

To some extent the English game had again become stereotyped, albeit into a new pattern. However, the visit of Hungary to Wembley in November 1953 was to act as a rude awakening. Not only were the Hungarians blessed with some fine ball players, but their centre forward, Hidegutti, played much deeper than his English counterparts. The two inside forwards, Puskas and Koscis, played as a twin spearhead and England's defensive formation was all over the place. The centre half was drawn out of position trying to mark an almost non-existent centre forward and the two wing halves had never before had to deal with twin strikers. Shortly afterwards when Don Revie played as a deep lying centre forward for Manchester City in League football the move was again effective. The numbers on the players shirts began to mean little in terms of their playing position.

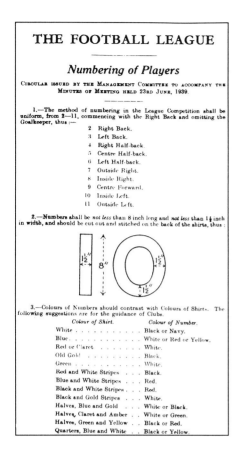

The modern method of numbering of players
was not introduced until 1939.

The move was further reinforced by Brazil during the 1958 World Cup. In attack they still retained two fast wingers and played, as Hungary had done, with twin strikers. To support the strikers the deep lying centre forward was now helped by one of the wing halves to form a midfield and the four defensive players included two centre backs to counteract the twin strikers now employed by many teams. The 4-2-4 system had arrived and was copied almost wholesale into English football. The problem now was, of course, that the Brazilians had developed the system to best suit the skills of players they had available. Had other players been available with different skills then a different system might well have been adopted.

Needless-to-say the new style did not necessarily suit all of the English League clubs. In order to keep pace with the new style of play the players needed to be fitter and make-up for some natural deficiencies by 'outworking' or 'outrunning' their opponents. Players were expected to be much more mobile and to work harder than their counterparts of 10 years earlier.

Sometimes revolutions start in the most unexpected of places. Suffolk had never really featured on the football map of Britain and yet, it was to do so with the success of Ipswich Town. Alf Ramsey had been appointed Ipswich manager in 1955 and in 1956-57 they gained promotion from Division 3 South to Division 2. Four years later they were promoted to Division 1 and were League Champions at their first attempt. Ramsey had taken one of his wingers out of the game and replaced him with Jimmy Leadbetter who wore the No. 11 shirt. Leadbetter was no winger, however. He was there to provide the twin strikers with a string of accurate passes so much so that in the season that the League Championship was won the Ipswich strikers Andy Crawford and Ted Phillips scored 61 goals between them. The success was due to the tactical problem set to opposing defences. This time the right back was drawn out of position searching for a non-existent left winger.

Early in 1962 Alf Ramsey became manager of England and immediately realised he had a problem. He felt that, at that particular time, English football lacked wingers capable of playing at the very highest International level. He, therefore, decided to abandon the idea of playing wingers altogether and build on the strength he believed he had in midfield. Now neither opposing full back had a formal winger to mark although Ramsey encouraged his own full-backs to move forward whenever they had the opportunity. Four years later for the first and, so far, only time England won the World Cup.

With the demise of the traditional English wingers, of course, went the remnants of the traditional old ball-playing dribbling game.

With the modern all–action midfield game the ability to take on and beat an opposing player is less important and, indeed, is almost positively discouraged by some coaches. Many critics of the modern game bemoan the loss of the great individual ball–playing footballers and yet it is interesting to note that back in 1930s Herbert Chapman too was convinced that the game had lost its great individuals and personalities. Yet one only has to listen to the crowd reaction when these traditional dribbling skills occasionally reappear to realise that this is the one aspect of the game more than any other that creates excitement.

England's World Cup victory inevitably led to League clubs using the same system. Unfortunately, however, this merely led to a crowded midfield with little goalmouth action. In 1970–71 Liverpool finished 5th in Division 1 scoring only 42 goals, but conceding only 24. The two–legged European competitions did not help much either. It rapidly became apparent that the object of such games was to concede as few goals as possible in the away leg.

Strangely, another football revolution started with a small, previously unsuccessful, team at Watford. Watford had moved from Division 4 (as Champions) in 1978 to Division 1 in 1982–83. Their style caused some consternation in football circles.

It was based on the long–ball game (used so effectively by Wolves, and others, during the 1950s) with two strikers and two wide forwards playing almost as wingers. Their game seemed to clash with modern thinking. If a player is capable of playing a long ball out of defence to one of his forwards then the midfield is by–passed. Many coaches had developed the midfield part of the game but these tactics excluded them. Yet nothing is wrong with the fine accurate pass. The obvious result of these developments is that teams should play a system best suited to the skills of the players they have available.

Unfortunately, the modern game demands success and it is difficult for coaches and managers to make bold tactical changes when a run of poor results can lead to them losing their jobs. It is easier for coaches to develop a style which prevents opposing teams playing than to develop a creative style of their own when resources are limited. Fortunately, changes to the playing system will inevitably occur from time to time as coaches search for a tactical advantage over their opponents. For example, in the 1990 World Cup England looked a more effective side whilst playing a sweeper in front of the back four. Sometimes tactical revolutions have started with 'unfashionable' clubs and, who knows, this could well happen again. It is to be hoped that, whatever new styles and tactics develop, players with some of the traditional ball–playing skills will be allowed to flourish.

10513–70   LONDON LIFE   FOOTBALL, CHELSEA v. ASTON VILLA AT STAMFORD BRIDGE.   ROTARY PHOTO, E.C.
THE IMMENSE CROWDS OF ENTHUSIASTIC FOLLOWERS OF THE GAME RAPIDLY INCREASE WITH EACH SEASON

32

Football Grounds

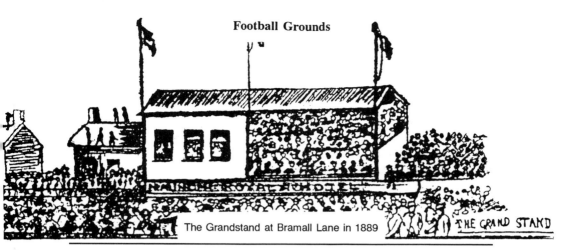

The Grandstand at Bramall Lane in 1889

THE GRAND STAND

Football grounds have been referred to as "Football's Cathedrals" and, to many a supporter, this they indeed are. However, the modern football stadium bears little resemblance to its primitive predecessor. For their first ground many clubs sought areas of waste land. Others used already established sports fields whilst the really lucky clubs, primarily those that had started life as a winter offshoot of a cricket club, were able to use part of the cricket pitch. In these latter cases players were able to change in the pavilion but in the vast majority of cases changing facilities were primitive (sometimes a tent) or non-existent. A local pub would also suffice. The pitches themselves were invariably dreadful – but more of that later. When a significant number of spectators started to watch the game in the 1870s the pitch was generally roped off to prevent spectators interfering with play although some of the wealthier clubs were able to erect a small fence.

Problems began to increase as the popularity of the game grew and with the arrival of professionalism. A professional had to be paid and hence an entrance fee had to be charged. The small box, passed around at half-time, for voluntary contributions was insufficient to keep clubs going. The answer, of course, was to enclose the entire playing area and its surrounds (so creating the first football grounds) and to allow entrance at limited points so that entrance fees could be collected.

However, if there were no natural slopes surrounding the pitch few spectators were able to see very much of the play once they were more than a few rows deep.

Obviously if clubs were to survive spectator facilities had to be improved and artificial banks were often erected to allow better viewing facilities. These banks, usually constructed from earth, cinders or waste, were the forerunners of today's terraces. Progressive clubs cut terraces into these banks but in most cases they were left as simple mounds. Other facilities were still primitive enough, however, most grounds providing no toilets, refreshments or crush barriers. Small stands or covered enclosures were often erected, usually along one of the touch lines for which an extra charge was made. These were for the benefit of the gentlemen spectators whilst the working man was expected to stand in the open behind one of the goals.

Slowly the standard of accommodation improved and newspapers during the 1880s give interesting glimpses of the state of English grounds. Extracts from the Football Field serve to illustrate. For example, by 1884 Burnley had – *erected a grandstand capable of seating 800 and, by rearranging natural earthworks, made sufficient standing for 2000 or more, and this week* [September] *they were erecting an uncovered stand covering two sides of the field and capable of accommodating 5000 people.*

Burslem Port Vale too had a grandstand which ......*strikes the eye. It is a brick structure, big enough to accommodate 1600, with a refreshment bar running underneath. Unfortunately it is ill–adapted for furnishing a view of the game, great ugly pillars interfering with the sight.*

Two of the best grounds appear to have been at Derby, where the football club shared facilities with the County Cricket Club, and at Preston. *The Deepdale ground is considered to be one of the best so far as the comfort of the spectator is concerned. There are raised platforms all around, which gradually rise in height to the back, and everybody in the cheapest part of the field has a good view of the game. The Committee of the Club have contracted for the roofing of the uncovered stand, so that one side of the ground will be entirely taken up with covered galleries. Then there is an enclosure for non–playing members. The touch line is close to the boundaries, and spectators have a near view of all the details of play. These arrangements, combined with good football and popular prices of admission, make the North End ground one of the best frequented football fields in the Kingdom.* Others were not so lucky!

Since many early grounds were created from wasteland the pitches themselves were diabolical. Little or (more usually) no attempt was made to level the playing surface or to drain it. Blackburn Rovers' first pitch (at Oozehead) had a pond almost in the middle of it. This was boarded over with planks and turfs placed on top and as such was used for the whole of the 1876–77 season. Planks were also used at the Drill Field, home of Northwich Victoria, to cover a small stream running alongside one touch line, so that corner kicks could be taken. Burslem Port Vale's pitch was described (in 1884) as completely devoid of grass and under water in several places. Appeals were inevitably lodged by visiting teams – often after a heavy defeat, but some of the playing surfaces were terrible. Even St. James' Park (Newcastle) had an 18 foot slope from one goalmouth to the other.

Many early League games were called off because the pitch was considered unplayable. However, so as not to disappoint the spectators, a friendly game was then played. No doubt this did little to help the playing surface.

Early League games played during the worst of the winter weather must have been almost farcical and some pitches achieved an unenviable reputation. West Bromwich Albion's Stoney Lane ground was considered the worst in Division 1. On the other hand the County Cricket Ground at Derby was one of the finest in England, as level as a billiard table; but Small Heath's Muntz Street ground was feared by most. When Wednesbury Old Athletic offered Small Heath £5 to reverse a local cup tie to the Wednesbury Oval Small Heath readily agreed and won 4–1. In 1891–92 Sheffield Wednesday offered £200 as compensation for the same favour in their FA Cup tie. Small Heath again agreed but this time the gamble failed as they lost 2–0.

The football correspondent of the Blackpool Gazette wrote (in 1900) that: *I have seen football played in many strange ways and in many strange places. I have seen men buried in chariot ruts that once beset the Darwen football ground and have vivid memories of Newton Heath football ground as it was in the days when officials of the Club, so it was said, studied in a class the art of restoring people from drowning. And I can remember one match played at Molineux grounds, when one side of the ground was lined with snow drifts 6 feet high, and when 4 players, after an exciting melee went into one of these drifts with such force that nothing was seen of them except 3 boots. But of all the terrible grounds I ever did see, the very worst is that on which the Blackpool club were supposed to give an exhibition of class football on Saturday last. The ground* [Raikes Lane] *was greasy, muddy, dirty, deceitfully damp and utterly vile.* The same correspondent obviously did not think much of Barnsley's pitch either claiming (hopefully somewhat exaggeratedly) that there were *legends of bygone players who, in exciting matches, slipped into slime yards deep, and whose uncovered remains lie below the surface of what is now a really fine playing field.*

By and large changing facilities appear to have matched the grounds themselves. Bradford City provided their players with a small hut near one corner of the pitch. They must have felt sorry for the visitors, however, as they made arrangements for the visiting team to change in an equally small back room of a nearby hotel. Grimsby Town solved their changing room problems by purchasing some second-hand bathing huts from Cleethorpes beech. I suspect these looked more romantic than they were practical. At Huddersfield an old tramcar served not only as a changing room but doubled up as a ticket office.

In many cases players walked several hundred yards through busy streets before and after the game. The return walk was no doubt unpleasant enough if they had lost. The referee, likewise, had to make his own way, but his journey was even more unpleasant if he could be blamed in any way for the defeat of the home team. The journey to the local railway station was then often undertaken at high speed followed by angry home supporters intent on doing him no good at all.

With the increasing popularity of football as a spectator sport many of the early grounds became hopelessly inadequate. The more progressive clubs saw an obvious advantage in moving to a new site, where better facilities were available both for the club and its supporters. Some clubs moved many times. For example, when Fulham eventually settled at Craven Cottage it was their ninth ground.

In the meantime the less wealthy clubs could ill-afford a move and had to do the best they could on their cramped sites many of which were rapidly becoming surrounded by terraced houses and factories. Here the priority was to survive but even that meant improvements had to be made. Survival, in many cases, meant making the best of "bumper" home gates in local Derbys and in FA Cup ties against bigger clubs. If these matches fell on an inclement day a huge slice of the club's income revenue would be lost.

Hence covered accommodation became critical. Indeed, even as late as the mid 1960s Wolves, in their match programme, proudly boasted "Covered Accommodation for 30,000".

One example of a club's attempts to maximise attendance at an FA Cup tie can be found in 1908–09 when Burnley were drawn at home to Manchester United on 6 March 1909. The Burnley Directors quickly took steps to enlarge the capacity of Turf Moor. Immediately after the home League game against Bolton Wanderers on 27 February the Star Stand was pulled down, enlarged and re-erected 12 yards further back from the pitch. In the meantime a new enclosure was formed in front of the new stand to hold 2,000 and altogether the ground capacity was increased to 35,000. All of this work was completed within a few days.

Of the original 12 founder members of the Football League only 3 [Stoke City (since 1878), Preston North End (since 1881) and Burnley (since 1883)] still play at the same site. In addition, of course, Everton played at Anfield. However, the honour of being the oldest senior club playing football continuously at the same venue appears to belong to Northwich Victoria who have used the Drill Field since 1875 (and possibly since 1874). It seemed likely that this distinction would disappear at the end of the 1990–91 season but the proposed re-development plans have so far not materialised.

Several now famous grounds were developed during the 1890s including Everton's Goodison Park in 1892. Goodison Park, built on a 30,000 sq.yd. piece of derelict wasteland, was proudly claimed to be finest football stadium of its era. The ambitious plans allowed for two uncovered stands holding a total of 8,000 spectators and a covered stand for 3,000. There were cinder banks to improve viewing and refreshment tents around the ground. The total cost of building Goodison Park, which had an initial capacity of 40,000, appears to have been about £4,000.

– Goodison Park in 1895 –

Manchester United moved to Old Trafford a few years later (1910). The original plans allowed for a capacity of 100,000 with seating for 12,000 and covered accommodation for 36,000. Construction costs, of course, had increased since 1892 but even so the work is reported to have been undertaken for only £30,000. Old Trafford included much improved facilities for the players as well as for the spectators. For example, there were fine dressing rooms, baths and a gymnasium. Another feature of the new ground was the quality of the pitch which was "fully turfed" and "as smooth as a billiard table". A sharp contrast with the playing surfaces at United's previous homes.

During the period 1919–1939 nine Football League clubs moved to new grounds. These ranged from some of the larger clubs such as Manchester City (one of their Hyde Road stands was removed and re-erected at the Shay, Halifax), Crystal Palace and Norwich City on one hand to "small town" clubs such as Durham City on the other. Clapton Orient contrived to move twice and, as mentioned earlier, in an attempt to survive South Shields moved to Gateshead changing their name in the process. South Shields had always suffered from the closeness of nearby glamorous Division 1 clubs and falling attendances had put their future in doubt. The move to Gateshead was bold enough and was welcomed in Gateshead. However, the same problems were to emerge at their new home.

Enemy activities during the second world war resulted in damage to several Football League grounds the most severe probably being that at Old Trafford. Manchester United were able to continue their League programme by sharing Maine Road for the first three post-war seasons. Hull City's Anlaby Road ground also suffered and they commenced their post-war activities at a new ground (Boothferry Park). Original plans for an 80,000 super stadium never really developed, however, and the ground has undergone significant changes since, including the building of a supermarket behind one goal. Sandheys Park, home of New Brighton, also suffered from bomb damage and the club moved to the Tower Ground (the earlier home of New Brighton Tower) in 1946–47. However, New Brighton's post-war survival in the Football League continued for only 5 post-war seasons before they failed to gain re-election being replaced by Workington (who were later to face the same fate themselves).

Only two other League clubs were to move until the mid 1980s. One of these, Port Vale, had grand plans for a new stadium at Burslem. The club purchased 18 acres of land (a former marl pit) and planned a stadium to hold 70,000. When opened in the autumn of 1950, however, the capacity was more like 40,000 and the main grandstand has never been completed to its original scale or design.

White Hart Lane, Tottenham, in the 1950's.

Many clubs, of course, continued to improve their existing grounds. A classic example must be Queens Park Rangers' Loftus Road ground which has been progressively re–built over a number of years so that all four sides now have covered accommodation with 17,000 seated. During the summer of 1981 Queens Park Rangers were responsible for an innovation in English football when they introduced an artificial playing surface. Such surfaces have some obvious advantages. Usable 7 days a week (and possibly on more than one occasion each day), playable in all weathers, and reproducible in their consistency over the whole of the playing surface they might have seemed the perfect answer to many club's prayers. Some also argued that players would become technically better on such surfaces. However, they were despised by others because of their 'unnatural' characteristics compared to grass, particularly the bounce of the ball. Queens Park Rangers, Luton Town and Oldham Athletic have already reverted to a turf surface and Preston North End will have to do so shortly in order to comply with the recent League rule banning them.

Little activity in finding new sites, however, took place until the 1980s when a number of clubs were forced to think again about their out–of–date grounds. In many cases to improve the present site was prohibitively expensive and other arrangements were sought.

The first major bombshell came in March 1983 when (the then) Oxford United Chairman, Robert Maxwell, announced that he and the Reading Chairman had discussed the merger of the two clubs. The idea behind the scheme was that the funds from the sale of the two grounds would be sufficient to build a new stadium (possibly at Didcot) with the new club to be known as Thames Valley Royals. The merger eventually failed after protests from both sets of supporters. The events of 1983 were quickly followed by two ground sharing schemes. The first of these involved Charlton Athletic where the vast East terrace at the Valley was rapidly crumbling. In addition, however, the owners of the land behind the West Stand gave the club notice that they were about to terminate the club's right to occupy the land.

Charlton endeavoured to find an alternative site in Greenwich but eventually had to settle on ground sharing scheme at Selhurst Park. They played their last game at the Valley on 21 September 1985. However, the move to Selhurst Park was never too popular with their supporters and eventually a possible return to the Valley was investigated. The return, although requiring a considerable amount of rebuilding work, was eventually approved and Charlton were due to play there again from the beginning of the 1990–91 season. However, slow progress in the alterations made this impossible and Charlton, having vacated Selhurst Park, had to seek a temporary ground sharing scheme with West Ham United at Upton Park in order to undertake their 1991–92 fixtures.

Bristol Rovers also found themselves in a difficult position at Eastville Stadium. Problems started in 1980 when the South Stand was so badly damaged by fire that its remains had to be demolished. Further problems arose two years later concerning their tenure at Eastville and eventually (in 1986) a ground sharing scheme with non–League Bath City, 15 miles away, was undertaken. Since moving the Rovers have spent nearly £1m on Twerton Park which has undoubtedly benefitted Bath City. In the meantime they are still hoping to move back to the Bristol area and by the end of October 1991 they had investigated 21 different possible sites. A similar problem has arisen with Maidstone United who have investigated 49 different sites in attempt to move back from Dartford to the Maidstone area.

Two small clubs, Scunthorpe United and Walsall, have recently taken the bold decision to move to new grounds. In both cases the money required was obtained by sale of their former grounds to supermarket chains. Both grounds have been built to the highest safety standards, and both have large car parks available. In Walsall's case there is sufficient parking for at least 1,500 cars with a separate car park for visiting supporters. The ground is within a corner kick of a main–line railway station with motorway exits within a few minutes journey.

The new ground cost about £4.5 M which represents a brave decision from a small club with little or no financial resources.

Not all clubs (or their supporters) were keen on moving although many now find themselves in difficult surroundings. In many cases grounds remain fenced in by terraced houses with little or no nearby car parking facilities and, even less likely, a nearby railway station. Although the grounds themselves can be improved little can be done outside the ground. The problems facing Wimbledon typify the problem. (One wag recently described Wimbledon as the only non–League club in Division 1). Plough Lane is unfortunately placed at an intersection of two busy roads. Road congestion is bad enough at the best of times without the additional load of football traffic on match days. In addition, there are no convenient rail services and, naturally, little nearby parking. The achievements of Wimbledon are considerable when these problems are considered. For example from seasons 1986–7 to 1989–90 they were the 6th most consistent side in Division 1 and this was achieved despite finishing as the Division 1 team with the lowest average home attendance in each of these seasons. At the beginning of the 1991–92 season they entered a ground sharing scheme at Selhurst Park. This, however, appears to have done nothing to improve their attendances some of which (during the 1991–92 season) have been as low as 3,000; many Division 3 clubs would be frightened by such low figures.

Another recent ground sharing scheme involved Chester City's temporary move to Macclesfield in time for the 1990–91 season which was sanctioned by the Football League for a maximum of two years. The Moss Rose ground, however, is over 40 miles from Chester and despite the provision of subsidised bus travel support is difficult. In their first home League game at Moss Rose Chester City attracted an attendance smaller than Macclesfield Town had for their first home Vauxhall Conference game. A few weeks later Chester folk were so outnumbered by visiting Stoke City's supporters that they suffered the indignity of being asked to remain in the ground until the Stoke supporters had left. A fate always reserved for away supporters. Worse was to follow when by the end of the season they had achieved 7 home attendances of less than 1,000 and had become the first Division 3 club to finish bottom of the average home attendance tables since the formation of Divisions 3 and 4 in 1958–59.

Several clubs have recently announced plans to give their grounds a significant face–lift including Tranmere Rovers, Nottingham Forest (£12 m.), Newcastle United (£16.5 m.), and Brighton (£18 m.). Other clubs are planning new grounds, but the financial problems are enormous. The cost of building a new ground to World Cup standards without financial assistance is surely beyond virtually all League clubs. Nevertheless too many grounds are now in desperate need of improvement if League status is to be maintained.

Significant activity can be anticipated during the 1990s not only in the modernisation of grounds but also to comply with the recommendations of the Taylor report. The Taylor report (issued in January 1990) requires all Division 1 and 2 League grounds to become all seater within 5 years and all Division 3 and 4 grounds by the end of the century. The judgement that seating must necessarily be safer than terracing is questionable but nevertheless the ruling will result in a fundamental change in the character of the game as far as supporters are concerned.

The ruling, of course, will also affect those Vauxhall Conference Champions who wish to gain League status from season 2000–01 onwards.

There can be little doubt that ground requirements for members of the Football League will tighten over the next few years. At the present time any club hoping to gain Vauxhall Conference status must meet a number of criteria. First, the stadium must have a capacity of at least 3,000 and be capable of being increased to 6,000 when Champions of the Conference with an overall potential capacity of 10,000 spectators for membership of the Football League. Secondly, there must be a minimum of at least 495 seats under cover (or 10% of the capacity whichever is greater) with a potential to increase to 1,000 seats (or 10% of the capacity whichever is greater). Thirdly, there must be covered standing accommodation for at least 1,000 spectators (unterraced banking is not acceptable as part of the capacity). Fourthly, a segregated standing area for visiting supporters must be available if required. There are several other requirements relating to other ground facilities and also with respect to the standard of floodlight illumination. It is questionable if all Football League clubs meet all of these requirements at the present time.

With spectator safety and ground facilities becoming more demanding in their requirements it seems possible that sometime in the near future a set of minimum criteria will be introduced which clubs will be required to meet before gaining promotion.

Craven Cottage, Fulham – due to become the latest ground 'casualty'.
(Photo: Dave Twydell)

The Supporters

A section of the Portsmouth crowd in 1911

There are few, if indeed any, sporting events that can rival a large crowd at an important football game for excitement. The game itself promotes the excitement. The cut and thrust of attacking the opponent's goal, the desperate defence of your own goal, the thunderous tackle, the speed and flow of the game all create, and add to, the excitement. Even the short stoppages such as the foul leading to a free kick and the corner kick all add to the excitement. It is a game of conflict – after all one team is trying to beat the other. The crowd is fiercely partisan too – it wants its own side to win, just how it achieves the victory is often of lesser importance.

There is no way that a football crowd is going to look like or behave like the visitors to the enclosure at a racecourse, or the sedate spectator on a balmy midweek summer afternoon politely applauding a gentle single at a cricket game.

The nature of the football crowd has, though, changed over the years. The early game was played, watched, organised, and administered by the educated classes with a strong sense of the sportsmanship ethic. The team was more important than any individual member of it and the game was played for the games' sake.

The result was unimportant; it was taking part that mattered. The ethic is typified by the response to the introduction of the penalty kick in 1891. Such a rule was unnecessary – no true sportsman would deliberately trip or push an opponent or deliberately handle the ball.

These "sportsmen" opposed the introduction of professionalism on several points. First, the professional would actually try and win. This was bad enough but such attitudes would destroy the amateur game. They could train and become fitter and more skilful players than amateurs and consequently the amateur players would no longer be able to compete at the very highest level. They also feared that the arrival of the professional would lead to the dominance of the 'big city' clubs who could afford to pay higher wages. The abolition of the maximum wage in 1961 was later to complete this particular process.

The arrival of professionalism approximately coincided with the arrival of the half–day Saturday holiday and the consequent arrival of the working man as a spectator. Such fans did not exactly match the sportsmanship ethic either. Their interest in the game, however, did much to increase the number of spectators and the popularity of football.

In order to watch a game most supporters had to rely upon an efficient public transport system in order to get to the game. Many would, of course, walk there, particularly if the ground was near to the town or city centre. Rail travel helped to bring supporters from nearby towns although with only a half–day holiday it was difficult to travel significant distances to away games except for local Derbys. By the time of the first League fixtures the game was already a colourful spectacle with supporters wearing the teams colours in the form of rosettes (often home made) or ribbons.

In the days before the formation of the Football League admission prices varied from club to club between about 3d. and 6d. with an extra charge for seated accommodation in a covered stand. Ladies were usually admitted half–price or, sometimes, without charge. In 1890 the Football League introduced a minimum charge of 6d. which remained in force until 1920. Virtually all clubs kept admission to part of their ground at this price although it would usually be behind one of the goals exposed to all the elements. Such spectators could expect to stand in pools of water often soaked by torrential rain and, in winter, often exposed to a bitterly cold wind. No wonder clubs were terrified of bad weather on the day of an important game as this would considerably reduce the attendance.

Between the two world wars the minimum charge became 1/- with seated (covered stand) accommodation costing between 3/- and 5/-, this rising in the late 1940s to 1/3 on the terraces. You could still watch football at these prices for most of the 1950s. By the mid 1960s admission prices had risen to 3/6 on the terraces with unreserved seating between about 6/- and 10/-. By the mid 1970s the terraces would cost about 50p with a seat in the stand between £1 and £2. Since this period the cost of watching the game has increased almost season by season until today's prices have been reached. Some clubs now operate a dual category pricing system with supporters having to pay extra when certain teams provide the opposition. In order to give some comparison with everyday life

the "shilling supporter" between the two wars could alternatively spend his shilling on a packet of cigarettes and would get a small amount of change if he spent it on a pint of beer.

There is no doubt that football crowds became increasingly working class during the late 1800s. These were tough people watching a rough tough game. Excursions on to the pitch were common enough and in many cases were merely an expression of excitement after a goal had been scored. Some pitch invasions were more serious, however, and these seemed to have been provoked by the tactics and rough play of the opponents or by dissatisfaction with the referee's decisions. Such incidents were fairly common. One such incident occurred at Walsall in 1891 in the local Derby between the local Town Swifts and Burton Swifts. During the game the home supporters were becoming increasingly irritated by the rough tactics of the Burton defence. The local favourite, centre forward "Sammy" Holmes, seemed to be the main target. He was well known for his sense of fair play and took rough play readily enough as part of the game. Eventually, even the gentle Holmes succumbed after a particularly thunderous tackle and raised his fist as a warning to his opponent. The crowd were already restless enough but when the referee went to send off Holmes pandemonium broke loose. It took fully 15 minutes to clear the pitch. The game did, however, restart but at the end of the game the referee needed a bodyguard to secure his safety. This incident was reported in the local press as purely part of the game and little was made of it. The reporter seemed to accept that these events were common enough and not worth any great attention. Today's headlines would be more sensational, however.

Although pitch invasions of one form or another seem to have been common enough the vast majority of League games were completed without incidents between opposing supporters. Opposing supporters seem to have been treated as objects of curiosity more than anything else.

They might expect to be jeered but there was also some good humoured banter between them.

The arrival of the full-day Saturday holiday during the inter-war years meant that much larger numbers of supporters could travel to away games and also travel from further afield to watch their favourite team at home. Public transport also improved and consequently attendances were increasing. The game was now an even more colourful spectacle with rival supporters trying to make more noise than their opponents. Rattles and bells were common place and added to the general pandemonium of noise.

The football supporter was still largely working class but naturally this varied from one place to another. Arsenal, for example, were well known in the 1930s as the club that attracted the wealthier middle class spectator, but in the industrial Midlands and Lancashire such spectators were less common.

Nevertheless the football crowd is remarkably heterogeneous and social inequalities rapidly disappear with the excitement of the game. Football crowds were also noted for their sense of humour. Any neutral attending a game would no doubt be taken by surprise by the partisan nature of the support and the general pandemonium greeting a goal by the home side. Unlike the post-war game there would be no organised chanting or singing. Violence against rival supporters did not appear to be widespread and when it did occur it seems to have been restricted to a minor scuffle.

One other interesting feature during the inter-war years was the rise of the "Supporters Clubs". Some of the motives behind their formation were admirable enough. For example, they would "stand-by" the club during "hard times", and organise excursions to away games. There was, however, a feeling that their formation was, in part, a "conspiracy" by the middle class supporter to try and reform the behaviour of the "shilling supporter" behind the goals.

The crowd at Huddersfield for this F.A.Cup semi-final between Millwall and Sunderland was so large, that thousands watched from the hillside upto half a mile away – the official attendance was 62,813.

There is little evidence that they achieved this latter objective. In the early post–war years there was a tremendous boom in football attendances. Many games were played before capacity crowds in all four Divisions. It was not uncommon to find the entrance gates closed well before the advertised kick off time. This era seems to have been largely free from crowd trouble although to some extent the closely packed terraces, which restricted movement of spectators during the game, prevented this. There was no attempt to segregate rival supporters who still seemed quite happy poking fun at one another and enjoyed the sense of rivalry with their neighbour.

Attendances began to slowly decline during the late 1950s and the arrival of "hooligans" at football matches grew from about the mid 1960s. Their arrival led to organised fighting at matches with attempts to gain the opponents 'end'. The exaggeration of early incidents by the popular press seemed to make matters worse rather than better. Clubs had to rapidly rethink their ground accommodation, and it became essential to segregate rival supporters. Unfortunately many of the antiquated grounds were, and still are, ill–equipped for segregation.

By the mid 1970s we find away supporters escorted from the railway station to the ground. The mid 1970s also saw a more disturbing aspect of hooliganism during a cup tie between Newcastle United and Nottingham Forest. With Forest leading a pitch invasion took place which seemed designed to prevent the completion of the game. Comparatively few such incidents of this type have occurred since and many clubs have erected perimeter fencing to prevent access to the pitch.

There can be little doubt that hooliganism (or violence) inside football grounds has decreased in recent years and that effective segregation of home and away supporters has been a considerable help in preventing this. Only a comparatively small number of arrests at football matches take place within the grounds themselves. There are also recent signs that the fans themselves dislike hooligans with chanting from the terraces letting hooligans know in no uncertain manner that they are not welcome.

There has been a widely held view that all seater stadiums would prevent hooliganism and restore a 'family atmosphere' to football. Coventry City's conversion of the Highfield Road ground into the first all seater stadium (reducing the overall ground capacity from 38,000 to 21,000 in the process) was a deliberate response to hooliganism. All games were made all–ticket, with tickets not available on match days. However, the arrangement failed and was abandoned in stages until by 1985 9,000 spectators could again stand on the terraces at Coventry.

It would be quite wrong to leave this section of the book with the view that violence at football games is widespread and a deterrent to the average 'decent' spectator. The majority of supporters who have watched League and non–league football have not seen an incidence of serious violence. It would be a serious distortion of fact to accuse football crowds of being violent, unruly mobs – they are not. Quite frankly it is possible to feel more threatened when travelling on the London Underground or walking through certain City streets late at night than at a football game.

General Overview of Attendances From 1888 to 1992

The arrival of League football in 1888 saw average attendances of just over 4,500. Prior to 1888 friendlies and cup ties had often attracted higher attendances than this. However, although this figure must have been disappointing it is not surprising that a new venture such as League football took a little time to establish itself.

The easiest way of gaining an overview of attendance figures from 1888 onwards is to examine the overall average figure for each Division of the Football League. The chart presented on page 140 shows these "Divisional Averages" for each Division and the way that they have changed over the seasons. The plots show a general increase until about 1950 followed by a corresponding period of decline.

During the period from 1888 to 1915 there was a steady increase in average attendances both in Division 1 and in Division 2 apart, that is, from the war-time season (1914–15) when a sharp decline occurred. (So significant was this decline that every League club experienced a decrease in their attendance figures).

Two factors make a contribution to this increase. First, some of the early member clubs (such as Accrington, the Burton clubs, Darwen, Gainsborough Trinity, Loughborough, and Northwich Victoria) were from small population centres and were comparatively poorly supported. As these clubs failed to gain re-election they were progressively replaced by clubs (such as Chelsea, Middlesbrough and Tottenham Hotspur) capable of achieving considerably higher attendance figures. This was not the only factor contributing to the overall increase, however. Many of the original founder members of Division 1 and Division 2 themselves experienced a significant rise in attendances. Notable in this respect were clubs such as Aston Villa, Birmingham, Liverpool, Manchester City, and Newcastle United.

The period from 1919 to 1939 is slightly more complex but nevertheless the general upward trend in Divisions 1 and 2 continued particularly towards the end of this period. There was an immediate post-war boom and the effect of the recession, with correspondingly lower attendances during the late 1920s and the early 1930s, is clearly seen.

The figures for Division 3, South and North, although different in appearance to those for Divisions 1 and 2 bear a remarkable resemblance to one another. Division 3 South was formed in the boom year of 1920–21 and Division 3 North one year later. In both cases an immediate slow decline set in. This might be explained, to some extent, by a decrease in the initial euphoria of gaining League status (an often repeated event). However, it appears that football at all levels experienced a sharp increase in attendances between 1919–20 and 1920–21. This view is supported by the fact that many Division 3 North clubs reported lower average attendances in 1921–22 (their first League season) than in 1920–21 (when they were non-League clubs).

Attendances in Division 3 North were always below those in Division 3 South. However, this does not represent a difference in popularity of the game in these geographical areas of the country. It simply reflects the fact that the clubs forming the new Southern Section came from larger population centres than the clubs forming the new Northern Section. The one up/one down promotion system allowed little change in the Divisional status of these clubs.

Divisional average attendances were again showing a level consistent with the general upward trend when season 1939–40 was abandoned. Following this trend after the war we find that attendances continue to increase until about 1950. Just as in 1919–20 there was a much discussed and documented post-war boom.

Thereafter, there has been a slow but general decline until the present time which, incidentally, sees attendances below those of the mid 1930s.

The period from 1888 to about 1950 then had seen a slow but general increase in Football League attendances. It would be necessary to study the social history of the country to find a detailed explanation of this increase. However, it clearly relates to the increased availability of first the half–day and then the full–day Saturday holiday together with an improving transport system. In addition the popularity of the game spread to larger sections of the population. Once a generation of supporters had taken their children to games they too became committed supporters. Family loyalties to a particular club are often very strong, even if later in life a supporter moves to a different part of the country. Add to these factors the excitement of the game and we have a recipe for increasing attendances. All of this, of course, raises the important question as to why attendances show a steady decline from about 1951 onwards.

The period from 1946 to 1950 saw most League (and for that matter most non–league) grounds filled almost to bursting point. Certainly attendances were well above those that would be allowed under the ground safety regulations in force today. Clearly a further upwards progression in attendances could not have been sustained without many major ground rebuilding programmes. However, the decline in attendances removed the immediate need for an expansion in football ground capacities.

There is no simple explanation for this decline. It is not linked to the Saturday holiday for example, or with transport. The present day network of motorways makes travel to away games comparatively straight forward as witnessed by the large number of cars displaying team colours on matchdays. The reason for the decline must lie elsewhere. Football is not the only pre–war leisure activity to have suffered a decline.

Many of us will well remember the long queues which used to assemble outside cinemas to watch even the most mediocre of films.

It is the use of leisure time itself which has changed. In a sense leisure activities have become more sophisticated and open to a wider section of the population. There is a greater competition for leisure time. Taking part in activities involving the whole family has replaced 'a day out with the lads'. Football as a spectator sport has stood up well to these changes in the use of leisure time. True attendances have declined from an all time high of 41,248,808 in 1948–49 to about 19,500,000 today but it could be easily argued that this decline is less than might have been expected. Football is still an exciting game attracting a large number of spectators.

One great influence on the game as a spectator sport has been television. Not only is it easier and more comfortable to watch sport at home on TV on a wet Saturday afternoon but televised football has probably influenced attendances in other ways. In pre–TV days there would be one opportunity a season to see a star player or a top team visit your local ground. Great names attracted huge crowds, but with the arrival of televised match highlights there were to be many opportunities to see these players, and their teams, in action but in the comfort of the home. Not only that, of course, but a rare occasion to see a player (or team) helped to give them a star status sometimes well above their real capabilities. In this sense TV may have done the game a dis–service by showing that players and teams were not really as good as their idealised image.

The loss of stature of the national team should not be over looked. It is difficult now, forty years later, to recall the invincibility associated with English football in the 1950s. True the national team had lost at home to the other home countries but no continental team had visited England and won. England could take on the world and beat them – until 25 November 1953 that is.

There can be no doubt that the 6–3 defeat by Hungary shook English football. Not only did we lose, but we were shown a different style of play better than our own by a team with far superior technical skills.

In true English fashion, however, this defeat was quickly dismissed. Given that we could play our strongest team we could show them a thing or two. So by the time of the return game in Budapest on 23 May 1954 the popular press (plus most supporters) were ready to take pleasure in a more representative scoreline. Unfortunately, this time the scoreline was even worse (1–7) and the belief that the national team were invincible and the best in the world was gone forever.

It is also tempting to blame the recent decline in attendances on problems such as hooliganism. No doubt some folk are deterred from watching football because of such problems. Although hooliganism is obviously a factor it would be naive to give it too much attention. Thankfully this problem is less noticeable at games now than it was a few years ago.

One factor which may also play a part in the general decline is the change in the style of play. There can be little doubt that modern football without "wingers" and "dribblers" and with a generally low standard of technical skill has lost a lot of its thrills especially in the penalty area. Could it be that a large number of supporters have simply voted with their feet?

There are several interesting features in the figures in the period from 1946 to 1992. As can be clearly seen on the chart from 1958–59 (when Divisions 3 and 4 were formed) Divisional average attendances in Division 3 continue very much at the same level as they were in Division 3 South and Division 4 very much at the level they were in Division 3 North. Together with Division 2, though, there is an unmistakable downward trend as, indeed, there is in Division 1. Division 1 is peculiar, however, in as much as it shows a marked "hump" between about 1966 and 1981.

This increase has often been attributed to England's victory in the 1966 World Cup. However, it is difficult to see the same effect in the other three Divisions and, consequently, other factors may also contribute to this feature.

The period from 1966 to 1981 (shortly after the abolition of the maximum wage in 1961) was a period when many of our 'town' teams were in decline. Clubs such as Blackburn Rovers, Blackpool, Burnley and Fulham, who were beginning to experience a serious decline in attendance figures, all left Division 1. Replacing them in Division 1 were a number of large, previously successful, clubs such as Leeds United (in 1964), Newcastle United (in 1965), Manchester City (in 1966), Wolverhampton Wanderers (in 1967) and, to a lesser extent Derby County (in 1969). Stoke City, Ipswich Town, Queens Park Rangers, and Birmingham City all had highly successful periods where they were well supported and in addition there were sustained high attendances at West Ham United, Manchester United and Liverpool. Towards the end of this period, however, a number of clubs who had been particularly well supported and had added to the boom, lost their status. These included West Ham United, Newcastle United, Queens Park Rangers, Derby County, and Wolverhampton Wanderers. There may be a "World Cup" effect superimposed on all of this. There was, no doubt, an additional attraction of seeing the World Cup stars in action. However, this boom was only experienced by a small minority of clubs, and then only in Division 1.

At many stages along each graph there is short term evidence for what might appear to be the start of a further decline or recovery in attendances. These changes, however, usually represent the interchange of well or poorly supported teams between Divisions at the end of each season. It is only when the overall picture can be viewed over many seasons that the general trends become more obvious. At the present time there is evidence that attendances are beginning to rise slightly but it is impossible to predict if this is just another short–term change. In particular, although they are not identical in every detail, all four Divisions have shown this recent increase and so, indeed and perhaps more importantly, have attendances at the non–league heart of the game such as in the Vauxhall Conference. Conference attendances first showed an upward turn in about 1984–85 (3 seasons before automatic promotion to Division 4 was introduced). This was followed by an increase in the attendances in the lower Divisions which has now also become evident in Division 1. If a sustained upward trend is underway at all levels it should be more clearly seen by about 1995.

It is interesting to collect together the average attendance data not only for the Football League but also for the Scottish Football League and for senior English non–League football. It is not easy to obtain accurate data for all of the different Leagues but the figures that are available for the 1990–91 and 91–92 seasons give some interesting comparisons:–

	1990–91	*1991–92*
Football League Div. 1	*22,681*	*21,622*
Scottish Premier	*15,722*	*11,850*
Football League Div. 2	*11,389*	*10,525*
Football League Div. 3	*5,153*	*5,423*
Football League Div. 4	*3,222*	*3,385*
Scottish League Div. 1	*2,051*	*2,055*
Vauxhall Conference	*1,429*	*1,218*
Scottish League Div. 2	*752*	*519*
Beazer Homes League		*551*
Diadora League		*509*
HFS Loans League		*349*

English Football League games clearly attract larger crowds than their corresponding Scottish counterparts, with the Scottish Second Division rather on a par with the second tier of the English non–league football pyramid. What would, of course, be interesting would be to compare these figures with those for other major European leagues. The only figures at hand at the time of writing are for the German Bundesliga where the average attendances were 21,801 and 7,271 for Divisions 1 and 2 respectively in 1990–91.

In order to make a more detailed analysis of attendances it is helpful to divide the total period from 1888 up to 1992 into convenient small sections.

1888–1898 The Early seasons – Everton dominate at home

There can be little doubt that Everton dominated the first 10 seasons, at least as far as home attendances were concerned. In most seasons they were head and shoulders above the rest. In the first 3 seasons Preston North End were the main challengers, but they were to be quickly replaced by Aston Villa. Away from home, as we shall see time and again, the situation was very different. The League Champions nearly always prove to be one of the major attractions by finishing in the top three in the average away attendance 'table'. Thus Preston North End, as befits their early dominance, were the top away attraction in the League's first two seasons, and finished in the top three in each of the first five seasons.

Sunderland, admitted to the League in 1891, were an immediate popular attraction, finishing Football League Champions in their first two seasons and again in 1894–95. Aston Villa finished as one of the top three most attractive away teams on no less than 6 occasions. League Champions three times and runners–up once, FA Cup winners twice and finalists once they were clearly a major attraction where ever they visited. Strangely, after such a dominant start, Everton were only to finish top of the average home attendance table on a further 3 occasions, and Preston North End have not been one of the top 3 most attractive visiting clubs since 1892–93.

1898–1904 Aston Villa Take Over

Aston Villa dominated attendances at home for the next 6 seasons very much as Everton had done for the first 10 seasons. Top "rivals" now though were Manchester City and Newcastle United.

The Villa also remained a great attraction away from home finishing top in the away table 3 times and second 3 times. No other club managed to match this type of consistency, although Sunderland's "team of all talents" obtained four top three away finishes. Aston Villa, twice League Champions, and once runners–up were obviously still going well, but new rivals were emerging. The same period saw Liverpool and Sheffield Wednesday gain their first Championships. Sheffield Wednesday were certainly an enigma as, although finishing Champions twice, their average home attendances were barely above the Divisional average.

Brown, Lockhead, Davies, Jackson, Smith Norgrove, Hughes, Buchan,
James, Coupe, Burgess, Eadie, Keiso, Bannister, Gould, Wynn,
Ramsey, Stewart, Chapelhow, Thornley, Furr, Ross, Dorsett, Conlin,
Jones, Wilkinson, Holford.

Manchester City 1909–10 Season:
Despite their great crowd-pulling power they were relegated the previous season.

1904–15 Chelsea and Spurs Impress

Our next period takes us through to the first of the two war–time breaks in the Football League programme. There is little doubt that this period began to see the first major shift in football power from the North and the Midlands to the South. The change was principally due to the election of two London clubs – Chelsea in 1905 and Tottenham Hotspur in 1908. There were many other new arrivals during this period but these two London clubs were to have a most dramatic impact.

Chelsea finished third in Division 2 in their first League season, a meritorious enough performance and finished 10th overall in the home attendance table. Since then only Tottenham Hotspur have made such an initial impact.

In 1907–08 Chelsea were to prove the top home attraction in the League attracting crowds the size of which the other London clubs could only dream about.

They were to prove the top home attraction on a further four occasions before the war enforced a break and were the first Division 2 team to finish top of the home attendance table (in 1911–12).

In their first season Spurs finished the 5th best home team and were second on a further 3 occasions. All of this was to have a major impact on attendances at rivals Woolwich Arsenal who suffered a significant slump. The demise of Arsenal was only prevented by the move to Highbury in 1913, with the consequent improvement in home attendances.

On the playing front some of the old faces were still there. Aston Villa with one League Championship and 4 runners–up spots, Newcastle United with three Championships and four FA Cup Final appearances together with Chelsea, were to dominate the period as far as top home attendances were concerned.

Away from home, however, Aston Villa were to appear in the top three on 9 occasions and Newcastle United, reflecting their playing successes, on 7 occasions. However, the biggest surprise was to come from two Lancashire town teams – Blackburn Rovers and Oldham Athletic. Blackburn Rovers twice finished Champions (in 1911–12 and 1913–14), a fine achievement. But what about Oldham? Elected to the League in 1907 they came from a Rugby League stronghold. Finishing 3rd in Division 2 in their first season they were to gain promotion to Division 1 in 1910 and finished 3rd in 1913–14. They looked certain Champions in 1914–15 when with two games remaining, including a game in hand, they were level on points with challengers Everton. Both games were at home first, to Burnley then to Liverpool. However, both were lost and Everton, gaining a draw from their last game at home to Chelsea snatched the title.

1913   GLOSSOP FOOTBALL CLUB   1914

Copyright Photo.   A. Wilkes, 46, Legge Street, West Bromwich.

BARNETT.   MONTGOMERY.   LITTLEWORTH.   HAMPTON.   STAPLEY.   DEARNLEY.   BERWICK.   CAUSER.   MR. MACEWEN.   CARNEY.
                                                                                                (Trainer)   (Manager)
        TURNELL.   BOWDEN.   DONCASTER.   BAMFORD.   KNIGHT.

Taylor, Warhurst, Day, Floyd, Webster.
Pattinson, Ward, Mettam, Jenkinson, Splevens, Boyle, Tellum, Magner.

Gainsborough Trinity 1909-10 Season: The worst supported team in the Football League.

The first 27 seasons of the Football League saw significant changes in its member clubs and their playing fortunes. By 1915 only Aston Villa, Blackburn Rovers and Everton of the original twelve clubs had avoided relegation. Accrington, of course, had disappeared after only 5 seasons. Of the eleven members of the Football Alliance who joined the Football League in 1892 only Birmingham, Manchester City, Manchester United, Nottingham Forest, and Sheffield Wednesday had maintained continuous membership. In attendance terms too there were significant variations of fortune.

The top clubs were already emerging, both at the turnstiles and in terms of their League status. Of those clubs who had been members of the Football League for at least 10 seasons the average home attendance at five clubs (Chelsea, Everton, Liverpool, Manchester City, and Newcastle United) never fell below the average of the Division in which they found themselves. On the other hand seven clubs (Barnsley, Blackpool, Burton Swifts/United, Gainsborough Trinity, Glossop, Stockport County, and Stoke) had not achieved an average home attendance greater than their respective Divisional averages in a single season.

1919–1929 Huddersfield Town's Remarkable Years

The resumption of football in 1919 saw a period of 10 seasons where no particular club dominated the attendance figures. Some of the pre-war "favourites" were still there or thereabouts. We find Chelsea four times, Newcastle United and Manchester City twice, and Liverpool and Arsenal both once, the top clubs at home. Away from home the most attractive teams were Aston Villa finishing in

the top three on 6 occasions, with Huddersfield Town (5 occasions), Sunderland and Newcastle United (both 4 occasions) running them close. On the playing front, however, Huddersfield Town emerged as the most consistent English League club. A hat trick of Championships (1923–1926), twice runners–up and once third, they also were once FA Cup winners and twice finalists.

A selection of action shots from the 1920's:

1. FA Cup Notts. County v. Sheffield Utd. (Jan 8th 1928) United's Anderson clears.
2. Burnley v. Manchester United. Beel (Burnley) scores one of his two goals in the 3–4 defeat.
3. 'Spurs v. Blackburn Rovers – The 'Spurs forward Osborne heads a goal at Tottenham.
4. Darlington v. Bradford –Darlington goalkeeper Archibald, fists the ball away from MacDonald.

1. Bradford City v. Nelson – Scottish Cap Tommy Cairns heads across the goal.
2. West Ham v. Sunderland – McInroy in the Sunderland goal thwarts West Ham's Watson.
3. Clapton Orient v. Manchester City in the FA Cup. Roberts of City, shoulder charges Evans.
4. Halifax Town v. Stockport County – Dixon, the Halifax centre–forward (centre) loses the ball.

Huddersfield Town, though, had hardly opened the 1919–20 season as potentially one of the strongest teams of the era. By early November 1919 it had become clear that they were in considerable financial difficulties. Their first 6 home games had attracted an average attendance of just over 4,000 – significantly less than any other League club. The Football League president, John McKenna (Chairman of Liverpool) was forced to observe that such attendances "were not conducive to retaining Football League membership" and it was clear that Division 2 football at Huddersfield could well be about to cease. Local loyalties tended much more towards rugby league than they did towards football.

A move to play at Elland Road, Leeds, was proposed (Leeds City having been expelled from the League one month earlier) with an amalgamation with the fledgling Leeds United club a definite possibility. The League Management Committee agreed to the proposal if that was what the club wished. News of the proposal, however, immediately led to protests in Huddersfield as a result of which the club were given a months grace to pay off their debts (about £25,000). Various deadlines and court proceedings followed before the club were eventually saved in June 1920. It is difficult to believe that whilst all of this was going on not only had the team gained promotion to Division 1 but they had also reached the FA Cup final! The club's fortunes took a further turn for the better when one year later Herbert Chapman was appointed manager, a position he was to hold until June 1925. When Chapman took over Huddersfield Town were probably best described as a moderate to poor Division 1 side. Not for long, however. They finished 3rd in 1922–23 followed by three consecutive Championships.

When Chapman left Huddersfield for Arsenal in 1925 he had moulded together a fine side strong enough to retain the League Championship and then finish runners–up in the following two seasons.

There are a few other noteworthy events during this period. The first of these concerns Cardiff City. Directly elected from the Southern League to Division 2 in 1920 they gained promotion in their first League season. They immediately finished 4th in Division 1 and in 1923–24 were runners–up behind Huddersfield Town. The following season they were FA Cup finalists eventually winning the FA Cup in 1927. In the meantime they had proved the top away attraction in 1923–24 and were among the top ten best home supported clubs between 1921 and 1924. Thereafter, though, their fortunes went into decline. They lost Division 1 status in 1929 and Division 2 status in 1931. Average home attendances fell from a peak of 32,760 in 1921–22 to only 7,008 in 1933. So serious was their decline that at the end of the 1933–34 season they finished bottom of Division 3 South and had to apply for re–election.

The second notable event occurred when Dixie Dean broke all goalscoring records in 1927–28. During his career with Everton Dixie Dean scored 349 goals in 399 League games, sixty of these coming in 1927–28. With such a prolific goalscorer in their team it is no surprise to find that Everton secured the League Championship and finished top of both the home and away Division 1 attendances tables. Surprisingly, though Everton did not have the top home average attendance that season. This distinction fell to Second Division Manchester City who thus became one of only 5 Division 2 sides to achieve this feat.

1929–1939 Arsenal Dominate

If the period from 1919 to 1929 had seen no particular team dominate League attendances the same most certainly cannot be said about the period from 1929 to 1939. At home Arsenal were to finish the best supported club on all but one occasion (1938–39 when they finished second to Aston Villa).

Away from home they finished top every season. As if to almost to symbolise their arrival as the new top club they were to beat Huddersfield Town in the 1929 FA Cup Final. In attendance terms Arsenal were almost in a league of their own.

Arsenal were perhaps fortunate to be in Division 1 at all in 1919 having been elected when the Division was enlarged to 22 clubs when finishing only 6th in Division 2. When Herbert Chapman joined them as manager in the summer of 1925 they were a struggling Division 1 side. However, by 1930-31 Chapman had repeated his achievements at Huddersfield and built an outstanding team. Finishing second the following year was to form the prelude to a famous hat-trick of Championships between 1932 and 1935. Chapman's untimely death in January 1934 left a team at Arsenal still of Championship quality; an almost exact repeat of achievements at Huddersfield a few years earlier. There can be little doubt that Arsenal were the team everyone wanted to watch during this period. In their Championship season of 1934-35 they attracted the highest gate of the season at 14 of the 21 grounds they visited. In 1932-33 and 1936-37 they attracted 13 highest attendances and the visit of Arsenal created new attendance records at many grounds.

Again there are several other notable events worthy of comment. One of these is most curious. At the end of the 1935-36 season Aston Villa and Blackburn Rovers were both relegated from Division 1. Previously these two clubs were the only founder members to have avoided relegation. Typically relegation seasons result in poor attendance figures not only at home but also away. Yet Aston Villa finished 2nd in the away attendance table. Perhaps there was a certain degree of curiosity in seeing the great Villa on their way down? Aston Villa were not the only great club to suffer during this period. Season 1933-34 saw Manchester United within one game of relegation to Division 3 North. Their last game of the season saw United travel to Millwall where only victory would save them from relegation. This they achieved (thus

relegating Millwall) but had they not have done so their subsequent fortunes could very well have followed a different path. Manchester United, in fact, recovered well from their poor season finishing Division 2 champions two seasons later.

At about the same time as these two famous clubs were experiencing variations of fortune Charlton Athletic were about to make a name for themselves. Finishing Division 3 South champions in 1934-35 they were promoted from Division 2, with Manchester United, in 1935-36 and then finished 2nd to Manchester City in Division 1 in 1936-37. This latter season, however, was also remarkable for their London rivals Brentford who were to finish third in the away attendance table. They too had risen from Division 3 South (in 1932-33) to Division 1 although in less spectacular fashion.

Spare a thought in passing for Newport County. Champions of Division 3 South in 1938-39 they were unable to take advantage of their elevated status due to the outbreak of hostilities. When the 1939-40 season was abandoned they had made a promising start gaining 3 points from 3 games, scoring 5 goals and conceding 4. However, in the 1946-47 campaign they lost all three of these same games scoring 4 goals but conceding 12.

During the period between 1919 and 1939 no fewer than 6 clubs succeeded in finishing all 20 seasons with an average seasonal home attendance higher than that of the Division in which they found themselves. These were Arsenal, Aston Villa, Chelsea, Everton, Millwall and Newcastle United. Consequently by 1939 founder members Everton had yet to experience an average home attendance below that of the average of the Division in which they found themselves and both Newcastle United and Chelsea had not done so since becoming League members in 1893 and 1905 respectively. At the other end of the scale Bournemouth, Bury, Blackburn Rovers, Gillingham, Huddersfield Town, Southend United, Southport, and Torquay United had all failed to achieve a single above average seasonal home attendance during this period.

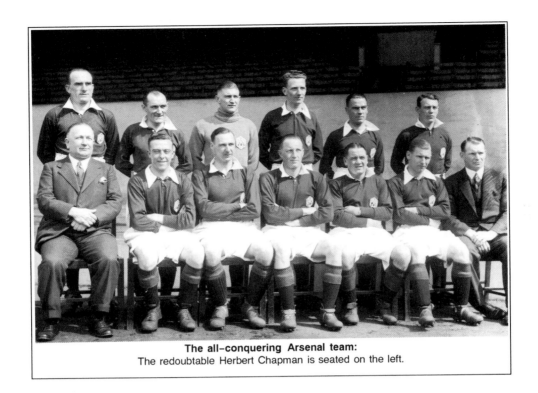

The all-conquering Arsenal team:
The redoubtable Herbert Chapman is seated on the left.

1946–1956 Matthews, Carter, and Lawton

S. MATTHEWS (STOKE CITY)   H. CARTER (SUNDERLAND)   T. LAWTON (EVERTON)

The first two post second world war seasons opened with the League Champions (Liverpool and Arsenal) finishing with the top average home Division 1 attendances.

However, in both cases Newcastle United, still in Division 2, outstripped them. Newcastle's average home attendance of 56,283 in 1947–48 set a new League record which has only been passed once since. Newcastle also finished top as a Division 1 team in 1948–49 followed in the next 3 seasons by Spurs and in the following two seasons by Arsenal.

Away from home Arsenal continued, at least to some extent, where they had finished off before the war with a further 5 top place finishes in this 10 season period. The surprise away team of this era, however, was Blackpool due, perhaps to no small extent, to the undoubted attraction of Stanley Matthews.

Matthews had spent the first post–war season with Stoke City who had duly finished 3rd in the away attendance listing. However, when Matthews was transferred to Blackpool the latter were to appear in the top three away listing on all but one occasion, finishing top 3 times and second four times. In season 1950–51 they became the only League club ever to attract over one million spectators to their away games. This is in stark contrast to their average home attendances over the same period. They finished well below the Division 1 average each season and were the worst supported Division 1 team at home on 3 occasions.

The transfer of Stanley Matthews from Stoke City to Blackpool was to have a curious effect on attendances at Stoke whenever Blackpool were the visitors. Stoke were relegated 6 seasons after the transfer but in 3 out of these seasons the visit of Blackpool was to attract the lowest or virtually the lowest gate of the season. Perhaps Stoke supporters could not bear to watch their former hero, or maybe they were none to happy about his transfer.

Stanley Matthews was not the only player to have been a major attraction during the early post–war seasons. Two others, Tommy Lawton and Raich Carter, were to have similar effects on attendances at Notts County and Hull City respectively. Both joined their new clubs in 1947–48 and both left at the end of the 1950–51 season. The table (top of column) illustrates the drawing power of such individuals at their club's home games in the early post–war boom years.

Season	Notts County	Hull City
1946–47	15,376	19,673
1947–48	25,380	24,010
1948–49	30,002	36,763
1949–50	35,176	37,319
1950–51	30,115	31,872
1951–52	26,525	29,210
1952–53	19,391	25,918
1953–54	16,237	20,995

December 27 1949 saw the largest number of spectators ever assembled to watch an English Football League programme. Altogether a total of 1,272,155 spectators watched the days football – an average of 28,913 per game. The attendances at each game were well above any that could be anticipated today and a large number of them exceeded the present day capacity of the grounds, some by a considerable amount:–

Division 1

Arsenal	v Manchester Utd.	65,133
Aston Villa	v Wolverhampton W.	64,937
Blackpool	v Burnley	31,074
Derby County	v Birmingham City	36,459
Fulham	v Everton	36,020
Liverpool	v Chelsea	58,757
Manchester City	v Huddersfield Town	50,195
Middlesbrough	v Newcastle United	53,802
Portsmouth	v Charlton Athletic	43,325
Stoke City	v Sunderland	41,685
West Bromwich Alb.	v Bolton Wanderers	41,746

Division 2

Blackburn Rovers	v Sheffield Wed.	30,636
Bury	v Bradford	22,700
Cardiff City	v Plymouth Argyle	32,499
Chesterfield	v Tottenham H.	26,341
Coventry City	v Leicester City	36,981
Hull City	v Brentford	48,447
Leeds United	v Barnsley	47,817
Queens Park R.	v Grimsby Town	22,994
Sheffield United	v Preston North End	50,586
Southampton	v Luton Town	26,928
Swansea Town	v West Ham United	25,721

Division 3 South				Division 3 North		
Aldershot	v Newport County	7,318		Bradford City	v Chester	21,246
Bristol Rovers	v Leyton Orient	19,786		Carlisle United	v York City	14,298
Ipswich Town	v Notts County	22,982		Doncaster Rovers	v New Brighton	23,381
Millwall	v Walsall	27,045		Gateshead	v Darlington	9,381
Northampton Town	v Port Vale	19,263		Halifax Town	v Stockport County	8,851
Nottingham Forest	v Norwich City	31,932		Hartlepools Utd.	v Barrow	6,910
Reading	v Bournemouth & B.A.	22,248		Lincoln City	v Crewe Alexandra	15,198
Southend United	v Exeter City	17,120		Oldham Athletic	v Mansfield Town	22,512
Swindon Town	v Brighton & Hove A.	18,872		Southport	v Rochdale	14,766
Torquay United	v Bristol City	12,258		Tranmere Rovers	v Rotherham United	15,670
Watford	v Crystal Palace	16,985		Wrexham	v Accrington Stanley	9,350

1956–1968 Manchester United Emerge

So far we have seen periods where, at least in attendance terms, certain teams have dominated and other periods where no particular team gained pre–eminence.

The period 1956–1968 saw the dominance at the turnstiles of Manchester United. Prior to 1956 United had never finished top of the home attendance table although they had finished top away from home from 1907 to 1911 and again in 1949–50. They clearly dominated the next 12 seasons, however. At home they finished top 6 times and were only out of the top 3 twice. Away from home they finished top 9 times and second three times. There were rivals, of course, notably Tottenham Hotspur (both home and away) and Everton and Liverpool at home. Nevertheless Manchester United had clearly taken over as the team everyone wanted to see. As often happens fortunes on the playing front were not so clear cut.

Manchester United did win the Championship 3 times, but Wolverhampton Wanderers and Liverpool both finished Champions twice with the remaining 5 Championships going to Burnley, Ipswich Town, Tottenham Hotspur, Everton, and Manchester City. Amongst these others two teams stand out – Burnley and Ipswich Town. Both came from relatively small population areas and Burnley in particular were not merely there to make up the numbers. They were widely reputed for the quality of their football and finished runners up once and third twice. In addition they won the FA Cup in 1961. Ipswich Town's Championship in 1961–62 took football by surprise. They had been Division 2 Champions the previous season and so became only the 4th club to achieve consecutive Division 2 and then Division 1 Championships. Liverpool (1904–06), Everton (1930–32) and Tottenham Hotspur (1949–51) were the others.

Manchester United pre–Munich Line–up February 1958.

(Left to right):
Duncan Edwards
Eddie Colman
Mark Jones
Ken Morgans
Bobby Charlton
Dennis Viollet
Tommy Taylor
Bill Foulkes
Harry Gregg
Albert Scanlon
Roger Byrne

1968-1974 Leeds United's Golden Era

These six seasons belong to Leeds United. Twice Champions, once runners up and three times third, twice FA Cup winners and once runners up. In any other era such consistency would have made Leeds the top club at the turnstiles. Yet Leeds' best placing at home was third in 1973–74. Away from home, of course, the picture was different. Finishing top in 1973–74 (and again in 1974–75) they finished second in all of the remaining seasons in this short period. Away from home the team they finished second to was Manchester United who also maintained their lead as the top home attended club (top on 4 occasions and 2nd twice).

Liverpool too were attracting large crowds finishing top twice, 2nd three times and 3rd once. They were poised to take over from Manchester United as the top attraction away from home.

Season 1972–73 saw a unique event when the Champions of all four Divisions (Liverpool, Burnley, Bolton Wanderers, and Southport) came from the same county. This season also saw Chelsea, for the first time since they had become members of the Football League in 1905, with an average home attendance below that of their Division, thus bringing to an end a remarkable run lasting 56 seasons.

Leeds United stars of the 1973-74 season: (L.to R., Top to bottom)
Harvey, Madeley, Cherry, Bremner, McQueen, Hunter,
Lorimer, Giles,Yorath, Jordan, Jones and Clarke.

1974–1992 Manchester United and Liverpool Well Ahead

The period from 1974 to date has been completely dominated by just two clubs – Manchester United and Liverpool. Home attendances have been completely dominated by Manchester United who have finished top on 16 occasions. (In 1974–75 they became the last Division 2 team to achieve this feat and the first since Tottenham Hotspur in 1949–50). The two remaining seasons they finished second to Liverpool.

Liverpool themselves in addition to finishing top twice finished second on fourteen occasions each time, of course to Manchester United. Only two other clubs, Tottenham Hotspur in 1981-82 and Arsenal in 1990-91, managed a top two place so complete has been the dominance of the big two.

The story away from home is the same except that now the roles of the two clubs are reversed. Liverpool have finished top on fourteen occasions and second four times whilst Manchester United have finished top three times and second ten times. Here, though, Leeds United did manage one top placing (in season 1974-75) before their fortunes declined somewhat. Three teams have all finished second - Tottenham Hotspur (twice), Arsenal, and Leeds United).

Apart from the big two, other teams well supported at home include Everton, Manchester City, and Arsenal. Support for Everton has been remarkably consistent. Although they have finished top of the home listing on 14 occasions, they did not have their first below average home attendance figures until 1975-76, a remarkable run lasting for 76 seasons from the formation of the League in 1888. Everton hold a further distinction presented to them by West Bromwich Albion's relegation to Division 3 at the end of 1990-91. They are now the only founder member who have maintained continual membership of the League never to have played below Division 2.

On the playing side it is curious that Manchester United have been relatively devoid of success despite their massive home support. Liverpool, for example, have finished Champions 10 times and runners-up 6 times during this period whilst Manchester United have never finished as Cjampions and have only finished runners-up three times. In fact during the first 8 seasons of this period one of the most consistent teams behind Liverpool was Ipswich Town. Although never Champions they finished second twice and third 3 times. They also won the FA Cup in 1978. Ipswich were the last of the "small town" teams to make an impact.

Since the re-commencement of League football in 1946 there have been 46 seasons of un-interrupted football, by far the longest peace-time period. Remarkably during the whole of this period the big two, Liverpool and Manchester United, have not had a below average seasonal home attendance. The next most impressive records belong to Arsenal and Everton who have both only had two below average seasons.

At the other end of the scale Gateshead (in 14 seasons), Rochdale, and Wimbledon (in 15 seasons) have not achieved an above average home attendance in any post-war season. Barrow (in 26 seasons), Cambridge United (in 22 seasons), Halifax Town, and Southport (in 32 seasons) have managed only one and Newport County (in 42 seasons) and Workington (in 26 seasons) only 2 above average seasons.

During the complete run of 93 seasons since 1888 only 9 different clubs have finished top of the overall average home attendance tables. Not surprisingly they are all "big city" clubs. Everton and Liverpool from Merseyside, the two Manchester clubs, Aston Villa from the Midlands and Newcastle United from the North East, and three London clubs Arsenal, Chelsea, and Tottenham Hotspur. Very few clubs who have joined the League since the formation of the sectional 3rd Divisions in the early 1920s have made a real impact. Ipswich Town have had a fairly successful period but even London based Wimbledon have struggled to gain significant support. Peterborough United started well in 1960-61, but at the end of 1991-92 only 2 out of the 12 new post-war clubs were in the top half of the home attendance tables. Clearly the "big city" clubs have taken over in support terms with the "town" teams struggling to compete effectively. If a new club joining the League were to make an impact they would, clearly, have to come from a large population area. At present the largest town (or city) without a League club is Salford but here competition from the two Manchester clubs would leave them in the same position as clubs such as Tranmere and Walsall with fierce competition from the local big glamorous clubs.

Support for a club is difficult to analyse. For example, Aston Villa finished 2nd in both the home and away attendance tables when relegated in 1935–36. Again their average home attendance when gaining promotion from Division 3 in 1971–72 (31,952) was higher than when they subsequently gained promotion from Division 2 three years later. Similarly, when Walsall applied for re-election on four successive occasions from 1951–52 to 1954–55 their average home attendances rose from 7,084 to 11,201 the latter being greater than when they won promotion to Division 3 in 1959–60 and to Division 2 one year later! Supporters are remarkably perceptive. If the data for each individual club is examined closely supporters seem to react in advance of their team's performance. There are numerous examples where support has grown in advance of promotion, sometimes by as much as three seasons. This could be explained by more supporters being attracted to an improving quality of football as the team strengthened. Also possible, although perhaps less likely, is that the increase in gate revenue enabled the club to build a better team. The reverse is often true of relegation with support falling away a season or two before the event. Sometimes a dramatic fall in support has preceded a catastrophic event such as at Accrington before their demise.

There are several clubs whose home attendances for the period from 1946 have closely followed the average attendance of the Division in which they have found themselves. They include Bradford City, Brentford, Gillingham, Mansfield Town, Peterborough (after an above average start), and Reading. The best example amongst the founder members is found with Bolton Wanderers whose attendance figures since 1888 have most closely followed those of their Division.

MANCHESTER UNITED

Back Row: Tommy Docherty (Manager), Stewart Houston, Stuart Pearson, Steve James, Pat Roche, Alex Stepney, Arnold Sidebottom, Jim Holton, Martin Buchan, Paul Bielby, Tommy Cavanagh (Trainer).
Front Row: Mick Martin, Sammy McIlroy, Alex Forsyth, Brian Greenhoff, Willie Morgan, Trevor Anderson, Jim McCalliog (now Southampton), Lou Macari, Gerry Daly, Tony Young.

The Manchester United team of the 1974/75 season was the last
Second Division side to top the seasonal attendance table

Season by season survey

Average attendances at home games 1888–1992

The main statistical section of this book presents the average home attendance for each League club, season by season, from 1888–89 to 1991–92. The records of attendances at Football League games can be divided into two distinct periods – before, and after, 1925. From 1925 onwards all League clubs have been required to return attendance data to the Football League after every home League game. It should be remembered that this data is required in order to calculate the levy due to the League and therefore only includes those spectators who paid for admission. However, at least this ensures the attendances for each club are returned on exactly the same basis and can be directly compared with one another.

Up until fairly recently the attendances have been recorded in hand–written ledgers and, prior to 1946, have not been totalled. Calculating the average home attendance for each club from these ledgers is straightforward but time consuming. In most post–war seasons the figures for each club have been totalled. In some cases errors in these totals have been revealed when checked with a pocket calculator. More serious than arithmetical errors, however, is the inclusion in these totals of attendances at abandoned games (on which a levy has also to be paid). Average attendances based on totals published by the Football League are, therefore, in error when ever there has been an abandoned game. Abandoned games have been excluded when calculating the average home attendance for each club presented later in this section. Since 1981 the League's attendance records have been fully computerised, although they still, of course, include abandoned games.

The period up to 1925, however, presents a very different problem. There is no unique source of attendance data for this period and correspondence with a selected number of clubs quickly revealed that those contacted have no records of their home (or away) attendances during this period. Between 1888 and 1925, I have therefore had to resort to information available in contemporary match reports. Very few clubs indeed appear to have issued actual attendance figures to the press during this period and, consequently, the figures reported in newspapers are at best rounded versions of attendances. At worst they are simply guesses made by the press or a club official. However, such figures are better than none at all and represent the only information available.

I found two sports papers (*The Football Field* and *The Athletic News*) enormously helpful as they carried match reports of all Division 1 games and many Division 2 and Division 3 games. For some games it has been possible to obtain attendances originating from more than one newspaper report. More often than not the figures quoted are in agreement, but when this is not the case, the average of the reported figures has been taken as the attendance for that particular game. It is frustrating that on occasions comments such as *'the best so far this season'*, *'good'*, *'poor'*, or *'thin'* appear, and it has been necessary to avoid the temptation to convert such comments into approximate attendances.

At the end of this process I was still short of data for some games. The next stage was to consult the local newspapers of both the home and away teams in the hope that they might give the missing data. Again it was frustrating to find that in some cases the local newspapers of neither club gave an attendance figure. It seems unlikely that it will ever be possible to establish figures for such games. However, despite these difficulties it has been possible to trace figures for all but 2,766 of the 143,199 League games that have been played up to the end of the 1991–92 season. I am hopeful that it may prove possible to fill in some of these gaps sometime in the future.

Since the data for the period 1888–1925 is based only on estimated attendances, the resulting average home attendances during this period have been rounded in order to allow for inaccuracies. Figures from 1925 onwards are, of course, presented to their full accuracy.

The average home attendances for each season are presented in numerical order irrespective of which Division the team were playing in that season. The second number in each column indicates each club's Divisional status. (This number has been omitted between 1888 and 1892 when there was only one Division). This format has the advantage of overlapping the figures from the various Divisions and allows overall placings for each club to be easily seen. The best supported team in each Division is presented in bold type.

No doubt readers will be interested in the fortunes of their favourite clubs through these attendance tables. Generally the average home attendance at each club reflects their playing fortunes and increases during successful seasons. Poorer seasons on the field result in poorer average attendances although there are instances of attendances rising during periods of adversity.

Attendances obviously vary during the course of a particular season, and for most clubs once promotion (or the League Championship) is no longer a possibility, attendances tend to decline as the season progresses. There will be higher attendances at Christmas and Easter matches and for local Derbys' but otherwise there is a definite downward trend. A promotion season is invariably well attended particularly when the promotion challenge is sustained throughout the season. The converse is usually, but not always, true of relegation.

Divisional status and success are not the only factors affecting attendances. The size of the local population is obviously a factor, but also important is the past history of success at that club which generates an interest in the game in that locality.

Also important, although hidden within average attendance figures, are the number of local Derby's. Clubs from large population areas, with a glamourous history, and several "big" local Derbys each season have a built-in advantage.

The main statistical section covering average home attendances is followed by a brief survey of the top supported clubs. This survey presents a quick guide not only to the best supported clubs in the Football League, but also to the best supported clubs in each Division. Individual match attendances not only allow the calculation of the average attendance for each club in their home games but also of their average away attendance. These latter figures give information on the most attractive visiting club each season. This information is presented in the third part of the statistical section. Finally, there is a survey taken at ten year intervals, of the number of season ticket holders at each club. These figures are mainly of "curiosity" value but, nevertheless, reveal some interesting additional information.

Special Notes:

1919–20: Attendances for Leeds City and Port Vale have been calculated separately.

1931–32: Games completed by Wigan Borough are included.

1961–62: Games completed by Accrington Stanley are included.

1973–74: The game between Scunthorpe United and Exeter City was not played and, therefore, is not included.
1991–92: Games completed by Aldershot are included.

The names of some League clubs have changed since 1888, in some cases more than once. The link with the modern name is usually obvious except perhaps for Birmingham City (formerly *Birmingham* and *Small Heath*), Manchester City (formerly *Ardwick*) and Manchester United (formerly *Newton Heath*).

Average Attendances at Home Games 1888–1992

SEASON 1888–89

7260	**Everton**	4200	Burnley
6280	Preston North End	4175	West Bromwich Albion
5505	Blackburn Rovers	3980	Wolverhampton Wanderers
5305	Bolton Wanderers	3610	Accrington
4555	Aston Villa	3450	Stoke
4300	Notts County	3050	Derby County

SEASON 1889–90

10110	**Everton**	5325	Bolton Wanderers
7650	Preston North End	4870	West Bromwich Albion
7205	Blackburn Rovers	3900	Derby County
5870	Aston Villa	3400	Notts County
5530	Wolverhampton Wanderers	3275	Stoke
5400	Burnley	3055	Accrington

SEASON 1890–91

11375	**Everton**	6240	Aston Villa
7805	Blackburn Rovers	5950	Sunderland
7580	Burnley	5845	Wolverhampton Wanderers
7580	Notts County	3920	West Bromwich Albion
7225	Preston North End	3270	Derby County
7190	Bolton Wanderers	2980	Accrington

SEASON 1891–92

10730	**Everton**	6100	Notts County
8225	Sunderland	5965	Derby County
7500	Bolton Wanderers	5105	Blackburn Rovers
7045	Aston Villa	4920	Darwen
6225	Preston North End	4850	Wolverhampton Wanderers
6195	West Bromwich Albion	3950	Stoke
6125	Burnley	3770	Accrington

SEASON 1892–93

13230 1	**Everton**	
10500 1	Sheffield Wednesday	
8075 1	Nottingham Forest	
7815 1	Sunderland	
7605 1	Aston Villa	
7475 1	Notts County	
7080 1	Newton Heath	
6805 1	Burnley	
6675 1	Preston North End	
5990 1	Derby County	
5970 1	Blackburn Rovers	
5790 1	Bolton Wanderers	
5520 1	Wolverhampton Wanderers	
5070 1	Stoke	

4665 1	West Bromwich Albion
4000 1	Accrington
3500 2	**Darwen**
3030 2	Ardwick
2550 2	Sheffield United
2500 2	Northwich Victoria
2435 2	Grimsby Town
2350 2	Small Heath
2225 2	Lincoln City
2125 2	Crewe Alexandra
2000 2	Burton Swifts
2000 2	Bootle
1310 2	Walsall Town Swifts
1200 2	Burslem Port Vale

SEASON 1893–94

13520 1	**Everton**
10665 1	Aston Villa
8730 1	Sheffield United
8550 1	Sheffield Wednesday
7280 1	Newton Heath
6890 1	Sunderland
6775 1	Nottingham Forest
6420 1	Blackburn Rovers
6300 1	Burnley
6255 1	Wolverhampton Wanderers
6050 2	**Woolwich Arsenal**
5800 1	Preston North End
5640 1	Derby County
5350 1	Bolton Wanderers
5215 2	Liverpool
5075 1	Stoke

5035 1	West Bromwich Albion
3900 2	Notts County
3700 1	Darwen
3525 2	Newcastle United
3410 2	Ardwick
3100 2	Walsall Town Swifts
3060 2	Small Heath
3000 2	Lincoln City
2800 2	Grimsby Town
2680 2	Crewe Alexandra
2450 2	Burslem Port Vale
2400 2	Burton Swifts
1450 2	Middlesbrough Iron.
1325 2	Rotherham Town
1325 2	Northwich Victoria

SEASON 1894–95

17420 1	**Everton**	
12015 1	Liverpool	
9625 1	Sheffield Wednesday	
8680 1	Aston Villa	
8250 1	Sunderland	
7910 1	Blackburn Rovers	
7510 1	Sheffield United	
7375 1	Bolton Wanderers	
6660 2	**Woolwich Arsenal**	
6400 2	Newton Heath	
6310 1	Preston North End	
6275 1	Small Heath	
6235 1	Burnley	
6000 2	Leicester Fosse	
5955 1	West Bromwich Albion	
5665 1	Nottingham Forest	

5300 1	Wolverhampton Wanderers
5045 2	Manchester City
4550 2	Notts County
4450 2	Bury
4390 1	Derby County
4155 2	Newcastle United
3875 1	Stoke
3650 2	Darwen
3530 2	Grimsby Town
3250 2	Burton Swifts
2600 2	Burton Wanderers
2475 2	Lincoln City
2300 2	Burslem Port Vale
2250 2	Rotherham Town
2200 2	Walsall Town Swifts
1800 2	Crewe Alexandra

SEASON 1895–96

16080 1	**Everton**	
12360 1	Aston Villa	
9535 1	Bolton Wanderers	
9480 2	**Manchester City**	
8975 1	Sheffield Wednesday	
8360 1	Derby County	
7810 1	Blackburn Rovers	
7800 1	Bury	
7600 1	Stoke	
7255 2	Newcastle United	
7200 2	Woolwich Arsenal	
6975 1	Preston North End	
6865 1	Sheffield United	
6625 1	Nottingham Forest	
6210 1	Sunderland	
6100 2	Leicester Fosse	

6065 1	Small Heath
6005 1	Wolverhampton Wanderers
5875 1	Burnley
5795 2	Liverpool
5660 1	West Bromwich Albion
5400 2	Newton Heath
3500 2	Grimsby Town
3400 2	Crewe Alexandra
3325 2	Notts County
2750 2	Burton Wanderers
2700 2	Darwen
2625 2	Lincoln City
2375 2	Burton Swifts
2200 2	Rotherham Town
2175 2	Loughborough
1625 2	Burslem Port Vale

15840 1	**Everton**	5680 1	West Bromwich Albion
12855 1	Aston Villa	5400 1	Stoke
12035 1	Liverpool	5250 1	Burnley
8360 1	Bolton Wanderers	5225 1	Nottingham Forest
8130 2	**Newcastle United**	5160 1	Sunderland
8080 1	Sheffield United	4775 2	Notts County
7995 1	Derby County	4495 2	Small Heath
7470 2	Manchester City	4345 2	Grimsby Town
7005 1	Blackburn Rovers	3950 2	Walsall
6900 1	Sheffield Wednesday	3800 2	Gainsborough Trinity
6865 1	Preston North End	2950 2	Blackpool
6600 1	Bury	2700 2	Burton Wanderers
6565 2	Woolwich Arsenal	2575 2	Burton Swifts
6445 2	Newton Heath	2350 2	Darwen
5945 1	Wolverhampton Wanderers	2275 2	Loughborough
5900 2	Leicester Fosse	1600 2	Lincoln City

17390 1	**Everton**	7025 1	Wolverhampton Wanderers
15870 1	Aston Villa	6685 1	Preston North End
12935 1	Liverpool	6380 1	Bury
11565 1	Sheffield United	6135 2	Newton Heath
11545 2	**Newcastle United**	6000 2	Leicester Fosse
10970 1	Sunderland	5420 2	Small Heath
9140 1	Sheffield Wednesday	4125 2	Burnley
8805 1	Derby County	3465 2	Grimsby Town
8190 1	Bolton Wanderers	3350 2	Luton Town
8060 1	Notts County	3200 2	Lincoln City
7845 1	Blackburn Rovers	2900 2	Walsall
7800 2	Manchester City	2500 2	Burton Swifts
7735 2	Woolwich Arsenal	2275 2	Darwen
7645 1	Nottingham Forest	2250 2	Gainsborough Trinity
7350 1	Stoke	2000 2	Loughborough
7070 1	West Bromwich Albion	1640 2	Blackpool

SEASON 1898–99

23045	**1**	**Aston Villa**	6355	1	Burnley
17390	1	Newcastle United	5770	1	Preston North End
15190	1	Everton	5470	2	Small Heath
14650	1	Liverpool	5330	1	Bury
12540	1	Sunderland	5020	1	West Bromwich Albion
11125	1	Notts County	4470	2	Woolwich Arsenal
9960	2	Manchester City	3710	2	Walsall
9870	1	Sheffield United	3575	2	New Brighton Tower
8920	1	Blackburn Rovers	3545	2	Grimsby Town
8815	1	Nottingham Forest	3250	2	Luton Town
8150	1	Sheffield Wednesday	3025	2	Loughborough
8000	**2**	**Leicester Fosse**	3000	2	Burton Swifts
7600	1	Stoke	2950	2	Lincoln City
7285	2	Newton Heath	2650	2	Barnsley
7110	1	Derby County	2625	2	Glossop North End
7085	1	Wolverhampton Wanderers	2600	2	Gainsborough Trinity
7075	1	Bolton Wanderers	2450	2	Blackpool
6500	2	Burslem Port Vale	1225	2	Darwen

SEASON 1899–1900

18765	**1**	**Aston Villa**	5880	1	Burnley
16445	1	Newcastle United	5735	1	West Bromwich Albion
15510	1	Manchester City	5205	2	Small Heath
13875	1	Everton	5020	1	Preston North End
11820	1	Liverpool	4875	2	Bolton Wanderers
11350	1	Sheffield United	4750	2	Lincoln City
11265	1	Sunderland	4460	2	Woolwich Arsenal
8655	1	Notts County	4005	1	Glossop
8255	1	Derby County	3800	2	Grimsby Town
7620	1	Nottingham Forest	3200	2	Walsall
7275	1	Stoke	3025	2	New Brighton Tower
7125	**2**	**Leicester Fosse**	2500	2	Chesterfield
6800	2	Sheffield Wednesday	2500	2	Barnsley
6780	1	Wolverhampton Wanderers	2000	2	Luton Town
6725	1	Blackburn Rovers	1750	2	Gainsborough Trinity
6400	1	Bury	1750	2	Burslem Port Vale
6175	2	Newton Heath	1750	2	Loughborough
6000	2	Middlesbrough	1500	2	Burton Swifts

SEASON 1900–01

17530 1	**Aston Villa**	
17135 1	Manchester City	
16855 1	Everton	
15575 1	Newcastle United	
15195 1	Liverpool	
14110 1	Sheffield United	
11695 1	Sunderland	
10925 1	West Bromwich Albion	
9815 1	Nottingham Forest	
9700 1	Bolton Wanderers	
9600 1	Sheffield Wednesday	
8945 1	Notts County	
8470 2	**Middlesbrough**	
7995 1	Derby County	
7650 1	Stoke	
7375 1	Bury	
6365 1	Wolverhampton Wanderers	
6225 1	Blackburn Rovers	

6170 1	Preston North End
6010 2	Woolwich Arsenal
5510 2	Small Heath
5500 2	Leicester Fosse
5480 2	Newton Heath
5125 2	Grimsby Town
3675 2	Lincoln City
3500 2	Stockport County
3275 2	Burnley
3200 2	Chesterfield
3075 2	Barnsley
3015 2	Walsall
2850 2	Glossop
2700 2	New Brighton Tower
2500 2	Burton Swifts
2300 2	Gainsborough Trinity
2300 2	Burslem Port Vale
2035 2	Blackpool

SEASON 1901–02

19580 1	**Aston Villa**
16825 1	Manchester City
16030 1	Everton
14715 1	Liverpool
14450 1	Newcastle United
13265 1	Small Heath
12905 1	Sunderland
12880 1	Sheffield United
10200 1	Bolton Wanderers
9765 1	Sheffield Wednesday
9430 1	Notts County
9275 2	**Middlesbrough**
9050 1	Derby County
8605 1	Nottingham Forest
7950 1	Blackburn Rovers
7870 1	Bury
7635 2	Woolwich Arsenal
7530 2	West Bromwich Albion

7280 1	Stoke
6525 1	Wolverhampton Wanderers
5955 1	Grimsby Town
5820 2	Bristol City
4555 2	Preston North End
4530 2	Newton Heath
4100 2	Leicester Fosse
4000 2	Doncaster Rovers
3600 2	Burslem Port Vale
3000 2	Lincoln City
3000 2	Stockport County
2800 2	Burton United
2800 2	Chesterfield
2575 2	Glossop
2450 2	Blackpool
2300 2	Barnsley
2225 2	Burnley
2025 2	Gainsborough Trinity

SEASON 1902–03

19790 1	**Aston Villa**	
17540 1	Newcastle United	
15715 2	**Manchester City**	
15645 1	Liverpool	
15430 1	Everton	
15305 1	Sunderland	
14465 1	West Bromwich Albion	
14015 1	Sheffield Wednesday	
12670 1	Middlesbrough	
11265 2	Manchester United	
11160 1	Sheffield United	
11110 2	Woolwich Arsenal	
10530 1	Bolton Wanderers	
9735 1	Derby County	
9540 1	Bury	
9440 1	Notts County	
8470 1	Nottingham Forest	
8080 1	Blackburn Rovers	

8050 1	Stoke
7655 2	Small Heath
6855 1	Wolverhampton Wanderers
6255 2	Bristol City
5800 2	Chesterfield
5800 2	Doncaster Rovers
5500 2	Leicester Fosse
5055 1	Grimsby Town
4300 2	Stockport County
4280 2	Preston North End
3700 2	Lincoln City
3650 2	Barnsley
3300 2	Burton United
2900 2	Gainsborough Trinity
2500 2	Blackpool
2400 2	Glossop
2300 2	Burslem Port Vale
1500 2	Burnley

SEASON 1903–04

20035 1	**Aston Villa**	
19870 1	Manchester City	
17845 1	Everton	
17775 2	**Manchester United**	
17565 1	Newcastle United	
15790 1	Sheffield United	
15725 1	Liverpool	
14335 1	Middlesbrough	
14285 2	Woolwich Arsenal	
13670 1	Sunderland	
12595 1	Sheffield Wednesday	
12340 1	West Bromwich Albion	
10765 1	Small Heath	
9910 1	Notts County	
9855 2	Bradford City	
9650 1	Derby County	
9395 1	Blackburn Rovers	
8910 1	Nottingham Forest	

8610 1	Stoke
8205 2	Preston North End
8195 2	Bolton Wanderers
7790 1	Bury
7710 1	Wolverhampton Wanderers
6250 2	Bristol City
5400 2	Leicester Fosse
4400 2	Grimsby Town
4100 2	Barnsley
4100 2	Burnley
4000 2	Chesterfield
4000 2	Lincoln City
3800 2	Stockport County
3300 2	Blackpool
3100 2	Burslem Port Vale
2900 2	Gainsborough Trinity
2500 2	Burton United
1400 2	Glossop

SEASON 1904–05

21605 1	**Newcastle United**	
19980 1	Woolwich Arsenal	
19155 1	Everton	
18715 1	Manchester City	
18390 1	Aston Villa	
15205 2	**Manchester United**	
14540 1	Small Heath	
14510 1	Sunderland	
14450 1	Sheffield United	
14315 2	Liverpool	
12880 1	Sheffield Wednesday	
12385 2	Bolton Wanderers	
11685 1	Middlesbrough	
11145 1	Blackburn Rovers	
11030 1	Nottingham Forest	
10700 2	Bradford City	
9795 1	Preston North End	
9145 1	Bury	

8915 1	Derby County	
8090 1	Notts County	
7470 1	Stoke	
7380 1	Wolverhampton Wanderers	
6935 2	Bristol City	
5900 2	Leicester Fosse	
4515 2	West Bromwich Albion	
4500 2	Gainsborough Trinity	
4400 2	Lincoln City	
4300 2	Chesterfield Town	
4260 2	Burnley	
4150 2	Barnsley	
4000 2	Blackpool	
3875 2	Grimsby Town	
3000 2	Doncaster Rovers	
2900 2	Burslem Port Vale	
2600 2	Burton United	
2380 2	Glossop	

SEASON 1905–06

22765 1	**Newcastle United**	
20735 1	Aston Villa	
19930 1	Bolton Wanderers	
18480 1	Liverpool	
17560 1	Manchester City	
16105 1	Woolwich Arsenal	
15920 1	Everton	
14560 2	**Manchester United**	
13685 1	Sheffield United	
13370 2	Chelsea	
13015 1	Sunderland	
12920 1	Blackburn Rovers	
12650 1	Middlesbrough	
11960 1	Birmingham	
11875 1	Sheffield Wednesday	
10485 1	Notts County	
10025 2	Leeds City	
9485 1	Preston North End	
9390 2	Bradford City	
9320 2	West Bromwich Albion	

9265 1	Nottingham Forest	
9140 1	Bury	
9070 2	Bristol City	
8610 1	Stoke	
7510 1	Derby County	
6525 2	Hull City	
6490 1	Wolverhampton Wanderers	
6175 2	Leicester Fosse	
5050 2	Stockport County	
4975 2	Burnley	
4900 2	Barnsley	
4300 2	Clapton Orient	
4230 2	Grimsby Town	
4150 2	Burton United	
4100 2	Chesterfield Town	
3750 2	Gainsborough Trinity	
3300 2	Burslem Port Vale	
3175 2	Blackpool	
3000 2	Lincoln City	
2600 2	Glossop	

SEASON 1906–07

33235 1	**Newcastle United**	
23835 1	Aston Villa	
21670 1	Manchester City	
20695 1	Manchester United	
19340 1	Everton	
18640 1	Liverpool	
18135 2	**Chelsea**	
15880 1	Middlesbrough	
15800 1	Woolwich Arsenal	
15685 1	Birmingham	
15450 1	Sunderland	
14960 1	Bolton Wanderers	
14920 1	Bristol City	
12265 1	Blackburn Rovers	
12155 1	Sheffield United	
11890 2	West Bromwich Albion	
11580 1	Bury	
11555 1	Sheffield Wednesday	
10835 2	Bradford City	
10290 1	Notts County	

10200 2	Leicester Fosse
10100 2	Nottingham Forest
9975 1	Preston North End
9965 2	Leeds City
7530 2	Hull City
7000 2	Clapton Orient
6980 1	Derby County
5890 2	Wolverhampton Wanderers
5605 1	Stoke
5275 2	Burnley
5100 2	Grimsby Town
4900 2	Chesterfield Town
4750 2	Barnsley
4650 2	Stockport County
3850 2	Lincoln City
3750 2	Burslem Port Vale
3600 2	Burton United
3000 2	Gainsborough Trinity
2940 2	Blackpool
2600 2	Glossop

SEASON 1907–08

31965 1	**Chelsea**	
27875 1	Newcastle United	
23255 1	Manchester City	
22315 1	Manchester United	
19520 1	Aston Villa	
17630 1	Everton	
17470 1	Sunderland	
17345 2	**Fulham**	
16905 1	Liverpool	
16605 1	Middlesbrough	
15875 2	Bradford City	
15265 1	Birmingham	
14515 1	Bolton Wanderers	
13765 1	Woolwich Arsenal	
13500 1	Sheffield Wednesday	
13270 1	Blackburn Rovers	
13245 1	Bristol City	
12890 1	Sheffield United	
12840 1	Nottingham Forest	
12775 2	Leicester Fosse	

11880 1	Bury
11265 2	West Bromwich Albion
10870 1	Preston North End
10780 2	Leeds City
10605 1	Notts County
10585 2	Oldham Athletic
9515 2	Derby County
9120 2	Wolverhampton Wanderers
7745 2	Hull City
7725 2	Burnley
7450 2	Clapton Orient
5825 2	Stoke
5500 2	Chesterfield Town
5275 2	Stockport County
4925 2	Barnsley
4575 2	Grimsby Town
4250 2	Gainsborough Trinity
3875 2	Lincoln City
3590 2	Blackpool
2300 2	Glossop

29300 1	**Newcastle United**	
29120 1	Chelsea	
23025 1	Everton	
21875 1	Bradford City	
20255 2	**Tottenham Hotspur**	
19665 1	Manchester City	
18945 1	Aston Villa	
18150 1	Manchester United	
17660 1	Liverpool	
16340 2	Fulham	
15525 2	West Bromwich Albion	
15235 1	Sunderland	
14745 1	Blackburn Rovers	
14050 1	Middlesbrough	
13025 1	Woolwich Arsenal	
12850 2	Bolton Wanderers	
12840 1	Sheffield Wednesday	
12790 1	Leicester Fosse	
12625 1	Sheffield United	
12295 2	Oldham Athletic	

12015 1	Bristol City
11350 2	Bradford
11090 1	Nottingham Forest
11055 2	Leeds City
10975 1	Bury
10825 2	Birmingham
10805 1	Notts County
10500 2	Clapton Orient
9210 1	Preston North End
8620 2	Wolverhampton Wanderers
8200 2	Hull City
6815 2	Burnley
6615 2	Derby County
5925 2	Stockport County
5650 2	Barnsley
5380 2	Gainsborough Trinity
5235 2	Grimsby Town
4975 2	Chesterfield Town
4970 2	Blackpool
3430 2	Glossop

28545 1	**Chelsea**	
27560 1	Tottenham Hotspur	
24825 1	Newcastle United	
21620 1	Liverpool	
21125 1	Aston Villa	
20640 1	Bradford City	
19110 1	Everton	
18740 1	Manchester United	
18540 2	**Manchester City**	
14300 2	Fulham	
13840 1	Sheffield United	
13805 1	Blackburn Rovers	
12445 1	Bolton Wanderers	
11780 2	Oldham Athletic	
11615 1	Sunderland	
11230 1	Middlesbrough	
10990 1	Bristol City	
10975 2	West Bromwich Albion	
10720 1	Sheffield Wednesday	
10395 1	Woolwich Arsenal	

10305 2	Bradford
10250 1	Notts County
10010 1	Nottingham Forest
9825 2	Leicester Fosse
9790 1	Bury
9205 2	Hull City
9110 1	Preston North End
8375 2	Derby County
8370 2	Birmingham
7950 2	Clapton Orient
7940 2	Wolverhampton Wanderers
7245 2	Leeds City
6555 2	Burnley
6550 2	Stockport County
6325 2	Lincoln City
5325 2	Barnsley
5325 2	Blackpool
4405 2	Grimsby Town
3600 2	Glossop
3250 2	Gainsborough Trinity

SEASON 1910–11

25055 1	**Newcastle United**	
24955 1	Manchester City	
24515 2	**Chelsea**	
24190 1	Manchester United	
23155 1	Tottenham Hotspur	
22705 1	Aston Villa	
18860 1	Everton	
16825 1	Liverpool	
16780 1	Bradford City	
16650 1	Sunderland	
15955 1	Middlesbrough	
15190 2	West Bromwich Albion	
14350 1	Blackburn Rovers	
14155 1	Oldham Athletic	
14140 2	Fulham	
13850 2	Birmingham	
12750 1	Notts County	
12595 1	Sheffield United	
11890 1	Sheffield Wednesday	
11675 2	Bradford	
11525 1	Woolwich Arsenal	
11025 1	Bristol City	
10435 2	Clapton Orient	
10360 1	Nottingham Forest	
10210 1	Bury	
9810 2	Bolton Wanderers	
9295 2	Leeds City	
9080 1	Preston North End	
8725 2	Derby County	
8515 2	Leicester Fosse	
8000 2	Hull City	
7715 2	Wolverhampton Wanderers	
7700 2	Burnley	
7110 2	Huddersfield Town	
5940 2	Blackpool	
5350 2	Lincoln City	
4700 2	Stockport County	
4680 2	Barnsley	
4300 2	Gainsborough Trinity	
3750 2	Glossop	

SEASON 1911–12

26295 2	**Chelsea**	
25030 1	**Tottenham Hotspur**	
24995 1	Newcastle United	
23655 1	Manchester City	
20710 1	Liverpool	
20480 1	Aston Villa	
19135 1	Bolton Wanderers	
19040 1	Manchester United	
18870 1	Everton	
17765 1	Blackburn Rovers	
17715 1	Bradford City	
17425 1	West Bromwich Albion	
14410 1	Sheffield Wednesday	
14215 1	Sheffield United	
14050 1	Middlesbrough	
14000 2	Burnley	
12960 2	Fulham	
12850 2	Bradford	
12745 2	Birmingham	
12555 1	Sunderland	
11800 1	Oldham Athletic	
11630 1	Woolwich Arsenal	
10985 1	Notts County	
10765 2	Wolverhampton Wanderers.	
10650 2	Clapton Orient	
10315 2	Derby County	
9365 2	Hull City	
9355 2	Nottingham Forest	
9265 2	Leicester Fosse	
9225 1	Preston North End	
9000 1	Bury	
7885 2	Leeds City	
7080 2	Bristol City	
6500 2	Stockport County	
6265 2	Barnsley	
6075 2	Huddersfield Town	
6045 2	Blackpool	
5250 2	Grimsby Town	
4325 2	Gainsborough Trinity	
2300 2	Glossop	

SEASON 1912–13

33555	**1**	**Chelsea**		12030	1	Notts County
26070	1	Aston Villa		11105	2	Bradford
24935	1	Newcastle United		10880	1	Oldham Athletic
23950	1	Manchester City		10675	1	Derby County
23865	1	Tottenham Hotspur		10005	2	Preston North End
23610	1	Manchester United		9835	2	Clapton Orient
22425	1	Liverpool		9395	1	Woolwich Arsenal
20920	1	Bolton Wanderers		8945	2	Bristol City
19945	1	Everton		8680	2	Wolverhampton Wanderers
18905	1	Sheffield Wednesday		8600	2	Lincoln City
18560	1	Blackburn Rovers		8290	2	Nottingham Forest
17940	1	Sunderland		7940	2	Leicester Fosse
16865	1	West Bromwich Albion		7885	2	Hull City
16035	**2**	**Birmingham**		6690	2	Barnsley
15785	1	Sheffield United		6375	2	Bury
14815	1	Bradford City		6145	2	Huddersfield Town
13405	2	Leeds City		5790	2	Grimsby Town
12970	2	Burnley		5695	2	Stockport County
12580	1	Middlesbrough		4410	2	Blackpool
12290	2	Fulham		2750	2	Glossop

SEASON 1913–14

37105	**1**	**Chelsea**		15845	2	Leeds City
28020	1	Tottenham Hotspur		14615	1	Middlesbrough
26805	1	Manchester City		14360	2	Fulham
25515	1	Manchester United		13155	1	Oldham Athletic
25350	1	Aston Villa		12970	2	Clapton Orient
25250	1	Everton		11945	2	Notts County
25055	1	Bolton Wanderers		10640	2	Wolverhampton Wanderers
24710	1	Newcastle United		10600	2	Bristol City
24315	1	Liverpool		9965	1	Derby County
22745	**2**	**Woolwich Arsenal**		9560	2	Hull City
22295	1	Blackburn Rovers		9365	2	Leicester Fosse
21820	1	Burnley		8440	2	Bury
21360	1	Sheffield Wednesday		8345	2	Grimsby Town
20865	1	Sunderland		8090	2	Nottingham Forest
20135	1	West Bromwich Albion		7800	2	Barnsley
19935	1	Sheffield United		7750	2	Lincoln City
17620	2	Birmingham		7000	2	Stockport County
17045	1	Bradford City		6880	2	Huddersfield Town
16265	1	Preston North End		6145	2	Blackpool
15995	2	Bradford		2670	2	Glossop

SEASON 1914–15

20205 1	**Manchester City**	
18540 1	Chelsea	
18530 1	Everton	
16805 1	Liverpool	
16120 1	Sheffield Wednesday	
14735 1	Sheffield United	
14545 1	Newcastle United	
13820 2	**Arsenal**	
13680 1	Aston Villa	
13580 1	Bolton Wanderers	
13365 1	Bradford City	
13270 1	Tottenham Hotspur	
13195 1	Bradford	
12740 1	Blackburn Rovers	
11950 1	Manchester United	
11825 2	Birmingham	
11415 1	Burnley	
10945 1	West Bromwich Albion	
10230 1	Sunderland	
9970 1	Notts County	

9060 1	Middlesbrough	
9045 1	Oldham Athletic	
8000 2	Preston North End	
7520 2	Wolverhampton Wanderers	
6900 2	Clapton Orient	
6835 2	Leeds City	
6570 2	Derby County	
6470 2	Fulham	
6455 2	Huddersfield Town	
6450 2	Bristol City	
5900 2	Grimsby Town	
5800 2	Nottingham Forest	
5625 2	Barnsley	
5000 2	Lincoln City	
4900 2	Bury	
4880 2	Hull City	
4850 2	Stockport County	
4235 2	Blackpool	
3600 2	Leicester Fosse	
1650 2	Glossop	

SEASON 1919–20

42615 1	**Chelsea**	
38390 1	Newcastle United	
34485 1	Arsenal	
34185 2	**Tottenham Hotspur**	
33500 1	Aston Villa	
29730 1	Liverpool	
29050 1	Everton	
29025 1	West Bromwich Albion	
26540 1	Manchester United	
25580 1	Sunderland	
25160 1	Manchester City	
24205 1	Sheffield United	
23715 2	Birmingham	
23300 1	Bolton Wanderers	
20930 1	Middlesbrough	
19530 1	Burnley	
19415 2	West Ham United	
18430 1	Sheffield Wednesday	
18110 1	Blackburn Rovers	
17200 1	Bradford City	
16875 2	Coventry City	
16215 1	Notts County	
15950 1	Preston North End	

14975 2	South Shields	
14530 2	Fulham	
14340 1	Bradford	
13940 2	Bristol City	
13725 1	Derby County	
13355 2	Leicester City	
13085 2	Clapton Orient	
12785 1	Oldham Athletic	
12780 2	Wolverhampton Wanderers	
12145 2	Stoke	
10880 2	Port Vale	
10150 2	Leeds City	
9735 2	Nottingham Forest	
9520 2	Hull City	
9310 2	Rotherham County	
9225 2	Bury	
9185 2	Huddersfield Town	
8790 2	Barnsley	
7475 2	Blackpool	
7420 2	Stockport County	
6675 2	Lincoln City	
6200 2	Grimsby Town	

41265 1	**Newcastle United**	
38520 1	Chelsea	
37215 1	Everton	
36010 1	Tottenham Hotspur	
35540 1	Arsenal	
35525 1	Manchester United	
35440 1	Liverpool	
35145 1	Aston Villa	
34400 1	Bolton Wanderers	
31535 1	Burnley	
31525 2	**Birmingham**	
31120 1	Manchester City	
28765 1	Sunderland	
28430 2	Cardiff City	
27930 1	Blackburn Rovers	
27915 1	West Bromwich Albion	
26920 1	Sheffield United	
23845 1	Middlesbrough	
22585 1	Bradford City	
22240 1	Huddersfield Town	
21310 1	Preston North End	
20870 2	West Ham United	
20745 2	Bristol City	
20545 2	Sheffield Wednesday	
20200 2	Wolverhampton Wanderers	
19185 2	Fulham	
18160 3	**Millwall**	
18075 1	Oldham Athletic	
17365 2	Coventry City	
17175 2	Leicester City	
16690 2	Clapton Orient	
16450 2	South Shields	
16275 2	Leeds United	

16235 1	Derby County	
16005 1	Bradford	
15490 2	Notts County	
15445 3	Portsmouth	
14430 3	Queens Park Rangers	
14000 2	Port Vale	
13885 3	Crystal Palace	
13465 3	Plymouth Argyle	
13370 3	Swansea Town	
13335 2	Nottingham Forest	
13315 2	Stoke	
12905 2	Rotherham County	
12835 2	Bury	
12585 3	Southampton	
12395 3	Bristol Rovers	
12300 3	Merthyr Town	
11370 2	Barnsley	
10245 2	Hull City	
9790 3	Grimsby Town	
9625 2	Blackpool	
9150 3	Luton Town	
9130 3	Swindon Town	
9010 3	Brighton & Hove Albion	
8905 2	Stockport County	
8760 3	Newport County	
8660 3	Brentford	
8600 3	Norwich City	
8450 3	Gillingham	
7240 3	Southend United	
7185 3	Reading	
7125 3	Northampton Town	
7125 3	Watford	
7050 3	Exeter City	

37545 1 Chelsea	11275 2 South Shields
36485 1 Tottenham Hotspur	**11050 3n Stockport County**
36105 1 Liverpool	10725 2 Derby County
34860 1 Newcastle United	10715 2 Rotherham County
32760 1 Cardiff City	10715 2 Port Vale
31700 1 Aston Villa	10500 2 Bradford
31175 1 Everton	10180 2 Hull City
29170 1 Arsenal	9835 2 Bury
28510 1 Manchester United	9810 2 Blackpool
26875 1 Birmingham	9525 3s Aberdare Athletic
25445 1 Sheffield United	9380 3s Charlton Athletic
25295 1 Bolton Wanderers	9115 3s Brentford
24200 1 Manchester City	8985 3s Merthyr Town
24150 1 Sunderland	8900 3s Gillingham
23640 1 Burnley	8850 3s Reading
23580 1 Blackburn Rovers	8750 3n Grimsby Town
23230 1 Middlesbrough	8650 3s Luton Town
22490 1 West Bromwich Albion	8275 3n Nelson
21815 1 Bradford City	8200 3n Halifax Town
20490 1 Preston North End	8070 3s Brighton & Hove Albion
20100 2 West Ham United	8000 3n Accrington Stanley
20005 2 Fulham	7885 3s Norwich City
17870 1 Huddersfield Town	7625 3n Wigan Borough
16680 1 Oldham Athletic	7600 3s Swindon Town
16650 3s Millwall	7550 3n Hartlepools United
15885 2 Leicester City	7400 3n Walsall
15315 2 Bristol City	7345 3s Newport County
15200 2 Stoke	7300 3n Darlington
14985 2 Coventry City	6825 3n Crewe Alexandra
14905 3s Plymouth Argyle	6785 3n Chesterfield
14650 2 Nottingham Forest	6725 3s Northampton Town
14345 2 Clapton Orient	6555 3s Southend United
14060 3s Portsmouth	6525 3n Tranmere Rovers
13855 2 Sheffield Wednesday	6145 3s Watford
13605 2 Wolverhampton Wanderers	5900 3n Wrexham
13570 2 Leeds United	5810 3s Exeter City
12335 2 Crystal Palace	5675 3n Barrow
12215 2 Notts County	5250 3n Stalybridge Celtic
11760 2 Barnsley	5075 3n Southport
11685 3s Swansea Town	5050 3n Ashington
11585 3s Bristol Rovers	4825 3n Lincoln City
11550 3s Queens Park Rangers	4550 3n Rochdale
11385 3s Southampton	2600 3n Durham City

33495 1	**Liverpool**	10700 3s	Bristol Rovers
31425 1	Tottenham Hotspur	10640 2	Barnsley
30905 1	Everton	10600 2	Derby County
30245 1	Arsenal	**10525 3n**	**Halifax Town**
30000 1	Chelsea	10315 3s	Queens Park Rangers
28550 1	Aston Villa	10155 3n	Wigan Borough
27475 1	Cardiff City	10080 3n	Bradford
27470 1	Birmingham	9980 2	Rotherham County
27085 1	Newcastle United	9885 2	Port Vale
23850 1	Manchester City	9210 2	Hull City
23070 1	Sunderland	9080 3s	Brighton & Hove Albion
22955 2	**Manchester United**	8665 3n	Chesterfield
21870 1	Bolton Wanderers	8595 3s	Luton Town
20145 1	Sheffield United	8495 2	South Shields
19845 2	Fulham	8445 3n	Grimsby Town
19450 1	Stoke	8350 3s	Norwich City
19065 1	Preston North End	8350 3s	Brentford
19040 2	Leicester City	8250 3s	Northampton Town
18855 2	West Ham United	8165 3s	Charlton Athletic
18755 1	Blackburn Rovers	7900 3s	Newport County
18315 1	West Bromwich Albion	7715 3s	Southend United
17855 1	Middlesbrough	7465 3s	Aberdare Athletic
16885 1	Burnley	7440 3n	Accrington Stanley
16690 2	Sheffield Wednesday	7225 3s	Watford
16480 3s	**Bristol City**	7095 3n	Nelson
15930 1	Nottingham Forest	7000 3s	Reading
15815 3s	Millwall	6440 3s	Swindon Town
15050 3s	Swansea Town	6440 3n	Walsall
15015 2	Clapton Orient	6280 3s	Gillingham
14885 1	Huddersfield Town	5935 3s	Exeter City
14190 2	Coventry City	5680 3n	Crewe Alexandra
13965 1	Oldham Athletic	5665 3n	Wrexham
13690 2	Bradford City	5655 3n	Tranmere Rovers
13310 2	Notts County	5460 3n	Rochdale
13135 2	Leeds United	5265 3s	Merthyr Town
12645 2	Southampton	5250 3n	Southport
12515 2	Wolverhampton Wanderers	4430 3n	Lincoln City
12440 2	Stockport County	4375 3n	Hartlepools United
12195 3s	Portsmouth	4300 3n	Ashington
11690 2	Blackpool	4045 3n	Darlington
11250 3s	Plymouth Argyle	3745 3n	Barrow
10880 2	Bury	3465 3n	Stalybridge Celtic
10720 2	Crystal Palace	2070 3n	Durham City

30895 1 Chelsea		
29950 1 Arsenal		
29185 1 Everton		
28420 1 Tottenham Hotspur		
28390 1 Liverpool		
28315 1 Aston Villa		
27145 1 Manchester City		
26920 1 Cardiff City		
26865 1 Newcastle United		
23475 1 Sunderland		
22580 1 Birmingham		
22080 1 West Ham United		
21740 1 Sheffield United		
21125 2 Manchester United		
20290 1 Bolton Wanderers		
18520 1 Blackburn Rovers		
18290 1 West Bromwich Albion		
17395 1 Huddersfield Town		
17335 2 Leicester City		
17285 1 Middlesbrough		
16870 2 Clapton Orient		
16765 3s Millwall		
16300 1 Preston North End		
16130 2 Sheffield Wednesday		
15335 1 Notts County		
15225 2 Fulham		
14995 2 Leeds United		
14890 1 Burnley		
14870 3s Swansea Town		
14515 3n Wolverhampton Wanderers		
14130 1 Nottingham Forest		
13745 2 Bradford City		
13680 2 Coventry City		
13270 2 Derby County		
12770 3s Portsmouth		
12285 2 Bristol City		
12275 2 Bury		
11765 2 Stoke		
11645 2 Blackpool		
11515 2 Stockport County		
10895 3s Plymouth Argyle		
10420 2 Southampton		
10365 2 Oldham Athletic		
10200 3s Queens Park Rangers		

10015 2 Port Vale
9945 2 Barnsley
9825 2 Crystal Palace
9425 3s Northampton Town
9300 3n Chesterfield
9255 3s Bristol Rovers
8925 2 Hull City
8855 2 South Shields
8795 2 Nelson
8555 3s Brighton & Hove Albion
8220 3s Reading
8210 3s Luton Town
8130 3s Norwich City
8000 3s Newport County
7800 3n Rotherham County
7620 3n Wigan Borough
7590 3n Grimsby Town
7300 3s Gillingham
7285 3n Doncaster Rovers
7280 3n Tranmere Rovers
7200 3s Swindon Town
6925 3s Merthyr Town
6915 3s Watford
6880 3n Bradford
6825 3s Brentford
6785 3s Southend United
6745 3s Charlton Athletic
6640 3n Wrexham
6570 3s Aberdare Athletic
6425 3n New Brighton
6255 3n Rochdale
6250 3s Bournemouth & B. Ath
5680 3s Exeter City
5660 3n Accrington Stanley
5570 3n Halifax Town
5315 3n Southport
5220 3n Lincoln City
5150 3n Ashington
5075 3n Walsall
4945 3n Darlington
4885 3n Crewe Alexandra
3965 3n Durham City
3870 3n Hartlepools United
3320 3n Barrow

29485 1 Arsenal	9750 3s	Charlton Athletic
29185 1 Liverpool	9635 2	Southampton
28975 2 Chelsea	9600 3s	Newport County
28195 1 Tottenham Hotspur	9595 2	Oldham Athletic
27995 2 Manchester United	9540 3s	Bristol Rovers
27965 1 Aston Villa	9035 2	South Shields
26915 1 Manchester City	9020 2	Hull City
26030 1 Everton	8925 2	Barnsley
24325 1 Newcastle United	8400 3s	Reading
22935 1 Bolton Wanderers	**8050 3n**	**Bradford**
22780 1 Birmingham	7900 3s	Brighton & Hove Albion
22715 1 Leeds United	7800 3s	Southend United
21630 1 Cardiff City	7500 3s	Luton Town
21115 1 West Bromwich Albion	7400 3s	Northampton Town
20970 1 Sheffield United	7370 3s	Norwich City
20885 1 West Ham United	7285 3n	Chesterfield
20455 2 Leicester City	7260 3n	Wigan Borough
20440 1 Sunderland	7010 3s	Brentford
19500 1 Bury	6800 3n	Lincoln City
17670 1 Huddersfield Town	6645 3n	Halifax Town
16685 2 Portsmouth	6630 3s	Exeter City
16655 2 Clapton Orient	6600 3s	Swindon Town
16375 2 Fulham	6400 3s	Aberdare Athletic
16340 1 Blackburn Rovers	6315 3n	Grimsby Town
16310 2 Derby County	6210 3n	Nelson
15890 1 Burnley	6100 3s	Watford
15630 1 Preston North End	5965 3n	New Brighton
15515 2 Wolverhampton Wanderers	5900 3s	Gillingham
15000 3s Millwall	5875 3n	Crewe Alexandra
14950 2 Sheffield Wednesday	5715 3n	Darlington
14250 2 Crystal Palace	5530 3n	Wrexham
13895 2 Middlesbrough	5475 3n	Tranmere Rovers
13350 1 Notts County	5380 3n	Doncaster Rovers
12775 2 Bradford City	5250 3s	Bournemouth & B. Ath.
12600 3s Swansea Town	5150 3n	Southport
12300 3s Plymouth Argyle	5110 3n	Accrington Stanley
12080 2 Stockport County	5060 3n	Rotherham County
11450 1 Nottingham Forest	5055 3n	Rochdale
11295 2 Coventry City	4810 3n	Walsall
11030 2 Stoke	4405 3n	Hartlepools United
11025 3s Bristol City	4300 3n	Barrow
10750 2 Blackpool	4200 3s	Merthyr Town
10700 2 Port Vale	3870 3n	Ashington
9900 3s Queens Park Rangers	2925 3n	Durham City

32355 2 Chelsea		9505 3n Coventry City
31614 1 Manchester City		9418 3n Grimsby Town
31471 1 Arsenal		9146 3s Brentford
29957 1 Newcastle United		9052 2 Darlington
27806 1 Tottenham Hotspur		8966 2 Nottingham Forest
27647 1 Manchester United		8612 3s Bristol Rovers
27240 1 Liverpool		8380 2 Hull City
26876 1 Everton		8109 3s Brighton & Hove Albion
26496 1 Aston Villa		8086 2 Stockport County
24692 1 Leicester City		8044 2 Barnsley
23661 2 Sheffield Wednesday		7545 3s Queens Park Rangers
21399 1 Sunderland		7515 3s Luton Town
21382 1 Leeds United		7427 3s Southend United
20437 1 Bolton Wanderers		7403 3s Charlton Athletic
20040 1 West Ham United		7325 2 South Shields
19569 1 Huddersfield Town		7036 3s Norwich City
19245 1 Sheffield United		6978 3s Northampton Town
19084 1 Birmingham		6808 3s Watford
17968 1 West Bromwich Albion		6653 3n Tranmere Rovers
17946 1 Cardiff City		6630 3s Swindon Town
17857 1 Burnley		6487 3n Nelson
17775 1 Blackburn Rovers		6334 3s Exeter City
16594 2 Fulham		6293 3s Gillingham
16314 2 Derby County		6030 3n Rochdale
16118 2 Swansea Town		5977 3s Newport County
15728 1 Bury		5967 3n Halifax Town
14952 3s Millwall		5910 3s Merthyr Town
14908 1 Notts County		5811 3n Wrexham
14705 2 Preston North End		5719 3n Chesterfield
14457 2 Portsmouth		5416 3n Rotherham United
14322 2 Wolverhampton Wanderers		5388 3s Bournemouth & B. Ath.
13728 3s Plymouth Argyle		5376 3n Wigan Borough
13259 2 Middlesbrough		5344 3n Lincoln City
12843 3n Bradford		5190 3n Doncaster Rovers
12767 3s Crystal Palace		4981 3n Crewe Alexandra
12765 3s Reading		4908 3n New Brighton
12757 2 Clapton Orient		4815 3s Aberdare Athletic
12144 2 Stoke City		4501 3n Hartlepools United
11962 3s Bristol City		4266 3n Southport
11959 2 Oldham Athletic		4248 3n Accrington Stanley
11833 2 Bradford City		3873 3n Ashington
10747 2 Port Vale		3368 3n Walsall
10606 2 Blackpool		2756 3n Barrow
9965 2 Southampton		2617 3n Durham City

36510	**1**	**Newcastle United**	
31416	1	Everton	
30848	**2**	**Manchester City**	
30054	1	Arsenal	
29861	2	Chelsea	
28502	1	Liverpool	
27393	1	Aston Villa	
26594	1	Tottenham Hotspur	
26138	1	Manchester United	
23718	1	Leicester City	
23061	1	Sheffield Wednesday	
22547	1	Sheffield United	
22030	1	Birmingham	
21828	2	Middlesbrough	
21603	1	Bolton Wanderers	
20666	1	Leeds United	
19536	1	Huddersfield Town	
19422	1	Burnley	
19396	1	Derby County	
18891	1	Blackburn Rovers	
18755	1	West Bromwich Albion	
18142	1	Sunderland	
18136	1	West Ham United	
17152	2	Preston North End	
16792	2	Portsmouth	
16360	**3s**	**Bristol City**	
16202	2	Fulham	
15447	1	Bury	
15424	1	Cardiff City	
14286	2	Swansea Town	
14173	3s	Millwall	
13389	2	Reading	
12929	2	Clapton Orient	
12764	2	Nottingham Forest	
12595	2	Bradford City	
12558	2	Grimsby Town	
12555	2	Oldham Athletic	
12246	2	Wolverhampton Wanderers	
11645	3s	Crystal Palace	
11302	2	Hull City	
10849	3s	Plymouth Argyle	
10736	2	Port Vale	
10507	**3n**	**Bradford**	
10498	2	Blackpool	
10311	3n	Stoke City	
10274	3s	Coventry City	
9837	2	Southampton	
9825	2	Notts County	
9713	3s	Brentford	
9551	3s	Brighton & Hove Albion	
9076	3s	Queens Park Rangers	
8998	3n	Stockport County	
8505	2	Barnsley	
8307	2	Darlington	
8274	3s	Swindon Town	
8145	3s	Bristol Rovers	
7817	3s	Luton Town	
7594	3n	Halifax Town	
7458	3s	Norwich City	
7201	3s	Exeter City	
7109	3s	Southend United	
6951	3s	Charlton Athletic	
6894	3s	Watford	
6668	3n	Tranmere Rovers	
6181	3n	Rochdale	
6053	3s	Northampton Town	
5952	3n	Nelson	
5890	3n	Chesterfield	
5453	3s	Bournemouth & B. Ath.	
5361	2	South Shields	
5334	3n	Doncaster Rovers	
5193	3s	Newport County	
5192	3n	Crewe Alexandra	
5080	3n	New Brighton	
5057	3n	Lincoln City	
4974	3s	Gillingham	
4728	3n	Walsall	
4703	3n	Wrexham	
4336	3n	Barrow	
4292	3n	Rotherham United	
4146	3n	Southport	
4100	3n	Accrington Stanley	
4037	3n	Wigan Borough	
3170	3s	Merthyr Town	
3020	3n	Hartlepools United	
2499	3s	Aberdare Athletic	
2328	3n	Ashington	
1814	3n	Durham City	

37468	**2**	**Manchester City**	
37461	**1**	**Everton**	
33546	2	Chelsea	
32505	1	Aston Villa	
30195	1	Newcastle United	
29975	1	Liverpool	
27434	1	Arsenal	
25555	1	Manchester United	
24758	1	Leicester City	
22752	1	Portsmouth	
22632	1	Middlesbrough	
22075	1	Sheffield Wednesday	
21928	1	Tottenham Hotspur	
21829	2	Leeds United	
21419	1	West Ham United	
21411	1	Sunderland	
21217	1	Birmingham	
19482	1	Sheffield United	
19383	1	Bolton Wanderers	
19306	1	Huddersfield Town	
19120	1	Blackburn Rovers	
17677	**3s**	**Millwall**	
17537	2	Preston North End	
17408	1	Burnley	
17381	2	West Bromwich Albion	
16243	1	Derby County	
16121	2	Fulham	
15845	2	Bristol City	
15608	1	Bury	
15607	1	Cardiff City	
15298	2	Wolverhampton Wanderers	
14395	2	Stoke City	
13893	2	Oldham Athletic	
13514	**3n**	**Bradford**	
13262	2	Clapton Orient	
12180	3n	Bradford City	
12153	2	Swansea Town	
11421	2	Blackpool	
11237	2	Grimsby Town	
11215	2	Reading	
11121	2	Port Vale	
11065	2	Notts County	
10946	3s	Crystal Palace	
10478	2	Nottingham Forest	

10407	3s	Queens Park Rangers
10177	2	Southampton
10095	3s	Northampton Town
9994	3s	Plymouth Argyle
9388	3s	Coventry City
9049	2	Hull City
8734	3s	Charlton Athletic
8418	3n	Stockport County
8352	2	Barnsley
8233	3s	Norwich City
7630	3s	Brighton & Hove Albion
7574	3n	Doncaster Rovers
7530	3s	Luton Town
7331	3s	Brentford
7193	3s	Watford
6876	3s	Exeter City
6843	3s	Bristol Rovers
6685	3s	Swindon Town
6580	3s	Walsall
6401	3n	Halifax Town
6201	3n	Lincoln City
6128	3s	Southend United
5893	3n	Tranmere Rovers
5386	3n	Barrow
5379	2	South Shields
5290	3s	Bournemouth & B. Ath.
4990	3n	Darlington
4881	3s	Gillingham
4741	3n	Accrington Stanley
4603	3n	Rotherham United
4533	3s	Newport County
4252	3n	Wrexham
4222	3n	Rochdale
4175	3s	Torquay United
4012	3n	New Brighton
3964	3n	Nelson
3932	3n	Crewe Alexandra
3918	3n	Chesterfield
3784	3n	Southport
3630	3n	Wigan Borough
3563	3n	Hartlepools United
2745	3s	Merthyr Town
2176	3n	Ashington
1759	3n	Durham City

31715 1	**Manchester City**	11636 2	Blackpool
31667 1	Newcastle United	11478 3s	Charlton Athletic
29583 1	Aston Villa	11201 2	Swansea Town
29513 1	Everton	10658 3s	Plymouth Argyle
28257 1	Liverpool	10208 2	Port Vale
28017 2	**Chelsea**	10131 3s	Northampton Town
27113 1	Sheffield Wednesday	10090 3s	Luton Town
26690 1	Arsenal	10065 2	Hull City
25196 1	Sunderland	9712 3s	Watford
24414 2	Tottenham Hotspur	9495 2	Nottingham Forest
23773 1	Leicester City	8159 3s	Brentford
23659 1	Manchester United	7846 2	Barnsley
22402 1	Leeds United	7796 3n	Carlisle United
22395 1	Sheffield United	7549 3s	Bristol Rovers
20643 1	Birmingham	7245 3s	Norwich City
20308 2	Millwall	7055 3n	Wigan Borough
20225 1	Portsmouth	6941 3n	Wrexham
19989 1	West Ham United	6871 3s	Brighton & Hove Albion
19419 1	Bolton Wanderers	6733 3n	Doncaster Rovers
18724 2	Middlesbrough	6527 3s	Walsall
18551 3n	**Bradford City**	6128 3n	Lincoln City
18250 3s	**Fulham**	6039 3n	Barrow
17240 2	Bradford	5960 3s	Southend United
17239 1	Burnley	5743 3s	Exeter City
16866 1	Derby County	5554 3s	Bournemouth & B. Ath.
16841 1	Blackburn Rovers	5455 3s	Swindon Town
16720 1	Huddersfield Town	5355 3n	Rochdale
15584 3s	Crystal Palace	5298 3n	Halifax Town
15256 1	Cardiff City	5125 3n	Tranmere Rovers
15211 2	Preston North End	4944 3n	Nelson
15090 2	Notts County	4919 3s	Torquay United
14875 2	Southampton	4710 3n	South Shields
14507 1	Bury	4660 3n	Rotherham United
14371 2	Bristol City	4610 3s	Gillingham
14353 3s	Coventry City	4398 3n	Accrington Stanley
14086 2	Wolverhampton Wanderers	4312 3n	New Brighton
13666 2	Stoke City	4100 3n	Chesterfield
13487 3s	Queens Park Rangers	4034 3n	Southport
13206 2	Oldham Athletic	4029 3s	Newport County
13182 2	West Bromwich Albion	4026 3n	Crewe Alexandra
12295 2	Grimsby Town	3691 3n	Darlington
12172 2	Clapton Orient	3360 3n	Hartlepools United
11947 3n	Stockport County	3154 3s	Merthyr Town
11639 2	Reading	1666 3n	Ashington

35537	**1**	**Arsenal**	11201	2	Bristol City
33339	1	Manchester City	10960	3s	Queens Park Rangers
32989	1	Everton	10435	2	Bury
32559	1	Newcastle United	9967	3s	Clapton Orient
30219	1	Liverpool	9904	3s	Norwich City
27799	**2**	**Chelsea**	**9542**	**3n**	**Stockport County**
27726	1	Aston Villa	9176	3n	Port Vale
25588	1	Sheffield Wednesday	8993	2	Nottingham Forest
24553	1	Sunderland	8833	3s	Northampton Town
21834	2	Tottenham Hotspur	8477	3s	Brighton & Hove Albion
21344	1	Leicester City	8227	3s	Watford
20398	1	Birmingham	7771	2	Hull City
20127	1	West Ham United	7612	3s	Luton Town
19916	1	Leeds United	7169	3s	Bristol Rovers
19711	1	Sheffield United	6921	2	Barnsley
19172	1	Middlesbrough	6821	3s	Southend United
18714	1	Blackburn Rovers	6592	3s	Exeter City
18685	2	Millwall	6271	3s	Bournemouth & B. Ath.
18599	1	Manchester United	6060	3n	Carlisle United
18495	1	Portsmouth	5607	3s	Walsall
18047	1	Bolton Wanderers	5421	3s	Swindon Town
17694	2	Oldham Athletic	5259	3n	Lincoln City
16366	2	Bradford City	5247	3n	York City
15977	1	Derby County	5049	3s	Gillingham
15767	1	Huddersfield Town	4828	3n	Crewe Alexandra
15489	**3s**	**Fulham**	4751	3n	Chesterfield
15233	3s	Plymouth Argyle	4709	3n	Hartlepools United
14726	1	Burnley	4708	3n	Wrexham
14724	1	Grimsby Town	4652	3n	Doncaster Rovers
14484	2	Wolverhampton Wanderers	4632	3n	Tranmere Rovers
14056	2	Blackpool	4614	3n	Rotherham United
13921	2	Bradford	4512	3n	Barrow
13666	2	Charlton Athletic	4376	3n	Wigan Borough
13455	3s	Crystal Palace	4307	3n	New Brighton
13274	2	West Bromwich Albion	4271	3s	Torquay United
12985	3s	Coventry City	4237	3n	Darlington
12944	2	Cardiff City	4236	3n	Accrington Stanley
12123	3s	Brentford	3918	3s	Newport County
12101	2	Swansea Town	3797	3n	Halifax Town
12073	2	Southampton	3485	3n	Southport
11831	2	Reading	3440	3n	Rochdale
11523	2	Stoke City	3362	3n	Nelson
11415	2	Preston North End	3300	3n	South Shields
11333	2	Notts County	2503	3s	Merthyr Town

37106 1	**Arsenal**	8813 2	Bury
35808 1	Chelsea	8785 3s	Queens Park Rangers
30781 1	Aston Villa	8337 3s	Norwich City
28148 2	**Tottenham Hotspur**	8267 2	Cardiff City
26849 1	Manchester City	8264 2	Nottingham Forest
26151 1	Newcastle United	8236 3s	Brentford
26086 1	Liverpool	7846 3s	Northampton Town
26039 2	Everton	**7737 3n**	**Lincoln City**
22015 1	Sunderland	7358 3n	Tranmere Rovers
19911 1	Sheffield Wednesday	7119 3s	Brighton & Hove Albion
19816 2	West Bromwich Albion	6937 3n	Stockport County
19469 1	Sheffield United	6860 2	Barnsley
19262 2	Plymouth Argyle	6718 3s	Luton Town
19135 1	Birmingham	6607 3s	Bristol Rovers
18779 1	Portsmouth	6550 3n	Hull City
18505 1	West Ham United	6447 3s	Watford
17108 1	Blackpool	6275 3n	Chesterfield
17075 1	Leicester City	6008 3n	Wrexham
16860 1	Middlesbrough	5938 3n	Gateshead
15701 1	Blackburn Rovers	5838 3n	Carlisle United
15701 1	Bolton Wanderers	5804 3s	Southend United
15040 1	Derby County	5669 3n	Barrow
14689 2	Millwall	5471 3s	Clapton Orient
14195 2	Bradford City	5417 3n	Wigan Borough
13929 1	Huddersfield Town	5375 3s	Bournemouth & B. Ath.
13631 2	Bristol City	5322 3n	Rotherham United
13385 1	Leeds United	5291 3n	Halifax Town
13181 3s	**Crystal Palace**	5091 3s	Walsall
13082 1	Grimsby Town	5030 3s	Gillingham
12702 2	Preston North End	4950 3s	Exeter City
12257 3s	Notts County	4911 3s	Swindon Town
12150 2	Southampton	4373 3s	Torquay United
11685 1	Manchester United	4176 3n	Doncaster Rovers
11493 2	Burnley	3906 3n	York City
11434 2	Stoke City	3478 3n	Southport
11313 2	Oldham Athletic	3438 3n	Hartlepools United
11051 2	Bradford	3382 3n	New Brighton
10875 2	Charlton Athletic	3340 3n	Darlington
10825 3s	Fulham	3338 3n	Crewe Alexandra
10506 2	Swansea Town	3191 3n	Accrington Stanley
10442 2	Port Vale	3162 3n	Rochdale
10426 2	Wolverhampton Wanderers	2840 3s	Newport County
10327 3s	Coventry City	2375 3n	Nelson
9318 2	Reading	2315 3s	Thames

40547 1	**Arsenal**	
35451 1	Everton	
32230 1	Chelsea	
31509 1	Aston Villa	
30366 1	Newcastle United	
24459 1	West Bromwich Albion	
24173 1	Manchester City	
23131 1	Sunderland	
22809 2	**Tottenham Hotspur**	
22742 1	Liverpool	
21241 2	Wolverhampton Wanderers	
20795 1	Sheffield United	
19627 1	Birmingham	
19520 2	Plymouth Argyle	
19239 1	West Ham United	
17647 3s	**Fulham**	
17478 1	Portsmouth	
17478 1	Blackpool	
17145 1	Sheffield Wednesday	
16241 1	Leicester City	
15843 1	Bolton Wanderers	
15132 3s	Crystal Palace	
15025 2	Millwall	
14079 2	Leeds United	
14059 2	Bradford City	
13890 1	Middlesbrough	
13303 3s	Queens Park Rangers	
13176 1	Blackburn Rovers	
13142 1	Derby County	
13011 2	Manchester United	
13010 1	Huddersfield Town	
12978 2	Bradford	
12278 2	Stoke City	
12235 3s	Coventry City	
11968 1	Grimsby Town	
11965 2	Notts County	
11929 2	Charlton Athletic	
11347 3s	Brentford	
10892 3s	Norwich City	
10880 2	Southampton	
10473 2	Chesterfield	
9756 2	Swansea Town	
9752 2	Nottingham Forest	
9666 2	Preston North End	

9629 3s	Reading	
9550 2	Port Vale	
8594 2	Bury	
8579 3n	**Lincoln City**	
8410 2	Burnley	
8389 2	Oldham Athletic	
8372 3s	Watford	
8120 3s	Brighton & Hove Albion	
8061 2	Bristol City	
7986 3s	Southend United	
7952 3n	Chester	
7943 3n	Gateshead	
7684 3s	Cardiff City	
7593 3s	Clapton Orient	
7330 3s	Mansfield Town	
7279 3s	Bristol Rovers	
7027 3s	Luton Town	
6695 3n	Hull City	
6535 3s	Northampton Town	
6413 3n	Wrexham	
6257 2	Barnsley	
6257 3s	Exeter City	
6002 3n	Crewe Alexandra	
5856 3n	Tranmere Rovers	
5811 3n	Barrow	
5747 3s	Bournemouth & B. Ath.	
5357 3s	Gillingham	
5147 3n	Stockport County	
5027 3s	Swindon Town	
4980 3n	Southport	
4689 3n	Carlisle United	
4330 3n	York City	
4195 3n	Halifax Town	
4064 3n	Rotherham United	
3960 3n	Hartlepools United	
3903 3n	Doncaster Rovers	
3718 3s	Torquay United	
3521 3n	Accrington Stanley	
3490 3n	Walsall	
3205 3n	Darlington	
3132 3n	Wigan Borough	
3070 3n	Rochdale	
2913 3n	New Brighton	
2623 3s	Thames	

41958 1 Arsenal	9480 2	Chesterfield
33205 2 Tottenham Hotspur	9406 2	Bury
32249 1 Aston Villa	9401 2	Burnley
31485 1 Chelsea	9064 2	Southampton
27104 1 Wolverhampton Wanderers	8876 2	Port Vale
26412 1 Everton	8636 3s	Bristol City
25992 1 Newcastle United	8357 2	Grimsby Town
24254 1 Manchester City	8254 2	Oldham Athletic
23382 1 Liverpool	8136 3n	Chester
22792 1 West Bromwich Albion	7707 3s	Queens Park Rangers
21336 2 Fulham	7665 3s	Exeter City
20149 2 Manchester United	7410 3n	Wrexham
18102 1 Portsmouth	7297 3s	Watford
17465 2 Plymouth Argyle	7008 3s	Cardiff City
17254 1 Sunderland	6597 3s	Gillingham
17114 1 Leeds United	6361 3s	Brighton & Hove Albion
16894 1 Birmingham	6083 3s	Southend United
16822 1 Leicester City	6064 3s	Clapton Orient
16704 1 Sheffield Wednesday	6056 3s	Northampton Town
16324 1 Blackpool	5824 3s	Luton Town
16244 2 West Ham United	5522 3n	Mansfield Town
15858 2 Stoke City	5279 3n	Walsall
15047 1 Derby County	5262 3n	Doncaster Rovers
14622 2 Bradford City	5210 3n	Stockport County
14296 1 Sheffield United	5210 3n	Carlisle United
13807 2 Millwall	5140 3s	Aldershot
13300 3s Brentford	5115 3n	Barnsley
13203 1 Bolton Wanderers	4954 3n	Halifax Town
12944 1 Blackburn Rovers	4920 3n	Crewe Alexandra
12938 2 Charlton Athletic	4905 3s	Swindon Town
12479 3s Coventry City	4822 3s	Bournemouth & B. Ath.
12157 1 Middlesbrough	4669 3n	Rochdale
11965 1 Huddersfield Town	4401 3s	Newport County
11015 2 Notts County	4382 3n	Gateshead
10930 3s Norwich City	4348 3n	York City
10877 3s Crystal Palace	4200 3n	Tranmere Rovers
10553 2 Bradford	4115 3n	Southport
10221 2 Preston North End	3991 3s	Torquay United
10184 2 Nottingham Forest	3931 3s	Rotherham United
10097 3n Hull City	3835 3n	Barrow
9984 3s Bristol Rovers	3740 3n	Hartlepools United
9840 3s Reading	3267 3n	New Brighton
9758 2 Lincoln City	2933 3n	Accrington Stanley
9566 2 Swansea Town	2520 3n	Darlington

40750 1	**Arsenal**	10051	2	Port Vale
33730 1	Tottenham Hotspur	10022	3s	Queens Park Rangers
30557 1	Aston Villa	9979	2	Southampton
30058 1	Manchester City	9912	3s	Reading
29429 1	Liverpool	9761	3n	Barnsley
29183 1	Chelsea	9616	2	Bury
27165 1	Everton	9147	3s	Bristol City
24681 1	Wolverhampton Wanderers	9119	3s	Clapton Orient
24142 1	Newcastle United	9114	3s	Swindon Town
23087 1	Stoke City	8944	3n	Stockport County
22197 1	Birmingham	8824	2	Oldham Athletic
20102 1	West Bromwich Albion	8204	2	Swansea Town
18666 1	Derby County	7959	3s	Cardiff City
18464 2	**West Ham United**	7941	3s	Luton Town
18349 1	Leicester City	7154	3n	Halifax Town
18338 2	Manchester United	7039	2	Lincoln City
18269 1	Sunderland	6609	3n	Chester
18243 1	Portsmouth	6602	3s	Watford
16723 2	Fulham	6338	3s	Brighton & Hove Albion
16377 2	Brentford	6271	3s	Northampton Town
16309 2	Blackpool	6228	3n	Walsall
16020 1	Sheffield Wednesday	6066	3s	Newport County
15926 2	Plymouth Argyle	6000	3n	Doncaster Rovers
15901 1	Sheffield United	5916	3s	Exeter City
15429 1	Leeds United	5896	3s	Gillingham
14978 2	Preston North End	5866	3s	Southend United
14515 1	Huddersfield Town	5840	3n	Wrexham
14093 3s	**Coventry City**	5305	3s	Bournemouth & B. Ath.
14091 2	Millwall	5156	3n	Mansfield Town
14005 1	Blackburn Rovers	4926	3n	Tranmere Rovers
13767 2	Bolton Wanderers	4561	3n	Barrow
13586 3s	Norwich City	4542	3s	Aldershot
12634 1	Middlesbrough	4452	3n	Carlisle United
11826 2	Notts County	4361	3n	York City
11403 2	Burnley	4213	3n	Rotherham United
11358 3s	Bristol Rovers	4186	3n	Crewe Alexandra
11129 2	Bradford	4001	3n	New Brighton
11040 2	Bradford City	3823	3n	Rochdale
10996 3s	Crystal Palace	3687	3n	Hartlepools United
10852 2	Grimsby Town	3606	3n	Darlington
10574 3n	**Chesterfield**	3352	3s	Torquay United
10574 3s	Charlton Athletic	3218	3n	Gateshead
10562 2	Hull City	2989	3n	Accrington Stanley
10192 2	Nottingham Forest	2889	3n	Southport

46252 1 Arsenal	9088 2 Southampton
34824 1 Manchester City	8882 3n Halifax Town
34389 1 Tottenham Hotspur	8870 3s Bristol City
33241 1 Aston Villa	8869 2 Barnsley
32342 1 Chelsea	8758 2 Bradford
26232 1 Everton	8685 3s Luton Town
25397 1 Sunderland	8652 3s Clapton Orient
25198 1 Liverpool	8588 2 Bradford City
23734 2 West Ham United	8463 2 Port Vale
23729 1 Wolverhampton Wanderers	8332 2 Swansea Town
22871 2 Manchester United	7934 2 Hull City
22349 1 Stoke City	7734 3s Watford
22277 1 West Bromwich Albion	7576 2 Oldham Athletic
21790 1 Birmingham	7362 3n Tranmere Rovers
21472 1 Preston North End	7352 3n Stockport County
20342 2 Bolton Wanderers	7344 3s Queens Park Rangers
20081 2 Newcastle United	7304 3s Swindon Town
19251 1 Derby County	6967 3n Chester
18568 1 Sheffield Wednesday	6729 3s Southend United
18062 2 Brentford	6570 3s Brighton & Hove Albion
17995 1 Portsmouth	6420 3s Northampton Town
17994 1 Leicester City	6381 3n Rotherham United
17160 2 Fulham	5645 3n Walsall
15713 3s Charlton Athletic	5614 3n Mansfield Town
15702 2 Blackpool	5524 3n Wrexham
15060 3s Coventry City	5375 3s Bournemouth & B. Ath.
15024 1 Huddersfield Town	5289 3s Gillingham
14927 1 Leeds United	5227 3n Lincoln City
14376 1 Middlesbrough	5186 3s Newport County
14166 2 Sheffield United	5053 3n Chesterfield
13787 2 Plymouth Argyle	5009 3s Exeter City
13706 1 Grimsby Town	4593 3n Rochdale
13357 3s Crystal Palace	4554 3n Darlington
13353 2 Norwich City	4196 3n Crewe Alexandra
13166 1 Blackburn Rovers	4105 3s Aldershot
12018 2 Nottingham Forest	4063 3n Carlisle United
11021 3s Millwall	3902 3n York City
10980 2 Notts County	3859 3n Barrow
10825 2 Burnley	3455 3n New Brighton
10761 3n Doncaster Rovers	3442 3s Torquay United
9908 3s Cardiff City	3256 3n Gateshead
9499 2 Bury	3114 3n Hartlepools United
9345 3s Reading	2785 3n Accrington Stanley
9302 3s Bristol Rovers	2500 3n Southport

41960 1 Arsenal	9811	3s Reading
40864 1 Aston Villa	9671	3s Bristol City
34977 1 Chelsea	9528	3s Cardiff City
33577 1 Manchester City	9241	2 Bury
33183 2 Tottenham Hotspur	8966	2 Swansea Town
30378 1 Sunderland	**8872**	**3n Tranmere Rovers**
29118 1 Everton	8716	2 Bradford City
27265 1 Liverpool	8401	3n Chesterfield
26868 1 Bolton Wanderers	8338	3s Watford
26070 2 Manchester United	8322	3s Bristol Rovers
25468 2 West Ham United	7787	2 Port Vale
25287 1 Brentford	7659	3s Brighton & Hove Albion
24824 1 Wolverhampton Wanderers	7586	3s Clapton Orient
24501 1 Birmingham	7320	3s Notts County
23110 1 West Bromwich Albion	7283	3s Southend United
22026 2 Charlton Athletic	7232	3s Bournemouth & B. Ath.
21586 1 Stoke City	7165	3n Stockport County
20932 1 Derby County	7101	3s Swindon Town
19511 1 Preston North End	7050	3s Northampton Town
19483 2 Newcastle United	6654	3n Chester
19358 1 Portsmouth	6551	3n Walsall
19232 3s Coventry City	6481	3n Carlisle United
18771 1 Middlesbrough	6343	3n Halifax Town
18617 1 Leeds United	6009	3s Gillingham
18428 2 Sheffield United	5926	3n Rotherham United
18128 1 Sheffield Wednesday	5892	3s Newport County
16605 2 Norwich City	5869	3n Oldham Athletic
16562 2 Fulham	5713	2 Hull City
16310 2 Plymouth Argyle	5405	3n Lincoln City
15498 1 Blackburn Rovers	5200	3s Exeter City
15126 2 Leicester City	5066	3n Wrexham
15097 1 Huddersfield Town	4882	3n Mansfield Town
14122 2 Doncaster Rovers	4827	3n Rochdale
13729 2 Blackpool	4487	3s Aldershot
12995 3s Luton Town	4290	3n Hartlepools United
12613 3s Crystal Palace	4157	3n Crewe Alexandra
11496 1 Grimsby Town	4048	3s Torquay United
11113 3s Queens Park Rangers	3926	3n Barrow
10707 2 Nottingham Forest	3721	3n York City
10705 2 Southampton	3637	3n Darlington
10565 3s Millwall	3578	3n Gateshead
10402 2 Burnley	3351	3n Accrington Stanley
9891 2 Barnsley	3184	3n New Brighton
9844 2 Bradford	2637	3n Southport

43353 1 Arsenal	11514 1 Grimsby Town
37537 2 Aston Villa	**11011 3n Stockport County**
35872 1 Manchester City	10870 3s Crystal Palace
32414 1 Chelsea	10667 3s Brighton & Hove Albion
32332 1 Manchester United	10579 3s Bristol Rovers
31086 1 Charlton Athletic	10422 2 Bradford
30292 1 Everton	10293 3s Queens Park Rangers
28670 1 Sunderland	10045 2 Bradford City
25342 2 Tottenham Hotspur	9960 3s Northampton Town
24544 1 Brentford	9880 2 Swansea Town
24430 2 Newcastle United	9686 3s Bristol City
23798 1 Liverpool	9237 3s Watford
23787 1 Wolverhampton Wanderers	9086 3s Reading
22991 1 Birmingham	8781 3s Newport County
22744 2 Coventry City	8455 3s Swindon Town
22518 1 Bolton Wanderers	8049 3s Southend United
22390 1 Middlesbrough	8036 3s Bournemouth & B. Ath.
22261 1 Stoke City	8027 3s Clapton Orient
21742 1 West Bromwich Albion	7828 3n Chester
21136 2 Sheffield United	7298 3n Port Vale
21078 2 Plymouth Argyle	7139 3n Lincoln City
20704 2 West Ham United	7061 3n Hull City
20475 1 Derby County	7004 3s Gillingham
20257 2 Leicester City	6488 3n Carlisle United
19692 1 Portsmouth	6433 3n Oldham Athletic
19530 1 Sheffield Wednesday	6264 3n Mansfield Town
19009 3s Millwall	5999 3n Tranmere Rovers
18199 1 Leeds United	5799 3n Halifax Town
18045 1 Preston North End	5740 3n Hartlepools United
17921 2 Blackpool	5672 3s Walsall
17457 2 Fulham	5493 3n Wrexham
16254 2 Nottingham Forest	5423 3s Exeter City
16010 2 Norwich City	5257 3n York City
15812 1 Huddersfield Town	5104 3n Southport
15644 3s Cardiff City	4669 3n Rochdale
15315 3s Luton Town	4396 3n New Brighton
14821 2 Blackburn Rovers	4378 3n Darlington
14129 3s Notts County	4353 3n Rotherham United
13139 2 Chesterfield	4037 3n Barrow
13025 2 Southampton	4018 3s Aldershot
12903 2 Bury	3875 3n Crewe Alexandra
12041 2 Burnley	3754 3s Torquay United
12039 2 Barnsley	3733 3n Accrington Stanley
11697 2 Doncaster Rovers	2835 3n Gateshead

44045 1 Arsenal	**12373 3n Doncaster Rovers**
41950 2 Aston Villa	12354 3s Notts County
33975 1 Chelsea	12288 1 Grimsby Town
32670 1 Manchester City	12015 2 Swansea Town
31032 1 Wolverhampton Wanderers	11804 2 Barnsley
30324 1 Everton	11270 3n Hull City
28336 1 Charlton Athletic	11116 2 Bradford
27682 1 Liverpool	10529 3s Watford
26633 2 Manchester United	10164 3s Brighton & Hove Albion
26101 2 Tottenham Hotspur	10120 2 Bury
25825 2 Coventry City	9640 3s Swindon Town
25132 1 Sunderland	9584 3n Tranmere Rovers
25012 1 Bolton Wanderers	9249 3s Newport County
24970 1 Stoke City	9214 3n Oldham Athletic
24544 1 Birmingham	9183 3n Gateshead
24260 1 Middlesbrough	8960 3s Reading
23335 1 Brentford	8359 3s Bristol Rovers
23207 1 West Bromwich Albion	7904 3n Lincoln City
23124 2 Sheffield Wednesday	7835 3s Clapton Orient
23004 2 West Ham United	7621 3n Rotherham United
22827 1 Portsmouth	7416 3s Northampton Town
22758 3s Millwall	7279 3s Southend United
22671 1 Preston North End	7241 3s Mansfield Town
21927 2 Sheffield United	7119 3s Bournemouth & B. Ath.
21276 2 Newcastle United	6713 3n Port Vale
21264 1 Blackpool	6408 3n Carlisle United
21256 1 Leeds United	6245 3s Exeter City
20402 1 Leicester City	6011 3n Bradford City
20009 3s Cardiff City	5957 3n York City
18449 2 Plymouth Argyle	5465 3s Gillingham
17288 1 Derby County	5417 3n Chester
17216 2 Fulham	5393 3n Halifax Town
17004 1 Huddersfield Town	5374 3n Rochdale
16917 3s Bristol City	5298 3s Aldershot
16583 2 Southampton	5218 3n Hartlepools United
16086 2 Norwich City	5059 3n Southport
15836 2 Luton Town	4875 3n Darlington
14818 2 Nottingham Forest	4844 3n Wrexham
14779 2 Blackburn Rovers	4564 3s Walsall
14399 2 Stockport County	4532 3n Barrow
13871 2 Chesterfield	4347 3n Crewe Alexandra
13799 3s Queens Park Rangers	4344 3n Accrington Stanley
13501 3s Crystal Palace	4223 3n New Brighton
13394 2 Burnley	3877 3s Torquay United

39932 1 Aston Villa	11587 3n Doncaster Rovers
39102 1 Arsenal	11448 3s Newport County
35040 1 Everton	10843 2 Swansea Town
32693 2 Newcastle United	10669 3s Queens Park Rangers
31422 1 Liverpool	10511 3s Swindon Town
31291 2 Manchester City	10430 3s Bristol City
30999 1 Chelsea	10410 3s Notts County
30365 1 Manchester United	10175 2 Bury
29397 2 Tottenham Hotspur	10005 2 Bradford
29328 1 Wolverhampton Wanderers	9938 2 Tranmere Rovers
27387 2 Millwall	8933 3n Stockport County
27147 2 Sheffield Wednesday	8392 3s Brighton & Hove Albion
26022 2 Sheffield United	8375 3s Reading
25528 1 Birmingham	8001 3s Northampton Town
25141 1 Charlton Athletic	7999 3s Bristol Rovers
23630 1 Portsmouth	7943 3s Clapton Orient
23117 1 Brentford	7587 3s Port Vale
23073 1 Bolton Wanderers	7539 3s Watford
22535 1 Stoke City	7364 3s Walsall
21740 1 Sunderland	7262 3n Rotherham United
21534 1 Preston North End	7079 3n Bradford City
21184 1 Middlesbrough	6828 3n Oldham Athletic
20135 2 West Ham United	6354 3n Barrow
19506 2 Coventry City	6327 3n Hull City
19309 1 Leeds United	6138 3s Aldershot
19178 1 Blackpool	6110 3n Rochdale
19101 1 Derby County	6055 3s Exeter City
18679 2 Fulham	5963 3n Chester
18400 2 West Bromwich Albion	5936 3s Bournemouth & B. Ath.
18262 2 Blackburn Rovers	5910 3s Southend United
16735 2 Plymouth Argyle	5862 3n Southport
16490 1 Huddersfield Town	5760 3n Crewe Alexandra
16225 1 Leicester City	5699 3n Halifax Town
15327 2 Luton Town	5544 3n York City
14799 3s Crystal Palace	5184 3n Gateshead
14596 2 Southampton	5091 3n Lincoln City
14242 2 Norwich City	4996 3n Carlisle United
14217 3s Cardiff City	4888 3n Wrexham
13777 3n Barnsley	4770 3s Mansfield Town
13731 2 Burnley	4510 3n New Brighton
13272 2 Chesterfield	4164 3n Hartlepools United
13033 2 Nottingham Forest	3926 3s Torquay United
12064 1 Grimsby Town	3890 3n Darlington
11975 3s Ipswich Town	3419 3n Accrington Stanley

49379 2	**Newcastle United**	16220 1 Grimsby Town
45732 1	**Liverpool**	16012 3s Swindon Town
44550 1	Chelsea	15376 3s Notts County
43945 1	Manchester United	15339 3n Doncaster Rovers
43266 1	Arsenal	14876 2 Bradford
43254 1	Wolverhampton Wanderers	14764 2 Bury
40854 1	Everton	14703 2 Chesterfield
39283 2	Manchester City	14082 3s Crystal Palace
38944 1	Aston Villa	13155 3n Rotherham United
35912 1	Middlesbrough	13114 3s Ipswich Town
35301 1	Sunderland	12527 3s Bristol Rovers
34636 2	Tottenham Hotspur	12505 2 Newport County
32653 2	Birmingham City	12032 3s Reading
32401 1	Charlton Athletic	11173 3s Walsall
30863 1	Stoke City	10877 3n Oldham Athletic
30198 1	Portsmouth	10582 3s Port Vale
29537 1	Sheffield United	10440 3s Bournemouth & B. Ath.
28692 1	Bolton Wanderers	10263 3n Carlisle United
28604 3s	**Cardiff City**	10048 3s Leyton Orient
26851 2	Sheffield Wednesday	9912 3n Bradford City
26649 1	Preston North End	9690 3s Southend United
26423 2	West Bromwich Albion	8888 3s Exeter City
26367 1	Blackburn Rovers	8881 3n Stockport County
26049 1	Leeds United	8807 3n Wrexham
25856 2	Burnley	8343 3s Watford
25768 1	Brentford	8227 3s Brighton & Hove Albion
23783 2	Leicester City	8076 3n Tranmere Rovers
23708 1	Derby County	7951 3s Northampton Town
23695 2	Fulham	7614 3n Lincoln City
23375 2	Plymouth Argyle	7577 3n Rochdale
23278 2	West Ham United	7562 3n Hartlepools United
22764 2	Nottingham Forest	7029 3s Mansfield Town
21841 2	Millwall	6685 3n York City
21552 1	Blackpool	6671 3n Darlington
21039 2	Swansea Town	6542 3n Barrow
19975 2	Coventry City	6466 3n Chester
19813 1	Huddersfield Town	6286 3s Torquay United
19673 3n	**Hull City**	5927 3n New Brighton
19206 2	Barnsley	5785 3n Crewe Alexandra
18849 3s	Bristol City	4708 3n Southport
17238 2	Luton Town	4677 3s Aldershot
17138 3s	Norwich City	4480 3n Halifax Town
16597 2	Southampton	4412 3n Gateshead
16519 3s	Queens Park Rangers	3976 3n Accrington Stanley

56283	**2**	**Newcastle United**	17948	2	Luton Town
54982	**1**	**Arsenal**	17858	3s	Swansea Town
54890	1	Manchester United	17687	2	Bradford
47592	1	Chelsea	16854	3s	Bournemouth & B. Ath.
44299	1	Liverpool	16037	2	Bury
44205	1	Everton	16031	1	Grimsby Town
42888	1	Sunderland	15829	3s	Swindon Town
42725	1	Manchester City	15711	3s	Walsall
41431	1	Aston Villa	15372	2	Chesterfield
39636	1	Wolverhampton Wanderers	15036	3s	Bristol Rovers
38365	2	Birmingham City	14937	3s	Crystal Palace
37871	2	Cardiff City	14330	3n	Rotherham United
37679	2	Tottenham Hotspur	13610	3s	Reading
36253	1	Charlton Athletic	13569	3s	Port Vale
35858	2	Sheffield Wednesday	13345	3s	Leyton Orient
35094	1	Sheffield United	13234	3s	Ipswich Town
33901	1	Middlesbrough	13187	3n	Lincoln City
33621	1	Burnley	13128	3n	Carlisle United
31590	1	Stoke City	12950	3n	Oldham Athletic
31226	1	Portsmouth	11545	3n	Mansfield Town
30860	2	West Bromwich Albion	11506	3s	Watford
29506	1	Preston North End	11486	3s	Brighton & Hove Albion
29408	1	Bolton Wanderers	11303	3n	Wrexham
28493	2	Leeds United	11242	3s	Newport County
27883	1	Blackburn Rovers	10990	3n	Stockport County
27110	2	Leicester City	10129	3s	Southend United
27044	1	Derby County	10104	3n	Bradford City
25548	1	Huddersfield Town	9900	3s	Exeter City
25380	**3s**	**Notts County**	9006	3n	York City
25197	1	Blackpool	8862	3n	Tranmere Rovers
24875	2	West Ham United	8571	3s	Northampton Town
24247	2	Nottingham Forest	8124	3n	Rochdale
24010	**3n**	**Hull City**	8034	3n	Southport
23341	2	Brentford	7847	3n	Chester
23081	2	Plymouth Argyle	7814	3n	Barrow
22317	2	Doncaster Rovers	7544	3n	Crewe Alexandra
22288	2	Coventry City	7508	3n	Halifax Town
22273	3s	Queens Park Rangers	7485	3n	Hartlepools United
21823	2	Millwall	7186	3s	Torquay United
21444	3s	Norwich City	6879	3n	Darlington
21437	2	Fulham	6729	3s	Aldershot
21262	2	Barnsley	6341	3n	Gateshead
20951	3s	Bristol City	6230	3n	Accrington Stanley
20789	2	Southampton	5229	3n	New Brighton

53839 1	**Newcastle United**	
51478 1	Arsenal	
48808 1	Manchester United	
48258 2	**Tottenham Hotspur**	
47320 1	Aston Villa	
46362 1	Chelsea	
45220 1	Sunderland	
45138 1	Everton	
44031 1	Liverpool	
43690 1	Wolverhampton Wanderers	
40216 1	Charlton Athletic	
38699 1	Manchester City	
38453 1	Birmingham City	
37082 1	Portsmouth	
36763 3n	**Hull City**	
35091 2	Cardiff City	
34387 1	Sheffield United	
34292 1	Middlesbrough	
34113 1	Bolton Wanderers	
33797 2	Sheffield Wednesday	
33395 2	West Bromwich Albion	
33226 1	Preston North End	
30384 2	Leicester City	
30290 1	Burnley	
30002 3s	**Notts County**	
29943 1	Stoke City	
29798 1	Derby County	
29327 2	Fulham	
29318 2	Leeds United	
25384 2	Southampton	
24882 1	Blackpool	
24629 3s	Millwall	
24325 3s	Norwich City	
24175 2	Nottingham Forest	
23354 2	West Ham United	
22820 2	Plymouth Argyle	
22755 2	Brentford	
22535 3s	Swansea Town	
22421 2	Blackburn Rovers	
22342 2	Coventry City	
22151 1	Huddersfield Town	
21628 2	Queens Park Rangers	
19305 2	Barnsley	
17796 2	Luton Town	

17729 3s	Brighton & Hove Albion	
17539 3s	Bristol Rovers	
16672 3s	Swindon Town	
16602 2	Grimsby Town	
16523 3s	Bristol City	
16360 2	Bury	
15975 3s	Bournemouth & B. Ath.	
15893 3n	Oldham Athletic	
15890 2	Lincoln City	
15588 3s	Reading	
14983 2	Bradford	
14874 3s	Crystal Palace	
14229 2	Chesterfield	
13842 3n	Doncaster Rovers	
13541 3n	Rotherham United	
13399 3s	Ipswich Town	
12444 3s	Leyton Orient	
12069 3s	Port Vale	
11878 3s	Newport County	
11312 3n	Mansfield Town	
11161 3s	Watford	
11129 3n	Carlisle United	
10916 3n	Stockport County	
10772 3s	Walsall	
10500 3s	Southend United	
10447 3n	Bradford City	
10412 3n	York City	
10234 3n	Darlington	
10143 3s	Exeter City	
9563 3n	Wrexham	
9211 3s	Northampton Town	
8914 3n	Halifax Town	
8796 3n	Hartlepools United	
8616 3n	Rochdale	
8298 3n	Tranmere Rovers	
7939 3s	Torquay United	
7637 3n	Southport	
7351 3s	Aldershot	
7311 3n	Crewe Alexandra	
7284 3n	Gateshead	
6959 3n	Chester	
6939 3n	Barrow	
6861 3n	New Brighton	
6001 3n	Accrington Stanley	

54111	**2**	**Tottenham Hotspur**	**18252**	**3n**	**Doncaster Rovers**
49001	**1**	**Arsenal**	18056	2	Grimsby Town
47785	1	Sunderland	16874	3s	Crystal Palace
46468	1	Newcastle United	16821	2	Bury
45783	1	Liverpool	16105	3s	Bristol Rovers
45466	1	Wolverhampton Wanderers	16036	2	Luton Town
43932	1	Everton	15885	2	Bradford
43282	1	Manchester United	15423	3s	Reading
42677	1	Aston Villa	15185	3n	Oldham Athletic
42238	1	Chelsea	14559	3s	Bournemouth & B. Ath.
40692	2	Sheffield Wednesday	14120	3s	Brighton & Hove Albion
39381	1	Manchester City	14075	3s	Swindon Town
38910	1	West Bromwich Albion	14047	2	Chesterfield
37319	2	Hull City	13320	3s	Ipswich Town
37004	1	Portsmouth	13158	3n	Bradford City
35407	1	Middlesbrough	12983	3s	Port Vale
35176	**3s**	**Notts County**	12792	3s	Northampton Town
34567	1	Charlton Athletic	12587	3s	Leyton Orient
34511	1	Birmingham City	12418	3n	Lincoln City
33030	1	Fulham	12166	3s	Watford
30764	2	Sheffield United	12128	3n	Mansfield Town
30266	2	Leicester City	12089	3s	Southend United
30203	2	Leeds United	12013	3n	Stockport County
29789	1	Bolton Wanderers	11800	3n	Carlisle United
28680	2	Cardiff City	11535	3s	Newport County
28164	2	Preston North End	10150	3n	Rotherham United
27631	1	Burnley	10117	3s	Exeter City
27215	1	Stoke City	10099	3s	Walsall
26336	1	Blackpool	9201	3n	Gateshead
26283	1	Derby County	9065	3n	Crewe Alexandra
23894	2	Southampton	9026	3n	Tranmere Rovers
23542	1	Huddersfield Town	8770	3s	Torquay United
23264	3s	Norwich City	8372	3n	Rochdale
22822	2	Coventry City	8343	3n	Wrexham
22613	2	Brentford	7829	3n	Southport
22351	2	Blackburn Rovers	7772	3n	York City
22233	2	West Ham United	7705	3n	Hartlepools United
22148	3s	Nottingham Forest	7317	3n	Darlington
21693	2	Plymouth Argyle	7098	3s	Aldershot
21571	2	Swansea Town	6941	3n	Halifax Town
21449	3s	Bristol City	6695	3n	Chester
20753	3s	Millwall	5946	3n	Barrow
19281	2	Queens Park Rangers	5891	3n	Accrington Stanley
18524	2	Barnsley	5457	3n	New Brighton

55509 1 Tottenham Hotspur	15973 3s	Reading
50474 1 Arsenal	15939 2	Grimsby Town
46651 1 Newcastle United	15105 2	Bury
42924 1 Everton	14333 2	Luton Town
41222 1 Sheffield Wednesday	13828 3s	Crystal Palace
39766 1 Sunderland	**13579 3n Oldham Athletic**	
39667 1 Chelsea	13130 3s	Ipswich Town
39616 1 Wolverhampton Wanderers	13077 2	Chesterfield
39008 1 Manchester United	12957 3n	Rotherham United
38369 1 Aston Villa	12730 3s	Bournemouth & B. Ath.
38294 1 Liverpool	12512 3n	Bradford City
36123 1 Middlesbrough	12256 3s	Gillingham
35016 2 Manchester City	12253 3n	Bradford
33142 1 Bolton Wanderers	11914 3s	Leyton Orient
32794 1 Portsmouth	11696 3n	Carlisle United
31872 2 Hull City	11506 3s	Newport County
31259 2 Preston North End	11163 3s	Brighton & Hove Albion
30957 1 West Bromwich Albion	10832 3s	Port Vale
30527 1 Fulham	10712 3s	Swindon Town
30115 2 Notts County	10573 3s	Colchester United
29293 1 Charlton Athletic	10440 3n	Lincoln City
28412 2 Cardiff City	10362 3s	Southend United
28296 1 Burnley	10308 3s	Northampton Town
27488 2 Sheffield United	10262 3n	Mansfield Town
27293 2 Leicester City	10006 3n	Stockport County
27141 1 Huddersfield Town	9869 3n	Tranmere Rovers
26694 2 Coventry City	9771 3s	Exeter City
26105 2 Leeds United	9615 3s	Watford
25791 1 Stoke City	9533 3n	Scunthorpe United
25595 1 Blackpool	9096 3n	Shrewsbury Town
24830 2 Blackburn Rovers	8803 3n	Wrexham
24550 2 Birmingham City	8788 3s	Walsall
24503 3s Norwich City	8500 3n	Gateshead
23259 1 Derby County	7805 3s	Torquay United
22838 2 Doncaster Rovers	7513 3n	York City
22636 3s Nottingham Forest	7492 3n	Hartlepools United
21816 2 Southampton	7349 3s	Aldershot
21540 2 West Ham United	7199 3n	Halifax Town
20161 3s Millwall	6736 3n	Crewe Alexandra
19593 2 Brentford	6519 3n	Rochdale
19398 2 Swansea Town	5951 3n	Chester
19159 2 Barnsley	5778 3n	Barrow
18457 3s Bristol City	5680 3n	Darlington
17763 3s Bristol Rovers	5650 3n	Southport
16866 2 Queens Park Rangers	4562 3n	Accrington Stanley
16542 3s Plymouth Argyle	4046 3n	New Brighton

51134 1	**Tottenham Hotspur**	
51030 1	Arsenal	
50476 1	Newcastle United	
42916 1	Manchester United	
41336 2	**Sheffield Wednesday**	
39932 1	Chelsea	
39853 1	Sunderland	
38641 1	Aston Villa	
38302 1	Manchester City	
38019 1	Liverpool	
37391 2	Everton	
35832 1	Bolton Wanderers	
34437 1	Wolverhampton Wanderers	
32936 1	Preston North End	
32523 1	Portsmouth	
31645 1	Fulham	
31185 2	Sheffield United	
29578 1	West Bromwich Albion	
29210 2	Hull City	
28945 2	Cardiff City	
28775 1	Middlesbrough	
28158 2	Nottingham Forest	
27609 1	Charlton Athletic	
26624 1	Burnley	
26525 2	Notts County	
26080 2	Leicester City	
25854 1	Blackpool	
25222 1	Stoke City	
24481 2	Birmingham City	
24285 2	Leeds United	
24250 1	Huddersfield Town	
23228 2	Blackburn Rovers	
23022 2	Brentford	
22548 2	Coventry City	
21949 1	Derby County	
21866 3s	**Norwich City**	
21078 2	Doncaster Rovers	
20359 2	West Ham United	
19375 3s	Millwall	
19236 3s	Plymouth Argyle	
19038 2	Southampton	
18770 2	Rotherham United	
18228 2	Swansea Town	
17831 3s	Brighton & Hove Albion	
17780 3s	Bristol City	
17369 3s	Bristol Rovers	
16545 2	Queens Park Rangers	
16284 2	Luton Town	
16153 3n	**Oldham Athletic**	
15867 2	Barnsley	
15455 3s	Reading	
14909 3n	Grimsby Town	
14873 3s	Crystal Palace	
14100 2	Bury	
13811 3n	Lincoln City	
12576 3s	Gillingham	
12101 3n	Bradford City	
12030 3n	Stockport County	
11767 3s	Northampton Town	
11558 3n	Bradford	
11487 3s	Leyton Orient	
11377 3s	Ipswich Town	
11272 3s	Port Vale	
10873 3s	Bournemouth & B. Ath.	
10564 3s	Swindon Town	
10100 3n	Carlisle United	
9917 3s	Newport County	
9799 3s	Shrewsbury Town	
9730 3n	Chesterfield	
9609 3s	Watford	
9569 3n	Mansfield Town	
9414 3s	Colchester United	
9265 3n	Hartlepools United	
8963 3s	Southend United	
8321 3s	Exeter City	
8303 3n	Scunthorpe United	
8161 3n	Wrexham	
7968 3n	York City	
7568 3n	Tranmere Rovers	
7564 3s	Torquay United	
7493 3s	Aldershot	
7084 3s	Walsall	
6939 3n	Barrow	
6745 3n	Halifax Town	
6679 3n	Workington	
6378 3n	Accrington Stanley	
6146 3n	Chester	
6114 3n	Gateshead	
6061 3n	Crewe Alexandra	
5452 3n	Southport	
5044 3n	Darlington	
4992 3n	Rochdale	

49191 1 Arsenal	16159	2 Southampton
44521 1 Newcastle United	15862	2 Doncaster Rovers
44106 1 Tottenham Hotspur	14504	3n Port Vale
43937 1 Chelsea	14298	3n Grimsby Town
42634 1 Sheffield Wednesday	13957	3s Watford
39971 1 Liverpool	13430	3s Coventry City
39767 1 Sunderland	13420	2 Bury
37933 1 Cardiff City	12484	3s Northampton Town
37571 1 Manchester United	12415	3s Crystal Palace
36608 1 Wolverhampton Wanderers	12401	3s Reading
34058 1 Manchester City	12205	3s Queens Park Rangers
32629 2 Everton	11558	3s Gillingham
32189 1 Aston Villa	11358	2 Barnsley
32066 1 Bolton Wanderers	10892	3n Bradford City
31578 1 Portsmouth	10768	3s Bournemouth & B. Ath.
31381 1 West Bromwich Albion	10562	3s Leyton Orient
31027 2 Sheffield United	10339	3s Exeter City
30586 1 Preston North End	10306	3n Wrexham
28480 1 Burnley	9949	3n Bradford
27883 1 Stoke City	9434	3s Ipswich Town
27764 2 Huddersfield Town	9326	3s Swindon Town
27077 1 Middlesbrough	9216	3n Chesterfield
26250 2 Leicester City	8868	3s Newport County
25918 2 Hull City	8697	3s Southend United
25835 1 Blackpool	8654	3n York City
25298 1 Charlton Athletic	8540	3s Shrewsbury Town
23411 3s Bristol Rovers	8245	3n Halifax Town
23345 2 Plymouth Argyle	8103	3n Carlisle United
23157 2 Blackburn Rovers	8074	3n Hartlepools United
23134 2 Fulham	8046	3s Colchester United
22816 2 Nottingham Forest	8006	3n Stockport County
21627 1 Derby County	7798	3n Tranmere Rovers
21121 3s Norwich City	7680	3n Mansfield Town
20469 2 Swansea Town	7407	3n Scunthorpe United
20432 2 Leeds United	7212	3n Workington
19797 2 West Ham United	6982	3s Torquay United
19747 2 Birmingham City	6822	3n Crewe Alexandra
19391 2 Notts County	6553	3s Aldershot
19291 3s Millwall	6200	3n Rochdale
18764 3s Bristol City	5992	3s Walsall
17928 3n Oldham Athletic	5839	3n Darlington
17474 2 Brentford	5761	3n Southport
17210 2 Luton Town	5616	3n Gateshead
16775 2 Lincoln City	5549	3n Accrington Stanley
16384 2 Rotherham United	5450	3n Barrow
16161 3s Brighton & Hove Albion	5271	3n Chester

50278 1	**Arsenal**	
46944 1	Chelsea	
45392 1	Newcastle United	
44493 2	**Everton**	
42505 1	Sunderland	
41641 1	Tottenham Hotspur	
40488 1	Liverpool	
38110 1	West Bromwich Albion	
36887 1	Manchester United	
36340 1	Wolverhampton Wanderers	
35220 1	Sheffield Wednesday	
34216 1	Bolton Wanderers	
32410 1	Cardiff City	
31313 1	Sheffield United	
30820 1	Huddersfield Town	
30155 1	Manchester City	
29985 1	Aston Villa	
28993 1	Portsmouth	
28982 2	Leicester City	
28803 1	Charlton Athletic	
28151 1	Burnley	
27888 1	Preston North End	
27002 1	Middlesbrough	
26123 2	Blackburn Rovers	
25416 1	Blackpool	
24662 2	Bristol Rovers	
22606 2	Fulham	
22603 2	Nottingham Forest	
22353 2	Birmingham City	
21810 2	Leeds United	
20995 2	Hull City	
20090 2	West Ham United	
19649 2	Plymouth Argyle	
18880 3s	**Brighton & Hove Albion**	
18580 3s	Norwich City	
18009 2	Stoke City	
17859 2	Oldham Athletic	
17596 3s	Bristol City	
17284 2	Derby County	
17197 2	Swansea Town	
16983 2	Doncaster Rovers	
16653 3n	**Port Vale**	
16237 2	Notts County	
15997 2	Luton Town	
15917 3s	Ipswich Town	
15626 2	Brentford	

14885 3s	Southampton	
14712 2	Lincoln City	
14009 2	Rotherham United	
13527 2	Bury	
13502 3s	Millwall	
12296 3s	Crystal Palace	
11856 3s	Watford	
11566 3s	Reading	
11218 3s	Leyton Orient	
10983 3s	Queens Park Rangers	
10753 3s	Swindon Town	
10602 3n	Bradford City	
10505 3s	Coventry City	
10333 3s	Gillingham	
10289 3s	Northampton Town	
9727 3s	Bournemouth & B. Ath.	
9578 3n	Grimsby Town	
9512 3n	Barnsley	
9344 3s	Exeter City	
9278 3s	Walsall	
9232 3n	Wrexham	
9188 3s	Shrewsbury Town	
9134 3n	Bradford	
8922 3s	Newport County	
8372 3n	Workington	
8246 3n	Scunthorpe United	
7957 3n	Chesterfield	
7712 3s	Colchester United	
7678 3n	Stockport County	
7603 3n	Mansfield Town	
7423 3n	Hartlepools United	
7372 3s	Southend United	
7321 3n	Accrington Stanley	
7111 3s	Torquay United	
6955 3n	Carlisle United	
6645 3s	Aldershot	
6212 3n	Tranmere Rovers	
6148 3n	Crewe Alexandra	
6121 3n	Rochdale	
5899 3n	Gateshead	
5636 3n	York City	
5587 3n	Barrow	
5548 3n	Halifax Town	
5503 3n	Chester	
4975 3n	Darlington	
4629 3n	Southport	

48260 1 Chelsea	14174	2 Bury
46394 1 Everton	13724	3s Millwall
43725 1 Arsenal	12837	3s Brighton & Hove Albion
43043 1 Sunderland	12385	2 Doncaster Rovers
42925 1 Newcastle United	**12160**	**3n Barnsley**
37248 1 Tottenham Hotspur	12067	2 Lincoln City
36911 1 Manchester United	11283	3s Queens Park Rangers
36477 1 Wolverhampton Wanderers	11201	3s Walsall
36215 2 Liverpool	11077	3s Brentford
35217 1 Manchester City	10798	3s Watford
31098 1 West Bromwich Albion	10731	3s Crystal Palace
31067 1 Leicester City	10385	3s Gillingham
29868 1 Portsmouth	9810	3s Bournemouth & B. Ath.
29578 1 Aston Villa	9766	3n Accrington Stanley
28370 1 Bolton Wanderers	9630	3n York City
26928 2 Blackburn Rovers	9293	3n Bradford City
26625 1 Preston North End	8961	3n Scunthorpe United
26141 1 Sheffield Wednesday	8799	3s Reading
25094 1 Burnley	8646	3n Chesterfield
24974 1 Huddersfield Town	8552	3n Darlington
24311 1 Cardiff City	8374	3s Newport County
24005 1 Charlton Athletic	8261	3n Grimsby Town
23959 1 Blackpool	8165	3n Bradford
23880 1 Sheffield United	8045	3s Exeter City
23116 2 Bristol Rovers	7883	3s Swindon Town
22219 3s Bristol City	7852	3s Northampton Town
21566 2 Fulham	7832	3n Hartlepools United
21387 2 Leeds United	7815	3s Southend United
21131 2 Stoke City	7796	3s Shrewsbury Town
21108 2 Middlesbrough	7760	3n Oldham Athletic
21052 2 Swansea Town	7758	3n Mansfield Town
20973 2 Birmingham City	7400	3s Colchester United
20869 2 Port Vale	7348	3n Stockport County
20299 2 West Ham United	7339	3n Wrexham
20285 2 Hull City	7055	3n Workington
19422 2 Plymouth Argyle	6942	3n Halifax Town
17311 2 Luton Town	6604	3s Torquay United
16895 2 Notts County	6202	3n Rochdale
16353 2 Rotherham United	6123	3s Aldershot
15621 3s Norwich City	5619	3n Carlisle United
15390 2 Ipswich Town	5390	3n Chester
15216 3s Leyton Orient	5374	3n Tranmere Rovers
14966 2 Derby County	4844	3n Gateshead
14724 3s Southampton	4785	3n Crewe Alexandra
14617 2 Nottingham Forest	4774	3n Barrow
14202 3s Coventry City	3507	3n Southport

42768 1 Everton		14721 2 Barnsley	
42034 1 Arsenal		13215 2 Lincoln City	
39254 1 Manchester United		12644 3s Walsall	
38042 1 Tottenham Hotspur		12469 2 Rotherham United	
37666 1 Newcastle United		12414 2 Doncaster Rovers	
37224 2 Liverpool		11919 2 Bury	
35888 1 Sunderland		11612 3s Southampton	
35185 1 Wolverhampton Wanderers		11062 3s Crystal Palace	
34141 1 Chelsea		10480 3s Northampton Town	
33683 1 Birmingham City		10302 3s Brentford	
32198 1 Manchester City		10291 3n York City	
29826 1 Aston Villa		10028 3s Southend United	
28134 2 Leicester City		10003 3n Bradford City	
27964 1 Bolton Wanderers		9271 3s Millwall	
26794 1 West Bromwich Albion		8946 3n Accrington Stanley	
26624 1 Cardiff City		8729 3n Chesterfield	
26575 2 Bristol City		8471 3s Shrewsbury Town	
26260 1 Portsmouth		8455 3s Queens Park Rangers	
26247 2 Sheffield Wednesday		8420 3s Gillingham	
26016 1 Blackpool		8168 3s Exeter City	
24872 1 Charlton Athletic		8108 3s Watford	
24657 1 Preston North End		8108 3s Reading	
24445 2 Leeds United		8035 3s Bournemouth & B. Ath.	
23860 2 Bristol Rovers		7702 3n Scunthorpe United	
23581 1 Sheffield United		7682 3n Mansfield Town	
23397 1 Burnley		7641 3s Colchester United	
23001 2 Blackburn Rovers		7640 3n Wrexham	
21455 1 Luton Town		7432 3s Swindon Town	
20024 1 Huddersfield Town		7412 3n Hartlepools United	
19850 2 Stoke City		7347 3n Stockport County	
19597 2 Fulham		7326 3n Bradford	
19487 2 Swansea Town		6989 3s Torquay United	
18985 2 Port Vale		6894 3n Carlisle United	
18688 3n Derby County		6640 3n Chester	
17866 2 Middlesbrough		6545 3s Newport County	
17679 2 West Ham United		6500 3n Tranmere Rovers	
17658 3s Coventry City		6473 3n Oldham Athletic	
17594 2 Plymouth Argyle		6235 3n Workington	
16225 2 Nottingham Forest		6194 3n Barrow	
16061 3s Leyton Orient		6044 3n Halifax Town	
15934 3n Grimsby Town		5626 3n Darlington	
15595 3s Norwich City		5606 3s Aldershot	
15489 3s Ipswich Town		5288 3n Crewe Alexandra	
15419 2 Hull City		5060 3n Southport	
15401 2 Notts County		4833 3n Rochdale	
15323 3s Brighton & Hove Albion		3287 3n Gateshead	

45481 1	**Manchester United**	
43280 1	Tottenham Hotspur	
41093 1	Arsenal	
36145 1	Sunderland	
35743 2	**Liverpool**	
35202 1	Newcastle United	
35076 1	Everton	
34956 1	Wolverhampton Wanderers	
32672 1	Leeds United	
32444 1	Birmingham City	
31732 1	Chelsea	
30624 2	Leicester City	
30487 1	Aston Villa	
30005 1	Manchester City	
28570 1	Sheffield Wednesday	
25219 1	Bolton Wanderers	
25024 1	Portsmouth	
23522 1	Preston North End	
23118 2	Nottingham Forest	
23091 2	Blackburn Rovers	
22746 1	West Bromwich Albion	
22493 1	Burnley	
22166 2	Bristol Rovers	
22146 2	Stoke City	
21961 1	Blackpool	
21803 2	Sheffield United	
21714 2	Bristol City	
21127 2	Middlesbrough	
20920 2	Fulham	
20550 1	Cardiff City	
20370 1	Charlton Athletic	
19611 3n	**Derby County**	
18667 2	West Ham United	
18262 1	Luton Town	
17524 2	Leyton Orient	
16585 2	Swansea Town	
15638 2	Notts County	
15331 2	Grimsby Town	
14861 2	Huddersfield Town	
14784 3s	**Southampton**	
14372 3s	Ipswich Town	
14046 2	Port Vale	
13686 3s	Coventry City	
12915 2	Barnsley	
12856 3s	Norwich City	
12821 3n	Bradford City	
12713 3s	Plymouth Argyle	
12375 2	Doncaster Rovers	
12081 3s	Crystal Palace	
12056 3n	Hull City	
11986 2	Bury	
11606 3s	Brighton & Hove Albion	
11545 3s	Millwall	
11482 3s	Brentford	
11347 3s	Walsall	
11180 2	Lincoln City	
10968 3s	Bournemouth & B. Ath.	
10744 2	Rotherham United	
9989 3n	Chesterfield	
9706 3n	Stockport County	
9549 3n	Wrexham	
9414 3n	York City	
9267 3s	Colchester United	
9261 3s	Newport County	
9239 3s	Queens Park Rangers	
9225 3n	Hartlepools United	
9219 3s	Watford	
9040 3n	Mansfield Town	
8832 3s	Reading	
8819 3s	Swindon Town	
8796 3s	Southend United	
8736 3n	Accrington Stanley	
8484 3n	Bradford	
8305 3n	Workington	
8273 3n	Oldham Athletic	
8158 3s	Northampton Town	
8014 3s	Torquay United	
7550 3s	Shrewsbury Town	
7430 3n	Carlisle United	
7037 3s	Gillingham	
6765 3s	Exeter City	
6472 3n	Chester	
6379 3n	Barrow	
6280 3n	Rochdale	
6227 3n	Scunthorpe United	
6118 3n	Halifax Town	
6061 3n	Tranmere Rovers	
5870 3n	Darlington	
5098 3s	Aldershot	
4918 3n	Crewe Alexandra	
4376 3n	Southport	
3875 3n	Gateshead	

46073 1 Manchester United	13084 3s Brentford
42942 1 Tottenham Hotspur	12624 3s Bournemouth & B. Ath.
39835 1 Arsenal	**12527 3n Bradford City**
39157 1 Everton	12180 3s Reading
38476 2 Liverpool	12112 3s Millwall
38430 1 Chelsea	12057 3s Swindon Town
37317 1 Wolverhampton Wanderers	11907 3s Coventry City
36241 1 Newcastle United	11775 3n Bury
36146 1 Sunderland	11190 3s Southend United
32756 1 Manchester City	11129 2 Doncaster Rovers
32419 1 West Bromwich Albion	10973 3n Hull City
31359 1 Leicester City	10457 3s Port Vale
31305 1 Nottingham Forest	10373 3n Tranmere Rovers
29553 1 Birmingham City	10179 2 Rotherham United
28842 1 Aston Villa	10147 2 Lincoln City
28499 1 Portsmouth	9994 3n Stockport County
25012 1 Preston North End	9677 3n Scunthorpe United
24920 1 Leeds United	9386 3s Queens Park Rangers
24854 2 West Ham United	9083 3n Wrexham
24398 2 Middlesbrough	8802 3s Walsall
24234 2 Fulham	8744 3n Bradford
22757 1 Sheffield Wednesday	8564 3s Colchester United
22708 2 Blackburn Rovers	8525 3n Carlisle United
22251 1 Burnley	8385 3n Chesterfield
22249 2 Charlton Athletic	8284 3s Watford
22091 2 Bristol City	8127 3s Northampton Town
22029 1 Bolton Wanderers	8099 3n Mansfield Town
21406 1 Blackpool	7853 3n Hartlepools United
20604 2 Bristol Rovers	7784 3s Exeter City
20511 2 Stoke City	7469 3n Oldham Athletic
20290 3s Norwich City	7270 3n York City
19830 2 Derby County	7187 3n Accrington Stanley
19662 3s Plymouth Argyle	7174 3s Newport County
19243 2 Sheffield United	7142 3s Shrewsbury Town
18419 1 Luton Town	7112 3s Torquay United
18285 2 Ipswich Town	7030 3s Gillingham
16420 3s Brighton & Hove Albion	6740 3n Chester
15711 2 Swansea Town	6654 3n Workington
15366 2 Cardiff City	6485 3n Halifax Town
14851 3s Southampton	6352 3n Rochdale
14839 2 Leyton Orient	5733 3n Barrow
14470 2 Notts County	5375 3n Darlington
14166 2 Grimsby Town	5000 3s Aldershot
14152 2 Huddersfield Town	4704 3n Gateshead
13969 2 Barnsley	4587 3n Crewe Alexandra
13229 3s Crystal Palace	3801 3n Southport

53258 1	**Manchester United**	13108 2	Grimsby Town
45227 1	Arsenal	12757 4	Port Vale
40857 1	Chelsea	12674 3	Reading
40453 1	Tottenham Hotspur	12377 2	Scunthorpe United
39458 1	Newcastle United	11855 4	Millwall
39171 1	Everton	11815 3	Tranmere Rovers
38439 1	Wolverhampton Wanderers	11359 3	Swindon Town
36749 2	**Liverpool**	11334 2	Lincoln City
33880 1	Aston Villa	11229 3	Southend United
32568 1	Manchester City	11212 2	Barnsley
31398 1	West Bromwich Albion	11133 3	Bradford City
30544 1	Blackburn Rovers	10680 3	Bournemouth & B. Ath.
28717 1	Nottingham Forest	10482 2	Rotherham United
28368 1	West Ham United	10338 3	Wrexham
27860 1	Leicester City	9529 3	Notts County
27772 2	Sunderland	9441 3	Bury
27659 1	Bolton Wanderers	9374 4	Exeter City
26982 2	Sheffield Wednesday	9255 3	Stockport County
26686 1	Birmingham City	9155 3	Queens Park Rangers
26260 2	Fulham	9050 4	Walsall
24905 1	Leeds United	9028 3	Chesterfield
24876 2	Middlesbrough	8467 3	Mansfield Town
24016 1	Portsmouth	8384 4	Watford
23733 1	Burnley	8124 4	York City
22926 3	**Plymouth Argyle**	8090 4	Northampton Town
22517 2	Brighton & Hove Albion	8081 4	Shrewsbury Town
22506 2	Bristol City	7756 3	Colchester United
22435 1	Preston North End	7443 4	Crewe Alexandra
21540 3	Southampton	7172 4	Carlisle United
21229 3	Norwich City	7016 4	Bradford
20860 1	Blackpool	6953 4	Chester
19872 1	Luton Town	6928 4	Gillingham
19580 2	Sheffield United	6665 3	Doncaster Rovers
18990 2	Derby County	6663 3	Halifax Town
17890 2	Bristol Rovers	6606 3	Newport County
17776 2	Cardiff City	6267 3	Accrington Stanley
17249 2	Stoke City	5499 4	Hartlepools United
16806 2	Charlton Athletic	5398 4	Torquay United
16330 4	**Coventry City**	5322 4	Oldham Athletic
14881 4	Crystal Palace	5042 4	Workington
14846 2	Huddersfield Town	5004 4	Darlington
14612 2	Swansea Town	4810 3	Rochdale
14375 3	Hull City	4325 4	Barrow
14261 2	Ipswich Town	4189 4	Aldershot
13924 3	Brentford	4142 4	Gateshead
13323 2	Leyton Orient	3388 4	Southport

47948 1	**Tottenham Hotspur**	
47288 1	Manchester United	
40788 1	Everton	
39423 1	Chelsea	
39341 1	Arsenal	
36244 1	Wolverhampton Wanderers	
36037 1	Newcastle United	
35637 1	Manchester City	
34257 2	**Aston Villa**	
32034 1	Sheffield Wednesday	
30271 1	Fulham	
30269 2	Liverpool	
28554 1	West Ham United	
27461 1	West Bromwich Albion	
27299 1	Blackburn Rovers	
27072 1	Birmingham City	
26978 1	Burnley	
26739 1	Nottingham Forest	
26402 3	**Norwich City**	
25998 1	Bolton Wanderers	
25550 2	Middlesbrough	
25399 1	Leicester City	
24552 1	Preston North End	
24183 2	Cardiff City	
22831 2	Sunderland	
21877 1	Leeds United	
21783 1	Blackpool	
20383 2	Plymouth Argyle	
18486 2	Bristol Rovers	
18331 2	Brighton & Hove Albion	
18054 2	Sheffield United	
18052 3	Southampton	
17755 2	Bristol City	
17067 1	Luton Town	
16348 3	Coventry City	
16156 2	Portsmouth	
15815 2	Derby County	
15687 2	Charlton Athletic	
15630 4	Crystal Palace	
15499 2	Hull City	
14773 2	Huddersfield Town	
14560 4	**Millwall**	
14506 2	Stoke City	
14355 2	Swansea Town	
13820 4	Notts County	
13768 2	Ipswich Town	

13250 2	Leyton Orient	
12869 2	Rotherham United	
12013 4	Watford	
11912 3	Brentford	
11464 3	Reading	
11157 4	Walsall	
11113 2	Scunthorpe United	
10734 2	Lincoln City	
10733 3	Port Vale	
10628 3	Bury	
10540 3	Grimsby Town	
10403 3	Bournemouth & B. Ath.	
10285 3	Queens Park Rangers	
10228 3	Swindon Town	
10163 3	Bradford City	
9965 3	Tranmere Rovers	
9931 3	Southend United	
9495 3	Wrexham	
8999 3	Shrewsbury Town	
8306 4	Northampton Town	
7962 4	Crewe Alexandra	
7812 3	Colchester United	
7507 3	York City	
7421 4	Exeter City	
7183 3	Mansfield Town	
6812 4	Torquay United	
6768 3	Halifax Town	
6578 3	Chesterfield	
6552 4	Stockport County	
6399 4	Bradford	
6315 3	Barnsley	
6241 3	Newport County	
6232 4	Gillingham	
5612 4	Barrow	
5454 4	Aldershot	
5421 4	Chester	
5308 4	Carlisle United	
5247 4	Doncaster Rovers	
4957 4	Oldham Athletic	
4651 4	Darlington	
4599 4	Rochdale	
4310 4	Workington	
4083 3	Accrington Stanley	
3646 4	Hartlepools United	
3563 4	Southport	
3412 4	Gateshead	

53124	**1**	**Tottenham Hotspur**	11044	3	Swindon Town
43448	1	Everton	10827	3	Walsall
37888	1	Manchester United	10681	4	Northampton Town
34318	1	Arsenal	10539	2	Leyton Orient
33599	1	Aston Villa	10207	3	Bury
30885	1	Wolverhampton Wanderers	9956	3	Queens Park Rangers
30156	1	Chelsea	9703	4	Millwall
29608	**2**	**Liverpool**	9702	3	Port Vale
29409	1	Manchester City	9549	2	Rotherham United
29229	1	Sheffield Wednesday	9460	3	Tranmere Rovers
26500	1	Newcastle United	9295	3	Grimsby Town
26051	2	Sunderland	9252	2	Stoke City
25775	1	Birmingham City	9209	4	Bradford
24710	1	West Bromwich Albion	9187	2	Scunthorpe United
24668	1	Nottingham Forest	8434	3	Hull City
24469	2	Norwich City	8107	3	Southend United
24056	1	Leicester City	8025	3	Shrewsbury Town
23827	1	Burnley	7811	3	Bournemouth & B. Ath.
23390	1	Cardiff City	7692	3	Reading
23014	1	Fulham	7447	3	Bradford City
21948	1	West Ham United	7429	2	Lincoln City
21670	1	Bolton Wanderers	7392	3	Brentford
19343	1	Blackburn Rovers	7311	4	Crewe Alexandra
19089	**4**	**Crystal Palace**	6900	4	York City
18715	1	Blackpool	6506	4	Stockport County
18665	2	Southampton	6378	4	Wrexham
18487	2	Sheffield United	6359	3	Barnsley
17613	2	Plymouth Argyle	6298	4	Aldershot
16804	1	Preston North End	6153	3	Torquay United
15859	2	Middlesbrough	6005	4	Gillingham
15522	2	Brighton & Hove Albion	5894	4	Darlington
15095	2	Ipswich Town	5548	3	Halifax Town
15028	2	Portsmouth	5439	3	Newport County
14888	2	Bristol Rovers	5180	3	Chesterfield
14203	4	Peterborough United	4962	3	Colchester United
14094	2	Derby County	4961	4	Exeter City
13443	2	Leeds United	4936	4	Mansfield Town
13434	2	Huddersfield Town	4892	4	Chester
12644	4	Oldham Athletic	4754	4	Doncaster Rovers
12599	**3**	**Watford**	4503	4	Southport
12574	2	Luton Town	4446	4	Carlisle United
12084	2	Swansea Town	4299	4	Barrow
11996	3	Coventry City	4091	4	Hartlepools United
11974	3	Notts County	3930	4	Rochdale
11488	3	Bristol City	3530	4	Accrington Stanley
11102	2	Charlton Athletic	3210	4	Workington

45576	**1**	**Tottenham Hotspur**
41432	1	Everton
39237	**2**	**Liverpool**
34447	1	Arsenal
33491	1	Manchester United
32986	2	Sunderland
32056	1	Aston Villa
28401	1	Sheffield Wednesday
27946	2	Newcastle United
27125	1	Burnley
27013	1	Chelsea
25733	1	West Ham United
25626	1	Manchester City
24803	1	Wolverhampton Wanderers
24401	1	Fulham
23533	1	Birmingham City
23517	1	Nottingham Forest
22863	1	Ipswich Town
22526	1	Sheffield United
21006	1	West Bromwich Albion
20241	2	Norwich City
19469	1	Leicester City
19294	1	Cardiff City
18618	1	Blackpool
17519	1	Bolton Wanderers
17481	**3**	**Crystal Palace**
16782	3	Portsmouth
15930	2	Derby County
15906	1	Blackburn Rovers
15810	2	Middlesbrough
15751	2	Stoke City
14751	2	Leyton Orient
14211	2	Charlton Athletic
13989	2	Plymouth Argyle
13763	2	Southampton
13607	2	Leeds United
13247	2	Huddersfield Town
13206	2	Brighton & Hove Albion
13067	2	Preston North End
12703	2	Walsall
12447	3	Bristol City
12392	3	Peterborough United
12174	2	Swansea Town
12096	2	Bristol Rovers
11762	4	Millwall
11622	3	Bournemouth & B. Ath.
11490	**4**	**Wrexham**
11324	4	Oldham Athletic
11242	3	Reading
11121	3	Queens Park Rangers
10899	3	Northampton Town
10609	3	Watford
10525	2	Luton Town
10518	2	Bury
10256	3	Coventry City
9829	2	Scunthorpe United
9697	3	Swindon Town
9469	3	Grimsby Town
9327	2	Rotherham United
8993	3	Port Vale
8871	3	Bradford
8483	3	Brentford
8352	3	Notts County
8079	4	Tranmere Rovers
7922	3	Southend United
7609	4	Mansfield Town
6887	3	Hull City
6664	4	Carlisle United
6591	3	Shrewsbury Town
6590	4	York City
6240	4	Bradford City
6143	4	Aldershot
6100	3	Barnsley
5868	3	Lincoln City
5656	4	Gillingham
5602	4	Darlington
5578	4	Chester
5428	4	Crewe Alexandra
5341	4	Colchester United
5023	3	Newport County
4982	3	Torquay United
4824	4	Stockport County
4670	3	Halifax Town
4471	4	Doncaster Rovers
4446	4	Barrow
4344	4	Exeter City
4321	4	Hartlepools United
4237	4	Chesterfield
4233	4	Southport
4024	4	Rochdale
3392	4	Workington
2688	4	Accrington Stanley

51603 1 Everton	11216 2 Grimsby Town
47342 1 Tottenham Hotspur	11121 3 Bristol City
42971 1 Liverpool	10365 2 Swansea Town
40883 2 Sunderland	10190 2 Rotherham United
40329 1 Manchester United	10137 3 Wrexham
32288 1 Arsenal	10041 3 Queens Park Rangers
31634 2 Newcastle United	9978 3 Southend United
31014 1 Aston Villa	9961 3 Brighton & Hove Albion
29376 2 Chelsea	9848 4 Mansfield Town
25841 1 Leicester City	9831 3 Bristol Rovers
25803 1 Wolverhampton Wanderers	9824 2 Walsall
25426 2 Stoke City	9763 3 Bournemouth & B. Ath.
25180 1 Burnley	9756 3 Watford
24790 1 Sheffield Wednesday	9070 2 Scunthorpe United
24683 1 Manchester City	8148 2 Luton Town
23621 1 West Ham United	8130 3 Port Vale
22775 1 Sheffield United	8077 3 Reading
22524 1 Birmingham City	7614 4 Tranmere Rovers
22086 1 Nottingham Forest	7502 4 Oxford United
21986 1 Fulham	7409 3 Bradford
20213 2 Leeds United	7350 3 Hull City
19406 1 Bolton Wanderers	7021 3 Barnsley
19197 2 Norwich City	7015 4 Gillingham
19044 1 Ipswich Town	6860 3 Notts County
18536 1 Blackpool	6573 4 Chesterfield
18531 1 West Bromwich Albion	6436 4 Crewe Alexandra
17098 3 Coventry City	6303 4 Doncaster Rovers
16545 2 Middlesbrough	5897 3 Shrewsbury Town
16406 1 Leyton Orient	5699 3 Carlisle United
16174 2 Huddersfield Town	5573 4 Aldershot
16043 2 Portsmouth	5542 4 Chester
16001 1 Blackburn Rovers	5309 3 Colchester United
15929 2 Plymouth Argyle	4872 4 Torquay United
15567 2 Cardiff City	4630 4 Lincoln City
15267 2 Southampton	4575 4 York City
14854 3 Crystal Palace	4541 4 Newport County
14312 4 Oldham Athletic	4414 4 Exeter City
13673 3 Swindon Town	4160 4 Darlington
13424 3 Northampton Town	4083 4 Barrow
13420 2 Charlton Athletic	4061 4 Stockport County
13225 3 Millwall	4015 4 Bradford City
12092 2 Derby County	3910 4 Hartlepools United
12016 3 Peterborough United	3561 3 Halifax Town
11694 2 Preston North End	3416 4 Southport
11418 4 Brentford	3306 4 Rochdale
11270 2 Bury	2852 4 Workington

49401 1	**Everton**	
45032 1	Liverpool	
44125 1	Manchester United	
43800 1	Tottenham Hotspur	
41258 2	**Sunderland**	
34793 1	Arsenal	
31305 1	Chelsea	
30315 1	Stoke City	
29938 2	Leeds United	
29435 2	Newcastle United	
26017 3	**Coventry City**	
24591 1	West Ham United	
24142 1	Leicester City	
23402 1	Sheffield Wednesday	
22574 1	Wolverhampton Wanderers	
22497 1	Nottingham Forest	
22346 1	Aston Villa	
22055 1	Birmingham City	
21654 1	Sheffield United	
21543 1	Blackburn Rovers	
21163 1	Fulham	
20552 1	West Bromwich Albion	
19755 1	Burnley	
18821 2	Preston North End	
18786 2	Middlesbrough	
18502 2	Swindon Town	
18283 2	Charlton Athletic	
18201 2	Manchester City	
17217 2	Southampton	
17204 3	Crystal Palace	
17018 1	Bolton Wanderers	
16540 1	Blackpool	
16294 2	Norwich City	
16044 1	Ipswich Town	
14681 2	Portsmouth	
13782 2	Cardiff City	
13001 2	Plymouth Argyle	
12705 2	Northampton Town	
12373 3	Oldham Athletic	
12120 2	Huddersfield Town	
11979 2	Derby County	
11883 3	Brentford	
11444 3	Watford	
10911 2	Swansea Town	
10826 3	Peterborough United	
10710 3	Bristol Rovers	

10501 3	Millwall	
10359 2	Leyton Orient	
10056 3	Port Vale	
9959 2	Rotherham United	
9912 3	Bristol City	
9902 4	**Gillingham**	
9830 3	Bournemouth & B. Ath.	
9515 2	Grimsby Town	
9484 3	Mansfield Town	
9318 4	Brighton & Hove Albion	
8536 3	Hull City	
8483 3	Southend United	
8434 3	Reading	
8346 4	Carlisle United	
8169 2	Bury	
7662 3	Queens Park Rangers	
7353 2	Scunthorpe United	
7308 3	Walsall	
7291 4	Exeter City	
7188 3	Luton Town	
7072 4	Tranmere Rovers	
7023 3	Wrexham	
6896 4	Oxford United	
6600 3	Shrewsbury Town	
6479 3	Barnsley	
6423 3	Notts County	
6355 4	Doncaster Rovers	
6182 4	Chester	
6003 4	Bradford	
5739 4	Bradford City	
5650 4	Lincoln City	
5501 3	Crewe Alexandra	
5366 4	Chesterfield	
5275 4	Aldershot	
5199 4	Torquay United	
5036 3	Colchester United	
4819 4	Workington	
4277 4	Stockport County	
4169 4	Hartlepools United	
3937 4	York City	
3800 4	Halifax Town	
3715 4	Newport County	
3371 4	Darlington	
3039 4	Barrow	
3020 4	Rochdale	
2964 4	Southport	

46521 1	**Manchester United**	
42062 1	Everton	
41138 1	Liverpool	
40637 1	Sunderland	
39391 1	Tottenham Hotspur	
37490 1	Leeds United	
37054 1	Chelsea	
35659 2	**Newcastle United**	
31327 1	Arsenal	
27426 1	Nottingham Forest	
26621 2	Coventry City	
25858 1	West Ham United	
25787 1	Stoke City	
22215 1	Aston Villa	
21499 1	Wolverhampton Wanderers	
20188 1	Sheffield Wednesday	
20006 1	Sheffield United	
19963 1	Leicester City	
19714 1	Birmingham City	
18848 1	West Bromwich Albion	
18641 1	Blackpool	
18232 2	Crystal Palace	
18207 2	Norwich City	
17907 4	**Brighton & Hove Albion**	
17563 1	Fulham	
17123 2	Southampton	
16110 1	Blackburn Rovers	
15739 1	Burnley	
15692 2	Middlesbrough	
15622 2	Preston North End	
15366 2	Northampton Town	
15269 2	Swindon Town	
14881 2	Plymouth Argyle	
14753 2	Manchester City	
14650 2	Bolton Wanderers	
14629 3	**Hull City**	
13820 2	Derby County	
13065 2	Charlton Athletic	
13058 2	Portsmouth	
12951 2	Ipswich Town	
12698 3	Bristol Rovers	
12194 3	Bristol City	
11656 4	Tranmere Rovers	
11323 3	Gillingham	
10789 3	Carlisle United	
10740 3	Brentford	

10587 2	Cardiff City
10467 2	Swansea Town
10021 3	Peterborough United
9753 2	Rotherham United
9644 2	Huddersfield Town
9451 3	Mansfield Town
9272 4	Millwall
8920 2	Leyton Orient
8744 4	Oxford United
8366 4	Bradford
8184 3	Oldham Athletic
8135 4	Doncaster Rovers
7784 2	Bury
7748 3	Bournemouth & B. Ath.
7659 4	Chester
7533 3	Reading
7421 3	Watford
7185 4	York City
7157 3	Southend United
7144 3	Grimsby Town
6754 3	Walsall
6663 3	Luton Town
6460 3	Exeter City
6131 4	Chesterfield
5884 4	Hartlepools United
5842 4	Wrexham
5756 4	Notts County
5739 4	Stockport County
5670 3	Queens Park Rangers
5635 3	Shrewsbury Town
5618 3	Scunthorpe United
5508 3	Port Vale
5178 3	Workington
4686 4	Rochdale
4648 4	Aldershot
4475 4	Lincoln City
4385 4	Torquay United
4292 4	Darlington
4273 3	Barnsley
4263 4	Crewe Alexandra
4219 4	Bradford City
4011 4	Newport County
3655 3	Colchester United
3204 4	Barrow
3006 4	Halifax Town
2870 4	Southport

46344 1	**Liverpool**	10096 2	Rotherham United
38769 1	Manchester United	9301 3	Oxford United
38498 1	Everton	9297 3	Walsall
38320 1	Tottenham Hotspur	9007 3	Bristol Rovers
35785 1	Leeds United	8943 3	Oldham Athletic
34488 1	Sunderland	8857 3	Reading
33793 1	Newcastle United	8504 4	Chester
31346 1	Chelsea	8416 3	Brentford
29036 1	Arsenal	8263 3	Queens Park Rangers
27739 2	**Manchester City**	8031 4	Tranmere Rovers
25370 2	Coventry City	7953 4	Darlington
24836 1	West Ham United	7802 4	Stockport County
23725 1	Nottingham Forest	7695 3	Watford
22828 3	**Hull City**	7694 3	Swansea Town
22503 1	Stoke City	7675 4	Luton Town
22366 1	Sheffield Wednesday	7667 2	Bury
22361 2	Wolverhampton Wanderers	7538 3	Southend United
22325 1	Leicester City	7492 3	Gillingham
21138 1	Fulham	7378 2	Leyton Orient
21063 1	Aston Villa	7239 3	Grimsby Town
19968 1	Burnley	7238 3	Peterborough United
19834 1	West Bromwich Albion	6329 3	Bournemouth & B. Ath.
19405 1	Sheffield United	6208 4	Torquay United
18919 2	Southampton	6087 3	Mansfield Town
18633 1	Northampton Town	6015 4	Port Vale
18322 2	Huddersfield Town	5921 3	York City
17297 2	Bristol City	5590 3	Exeter City
16185 1	Blackpool	5567 4	Wrexham
14983 2	Norwich City	5287 4	Bradford
14809 2	Crystal Palace	5181 3	Scunthorpe United
14644 2	Portsmouth	5151 4	Colchester United
14398 2	Birmingham City	5118 3	Shrewsbury Town
14151 2	Derby County	4995 4	Chesterfield
14023 2	Preston North End	4949 4	Notts County
13978 3	Millwall	4842 4	Hartlepools United
13513 1	Blackburn Rovers	4701 4	Barrow
13450 2	Middlesbrough	4510 4	Barnsley
13217 2	Plymouth Argyle	4257 4	Southport
13125 3	Swindon Town	4025 4	Bradford City
12799 3	Brighton & Hove Albion	3873 4	Crewe Alexandra
12473 2	Ipswich Town	3845 4	Lincoln City
12271 2	Charlton Athletic	3825 4	Aldershot
12067 2	Carlisle United	3263 3	Workington
12005 2	Bolton Wanderers	3069 4	Halifax Town
11005 2	Cardiff City	2974 4	Rochdale
10398 4	**Doncaster Rovers**	2636 4	Newport County

53854 1	**Manchester United**	
46388 1	Liverpool	
42606 1	Everton	
41988 1	Tottenham Hotspur	
35591 1	Chelsea	
35224 1	Leeds United	
32081 1	Newcastle United	
31773 1	Arsenal	
31731 1	Sunderland	
31282 1	Nottingham Forest	
31208 1	Manchester City	
30219 1	Sheffield Wednesday	
29271 1	West Ham United	
28269 2	**Coventry City**	
25933 1	Stoke City	
25527 1	Southampton	
24787 2	Wolverhampton Wanderers	
24463 1	Leicester City	
24430 1	Fulham	
24276 2	Hull City	
23342 1	West Bromwich Albion	
21628 1	Aston Villa	
20600 1	Sheffield United	
20508 1	Burnley	
19798 2	Birmingham City	
18100 2	Crystal Palace	
17586 3	**Middlesbrough**	
17283 1	Blackpool	
16190 2	Millwall	
16183 2	Bristol City	
15867 2	Derby County	
15859 2	Ipswich Town	
14969 2	Norwich City	
14904 2	Huddersfield Town	
14831 2	Portsmouth	
14721 2	Blackburn Rovers	
14350 2	Preston North End	
14281 2	Plymouth Argyle	
13235 2	Bolton Wanderers	
13157 3	Queens Park Rangers	
12611 2	Charlton Athletic	
12467 3	Swindon Town	
12310 2	Northampton Town	
11785 3	Brighton & Hove Albion	
11201 2	Carlisle United	
10344 2	Rotherham United	

10259 2	Cardiff City	
10253 3	Bristol Rovers	
9940 3	Oldham Athletic	
9820 4	**Stockport County**	
9385 3	Watford	
8594 3	Walsall	
8523 4	Wrexham	
8076 2	Bury	
8034 4	Southend United	
7906 3	Doncaster Rovers	
7839 4	Tranmere Rovers	
7800 3	Mansfield Town	
7405 3	Oxford United	
7141 3	Reading	
7040 3	Torquay United	
6727 4	Brentford	
6591 3	Darlington	
6548 3	Gillingham	
6488 3	Peterborough United	
6390 3	Swansea Town	
6035 4	Luton Town	
5981 3	Leyton Orient	
5965 3	Grimsby Town	
5778 4	Hartlepools United	
5770 4	Barrow	
5568 3	Colchester United	
5521 4	Barnsley	
5515 4	Southport	
5418 4	Crewe Alexandra	
5332 3	Bournemouth & B. Ath.	
5239 4	Scunthorpe United	
5156 4	Chester	
5115 4	Chesterfield	
5074 4	Port Vale	
4958 3	Shrewsbury Town	
4826 4	Bradford City	
4802 4	Bradford	
4483 4	Aldershot	
4354 4	Notts County	
4088 4	Lincoln City	
3990 4	Exeter City	
3886 4	Halifax Town	
3811 4	York City	
2869 4	Newport County	
2664 3	Workington	
2443 4	Rochdale	

57552	**1**	**Manchester United**
46983	1	Everton
46755	1	Liverpool
42608	1	Tottenham Hotspur
37239	1	Newcastle United
37223	1	Manchester City
36691	1	Leeds United
35979	1	Chelsea
35017	1	Wolverhampton Wanderers
34705	1	Coventry City
32715	1	Nottingham Forest
31896	1	Arsenal
31461	1	Sheffield Wednesday
30873	1	Sunderland
29843	1	West Ham United
28160	**2**	**Birmingham City**
25828	1	West Bromwich Albion
24665	1	Southampton
24528	1	Leicester City
22988	2	Portsmouth
22646	1	Sheffield United
22203	1	Fulham
21949	1	Stoke City
20914	2	Derby County
19785	2	Aston Villa
18906	2	Middlesbrough
18627	2	Ipswich Town
18419	2	Queens Park Rangers
17435	1	Burnley
17178	2	Blackpool
17141	2	Crystal Palace
16286	2	Norwich City
15935	2	Bristol City
15626	2	Hull City
15051	2	Preston North End
13945	2	Charlton Athletic
13635	**3**	**Swindon Town**
13531	2	Blackburn Rovers
13509	2	Millwall
13301	2	Cardiff City
12400	**4**	**Luton Town**
11553	2	Huddersfield Town
11487	2	Bolton Wanderers
10818	4	Barnsley
10669	2	Plymouth Argyle
10619	4	Southend United
10492	3	Brighton & Hove Albion
10414	2	Carlisle United
10365	2	Rotherham United
10214	4	Chesterfield
9119	3	Walsall
9096	3	Torquay United
8937	3	Northampton Town
8913	3	Watford
8325	3	Oxford United
8281	3	Bury
8237	3	Stockport County
8127	3	Reading
8105	3	Bristol Rovers
7852	4	Doncaster Rovers
7403	3	Tranmere Rovers
7341	4	Bradford City
6889	3	Peterborough United
6729	4	Wrexham
6692	4	Lincoln City
6675	3	Shrewsbury Town
6211	4	Brentford
6190	4	Hartlepools United
6062	3	Barrow
5983	3	Bournemouth & B. Ath.
5948	3	Mansfield Town
5917	4	Crewe Alexandra
5903	3	Southport
5855	4	Swansea Town
5770	3	Gillingham
5745	3	Oldham Athletic
5641	4	Notts County
5618	4	Aldershot
4886	4	Port Vale
4715	3	Orient
4578	4	York City
4502	4	Halifax Town
4415	4	Chester
4301	3	Grimsby Town
4026	4	Darlington
3992	3	Colchester United
3855	4	Exeter City
3845	3	Scunthorpe United
3609	4	Bradford
3326	4	Newport County
2292	4	Rochdale
2086	4	Workington

51169 1	**Manchester United**	
47348 1	Liverpool	
45958 1	Everton	
38423 1	Arsenal	
37613 1	Chelsea	
37455 1	Tottenham Hotspur	
36998 1	Leeds United	
34016 1	Newcastle United	
33750 1	Manchester City	
33223 1	Coventry City	
31125 1	West Ham United	
30714 1	Wolverhampton Wanderers	
28446 1	Leicester City	
27659 2	**Derby County**	
26866 1	Sheffield Wednesday	
26095 2	Birmingham City	
25426 1	Sunderland	
25096 1	West Bromwich Albion	
24920 1	Nottingham Forest	
24656 2	Aston Villa	
23593 1	Ipswich Town	
22492 1	Southampton	
21579 1	Queens Park Rangers	
21063 2	Middlesbrough	
19874 2	Crystal Palace	
19163 2	Portsmouth	
18984 1	Stoke City	
18055 3	**Swindon Town**	
17973 2	Charlton Athletic	
16870 2	Cardiff City	
16073 1	Burnley	
15480 2	Sheffield United	
15463 2	Bristol City	
15388 2	Millwall	
15123 2	Blackpool	
14896 3	Luton Town	
14221 2	Fulham	
14216 2	Hull City	
13750 2	Norwich City	
13576 3	Watford	
13215 2	Preston North End	
11637 2	Oxford United	
10840 3	Brighton & Hove Albion	
10617 2	Blackburn Rovers	
10599 3	Plymouth Argyle	
10559 4	**Southend United**	

10536 2	Bolton Wanderers	
10212 4	Doncaster Rovers	
10167 2	Huddersfield Town	
9459 3	Barnsley	
9212 2	Carlisle United	
9077 3	Rotherham United	
8285 3	Torquay United	
7912 4	Lincoln City	
7765 2	Bury	
7564 3	Bournemouth & B. Ath.	
7214 4	Bradford City	
7173 3	Stockport County	
7118 3	Bristol Rovers	
7049 3	Mansfield Town	
6790 3	Northampton Town	
6552 3	Reading	
6419 4	Brentford	
6273 4	Colchester United	
6164 4	Darlington	
6040 3	Tranmere Rovers	
5883 4	Chester	
5882 4	Aldershot	
5867 3	Walsall	
5695 3	Orient	
5670 4	Halifax Town	
5664 4	Swansea Town	
5618 4	Peterborough United	
5604 4	Wrexham	
5516 3	Shrewsbury Town	
5399 4	Rochdale	
5387 3	Gillingham	
5371 4	Exeter City	
5063 4	Chesterfield	
4804 3	Crewe Alexandra	
4778 4	Notts County	
4676 3	Barrow	
4361 4	Port Vale	
4200 3	Hartlepool	
4189 3	Southport	
3984 4	Grimsby Town	
3883 4	York City	
3862 3	Oldham Athletic	
3644 4	Scunthorpe United	
3273 4	Bradford	
2457 4	Newport County	
2370 4	Workington	

49862	**1**	**Manchester United**	10259	3	Fulham
49531	1	Everton	10234	3	Barnsley
43567	1	Liverpool	10041	2	Bolton Wanderers
40342	1	Chelsea	**9902**	**4**	**Wrexham**
37553	1	Newcastle United	9886	4	Chesterfield
36060	1	Tottenham Hotspur	9855	3	Reading
35924	1	Derby County	9388	2	Carlisle United
35758	1	Arsenal	9112	3	Plymouth Argyle
34613	1	Leeds United	8852	3	Bradford City
33930	1	Manchester City	8561	3	Doncaster Rovers
32043	1	Coventry City	8406	4	Swansea Town
31164	1	Wolverhampton Wanderers	8294	3	Rotherham United
30530	1	West Ham United	7773	4	Brentford
29901	1	Crystal Palace	7143	3	Mansfield Town
27877	1	West Bromwich Albion	6894	4	Port Vale
27345	**2**	**Aston Villa**	6884	3	Torquay United
25924	1	Sheffield Wednesday	6396	4	Southend United
25104	2	Leicester City	6109	4	Peterborough United
25004	2	Birmingham City	6109	3	Rochdale
24932	1	Nottingham Forest	6101	4	Aldershot
24165	1	Stoke City	6070	4	Lincoln City
22901	1	Southampton	5779	4	Notts County
21790	1	Sunderland	5594	4	Northampton Town
21501	2	Cardiff City	5428	3	Walsall
20715	1	Ipswich Town	5410	3	Bournemouth & B. Ath.
20075	2	Swindon Town	5401	3	Gillingham
19856	2	Middlesbrough	4920	4	Exeter City
17840	2	Sheffield United	4674	3	Halifax Town
17526	2	Huddersfield Town	4643	4	Colchester United
17525	2	Queens Park Rangers	4512	3	Bury
17223	2	Watford	4487	4	Chester
16452	1	Burnley	4424	4	Scunthorpe United
16274	2	Bristol City	4415	4	Grimsby Town
15695	2	Blackpool	4394	3	Tranmere Rovers
14928	2	Portsmouth	4357	4	Oldham Athletic
14808	**3**	**Luton Town**	4289	3	Shrewsbury Town
14711	3	Brighton & Hove Albion	4274	4	York City
13548	2	Preston North End	3649	3	Barrow
13215	2	Norwich City	3506	3	Stockport County
12693	2	Charlton Athletic	3428	3	Southport
12523	2	Blackburn Rovers	3345	4	Crewe Alexandra
11870	3	Bristol Rovers	3137	4	Bradford
11688	2	Millwall	2755	4	Newport County
11369	3	Orient	2744	4	Darlington
11230	2	Hull City	2563	4	Hartlepool
10812	2	Oxford United	2123	4	Workington

45459 1 Liverpool	9824 3 Brighton & Hove Albion
43945 1 Manchester United	9636 3 Chesterfield
43776 1 Arsenal	9546 4 Oldham Athletic
41090 1 Everton	9119 2 Orient
39545 1 Chelsea	8706 2 Bolton Wanderers
39204 1 Leeds United	8704 3 Plymouth Argyle
35650 1 Tottenham Hotspur	8676 4 Bournemouth & B. Ath.
31367 1 Derby County	8137 3 Wrexham
31041 1 Manchester City	8035 3 Swansea City
29962 1 West Ham United	8034 2 Blackburn Rovers
29735 1 Newcastle United	7885 3 Rotherham United
28604 1 Crystal Palace	6889 3 Reading
27608 1 Wolverhampton Wanderers	6867 3 Mansfield Town
26219 3 Aston Villa	6830 3 Barnsley
26039 1 Coventry City	6776 4 Brentford
25996 2 Leicester City	6597 4 Northampton Town
25692 1 West Bromwich Albion	6409 4 Southend United
25254 2 Sheffield United	5997 3 Bradford City
24203 2 Birmingham City	5837 3 Torquay United
23324 1 Nottingham Forest	5603 4 Colchester United
23228 1 Huddersfield Town	5499 4 Lincoln City
22267 1 Southampton	5437 3 Port Vale
21535 2 Cardiff City	5382 4 Aldershot
20472 1 Blackpool	5253 4 York City
20432 1 Ipswich Town	5212 3 Walsall
19905 1 Stoke City	5134 3 Halifax Town
19737 2 Hull City	5086 4 Chester
18534 2 Middlesbrough	5072 3 Shrewsbury Town
17353 2 Luton Town	4919 4 Cambridge United
16156 1 Burnley	4884 4 Peterborough United
16021 2 Swindon Town	4866 3 Rochdale
15788 2 Sheffield Wednesday	4703 4 Exeter City
15780 2 Sunderland	4329 4 Grimsby Town
14348 2 Watford	4265 3 Doncaster Rovers
14165 2 Bristol City	4241 3 Gillingham
13787 3 Preston North End	4007 4 Scunthorpe United
13759 2 Portsmouth	3993 3 Bury
13069 2 Queens Park Rangers	3949 3 Tranmere Rovers
12657 2 Norwich City	3271 4 Stockport County
12004 3 Fulham	3029 4 Crewe Alexandra
11313 3 Bristol Rovers	3011 4 Darlington
10981 2 Charlton Athletic	2860 4 Southport
10884 2 Oxford United	2549 4 Newport County
10757 4 Notts County	2459 4 Hartlepool
10657 2 Carlisle United	2333 4 Barrow
9861 2 Millwall	2209 4 Workington

47687	1	**Liverpool**	10817	2	Orient
45999	1	Manchester United	10799	3	Plymouth Argyle
40500	1	Arsenal	10461	4	Southend United
38833	1	Tottenham Hotspur	10430	2	Charlton Athletic
38783	1	Chelsea	9530	2	Oxford United
38573	1	Manchester City	9479	2	Carlisle United
37242	1	Everton	9340	3	Bristol Rovers
35637	1	Leeds United	8256	3	Blackburn Rovers
33189	1	Sheffield United	8173	3	Bolton Wanderers
33087	1	Derby County	8016	3	Oldham Athletic
32664	1	Newcastle United	7992	3	Chesterfield
32337	**2**	**Birmingham City**	7603	4	Lincoln City
31952	**3**	**Aston Villa**	7313	3	Rotherham United
30005	1	West Ham United	6412	3	Swansea City
28536	1	Leicester City	6099	4	Scunthorpe United
28221	1	Wolverhampton Wanderers	6083	3	Wrexham
26973	1	Crystal Palace	5988	3	Mansfield Town
25786	1	West Bromwich Albion	5677	3	Torquay United
24204	1	Stoke City	5597	3	York City
23724	1	Coventry City	5531	4	Reading
23037	2	Norwich City	5445	3	Walsall
21433	1	Nottingham Forest	5429	4	Colchester United
21191	1	Southampton	5412	4	Gillingham
20924	1	Ipswich Town	5341	3	Barnsley
17943	2	Middlesbrough	5265	3	Shrewsbury Town
17661	3	Brighton & Hove Albion	5115	4	Peterborough United
17087	2	Sheffield Wednesday	5042	3	Bradford City
16262	2	Millwall	4891	4	Cambridge United
15940	1	Huddersfield Town	4486	4	Northampton Town
15906	2	Sunderland	4387	3	Rochdale
15510	2	Cardiff City	4366	3	Port Vale
15225	2	Bristol City	4355	3	Tranmere Rovers
15136	2	Preston North End	4125	4	Doncaster Rovers
14367	2	Queens Park Rangers	4056	4	Aldershot
13972	2	Hull City	3857	4	Exeter City
13941	3	Notts County	3839	3	Halifax Town
13579	2	Swindon Town	3793	4	Hartlepool
13483	2	Blackpool	3502	4	Bury
12991	3	Bournemouth & B. Ath.	3462	4	Newport County
12893	2	Burnley	3254	4	Southport
11918	2	Portsmouth	3002	4	Chester
11738	4	Brentford	2552	4	Darlington
11384	2	Luton Town	2487	4	Workington
11315	**4**	**Grimsby Town**	2477	4	Stockport County
11147	2	Fulham	2307	4	Barrow
10908	2	Watford	2104	4	Crewe Alexandra

48623 1	**Manchester United**	9057	3	Plymouth Argyle
48127 1	Liverpool	**8917**	**4**	**Hereford United**
40246 1	Arsenal	8900	3	Bristol Rovers
36663 1	Birmingham City	8742	3	Brentford
35831 1	Leeds United	8256	3	Oldham Athletic
34471 1	Everton	8175	2	Huddersfield Town
32351 1	Manchester City	7606	2	Carlisle United
32318 1	Tottenham Hotspur	7329	3	Southend United
30174 1	West Ham United	6749	3	Watford
30167 1	Crystal Palace	6449	2	Orient
29766 1	Derby County	5723	3	Chesterfield
29722 1	Chelsea	5658	3	Charlton Athletic
28420 1	Norwich City	5615	3	Tranmere Rovers
27939 1	Newcastle United	5429	3	Port Vale
27689 2	**Aston Villa**	5321	4	Reading
24623 1	Coventry City	5010	4	Mansfield Town
24418 1	Wolverhampton Wanderers	4956	4	Exeter City
23800 1	Stoke City	4817	4	Newport County
23509 1	Sheffield United	4803	3	Walsall
22706 1	Leicester City	4761	4	Peterborough United
22603 2	Sunderland	4741	3	Rotherham United
22241 1	Ipswich Town	4547	4	Lincoln City
21427 1	West Bromwich Albion	4546	3	Wrexham
18118 1	Southampton	4442	4	Aldershot
17076 2	Sheffield Wednesday	4227	4	Cambridge United
14715 2	Queens Park Rangers	3793	3	York City
14167 2	Brighton & Hove Albion	3736	3	Scunthorpe United
14083 2	Burnley	3728	4	Stockport County
13928 3	**Bolton Wanderers**	3691	4	Hartlepool
12892 2	Bristol City	3580	4	Southport
12268 3	AFC Bournemouth	3498	4	Bradford City
11456 2	Cardiff City	3300	4	Torquay United
10849 3	Grimsby Town	3232	4	Colchester United
10782 2	Blackpool	3186	3	Rochdale
10701 3	Notts County	3186	4	Gillingham
10643 2	Luton Town	3104	3	Swansea City
10418 2	Middlesbrough	3004	3	Shrewsbury Town
10267 2	Swindon Town	2971	4	Bury
10267 2	Fulham	2963	4	Chester
10265 2	Millwall	2862	4	Barnsley
10199 2	Preston North End	2835	4	Northampton Town
9995 2	Nottingham Forest	2741	3	Halifax Town
9477 2	Portsmouth	2259	4	Doncaster Rovers
9233 2	Hull City	2059	4	Crewe Alexandra
9214 3	Blackburn Rovers	1697	4	Darlington
9197 2	Oxford United	1442	4	Workington

42712 1	**Manchester United**	
42332 1	Liverpool	
38666 1	Leeds United	
35351 1	Everton	
33048 1	Birmingham City	
32861 1	Newcastle United	
30756 1	Manchester City	
30212 1	Arsenal	
28394 1	West Ham United	
27788 1	Derby County	
26124 1	Tottenham Hotspur	
25983 1	Chelsea	
25609 1	Wolverhampton Wanderers	
24825 1	Leicester City	
24409 2	**Sunderland**	
23413 2	Aston Villa	
23280 1	Coventry City	
23023 1	Norwich City	
22917 1	Sheffield United	
22867 1	Queens Park Rangers	
22381 1	Ipswich Town	
22264 2	Middlesbrough	
21797 2	Crystal Palace	
21587 1	Stoke City	
21128 1	Southampton	
20634 1	Burnley	
15990 2	West Bromwich Albion	
15942 2	Bolton Wanderers	
14645 2	Sheffield Wednesday	
14416 2	Notts County	
14058 2	Bristol City	
13675 2	Portsmouth	
13026 3	**Bristol Rovers**	
12214 2	Luton Town	
12174 2	Preston North End	
11897 2	Nottingham Forest	
11793 2	Orient	
10864 3	Brighton & Hove Albion	
10714 2	Cardiff City	
10129 2	Fulham	
10120 2	Blackpool	
10118 3	Oldham Athletic	
9516 2	Millwall	
8981 3	AFC Bournemouth	
8824 4	**Peterborough United**	
8302 2	Oxford United	

8270 2	Carlisle United
8216 2	Hull City
8040 3	Hereford United
7743 3	Plymouth Argyle
7502 4	Gillingham
7432 3	Blackburn Rovers
7419 3	Grimsby Town
7299 2	Swindon Town
6885 3	York City
6683 3	Watford
6477 4	Reading
6472 3	Southend United
5957 3	Wrexham
5777 3	Chesterfield
5696 3	Huddersfield Town
5427 4	Colchester United
5424 4	Northampton Town
5306 3	Charlton Athletic
5235 3	Aldershot
5063 4	Brentford
4879 4	Bury
4789 3	Walsall
4377 3	Cambridge United
4254 4	Barnsley
4215 3	Tranmere Rovers
4186 4	Exeter City
3959 3	Port Vale
3930 4	Lincoln City
3797 4	Bradford City
3410 4	Rotherham United
3392 4	Torquay United
3160 4	Mansfield Town
3029 4	Scunthorpe United
3023 4	Newport County
2849 3	Halifax Town
2815 4	Swansea City
2721 4	Hartlepool
2682 4	Chester
2547 3	Southport
2502 3	Shrewsbury Town
2395 4	Doncaster Rovers
2380 4	Stockport County
2334 4	Darlington
1921 4	Crewe Alexandra
1890 3	Rochdale
1173 4	Workington

48389 2	**Manchester United**	
45966 1	**Liverpool**	
40021 1	Everton	
34822 1	Leeds United	
34614 1	Newcastle United	
32898 1	Manchester City	
30854 1	Birmingham City	
29931 2	Sunderland	
29872 1	West Ham United	
28605 1	Middlesbrough	
28315 1	Arsenal	
27654 2	Aston Villa	
27396 1	Chelsea	
27011 1	Stoke City	
26719 1	Derby County	
26458 1	Tottenham Hotspur	
24924 1	Ipswich Town	
23765 1	Leicester City	
23405 1	Wolverhampton Wanderers	
22555 1	Sheffield United	
22460 2	Norwich City	
20394 1	Queens Park Rangers	
19641 1	Burnley	
19100 1	Coventry City	
17396 1	Luton Town	
17274 3	**Crystal Palace**	
15910 2	Southampton	
14530 1	Carlisle United	
14061 2	Bristol City	
14060 3	Plymouth Argyle	
13800 2	Bolton Wanderers	
13453 2	Sheffield Wednesday	
13000 2	Nottingham Forest	
12651 3	Blackburn Rovers	
12492 2	Oldham Athletic	
12474 2	Portsmouth	
12424 2	West Bromwich Albion	
12222 2	Bristol Rovers	
11751 3	Brighton & Hove Albion	
10927 2	Notts County	
10809 2	Fulham	
10444 3	Charlton Athletic	
10112 2	Blackpool	
9568 3	Preston North End	
9143 2	Cardiff City	
8954 2	York City	

8583 2	Millwall	
8573 2	Hull City	
8446 3	Peterborough United	
8280 3	Swindon Town	
8261 2	Oxford United	
7605 2	Orient	
7331 3	Gillingham	
7230 3	Hereford United	
7204 4	**Mansfield Town**	
7017 3	Southend United	
6460 3	Watford	
6268 3	Walsall	
5988 3	AFC Bournemouth	
5962 3	Grimsby Town	
5795 4	Lincoln City	
5527 3	Bury	
5488 4	Rotherham United	
5428 3	Huddersfield Town	
5386 4	Reading	
5172 4	Brentford	
4937 3	Colchester United	
4745 4	Chester	
4646 4	Barnsley	
4615 3	Chesterfield	
4385 3	Aldershot	
4376 3	Wrexham	
4346 3	Port Vale	
4179 4	Northampton Town	
4125 4	Shrewsbury Town	
3435 4	Exeter City	
3191 4	Bradford City	
3021 4	Cambridge United	
2975 4	Doncaster Rovers	
2868 4	Torquay United	
2803 3	Tranmere Rovers	
2718 4	Newport County	
2681 3	Halifax Town	
2649 4	Crewe Alexandra	
2634 4	Hartlepool	
2239 4	Scunthorpe United	
2233 4	Darlington	
2099 4	Stockport County	
2070 4	Swansea City	
1737 4	Southport	
1507 4	Rochdale	
1481 4	Workington	

54750 1 Manchester United	7714 3 Swindon Town
41623 1 Liverpool	7693 4 Reading
38874 1 Aston Villa	7689 3 Millwall
34280 1 Manchester City	7607 3 Peterborough United
33060 1 Newcastle United	7344 3 Mansfield Town
31511 1 Leeds United	7069 3 Preston North End
31250 2 Sunderland	6901 2 Hull City
28350 1 Derby County	6736 2 Oxford United
28003 1 Birmingham City	6416 4 Northampton Town
27836 1 Tottenham Hotspur	6386 2 Orient
27417 1 West Ham United	6301 3 Gillingham
27115 1 Everton	6056 4 Doncaster Rovers
26945 1 Arsenal	5936 3 Bury
25366 1 Ipswich Town	5618 3 Walsall
23850 1 Queens Park Rangers	5580 3 Grimsby Town
23549 1 Sheffield United	5430 4 Huddersfield Town
23223 1 Middlesbrough	5413 2 York City
22951 1 Wolverhampton Wanderers	5219 3 Rotherham United
22760 1 Norwich City	5103 3 Chester
22314 1 Stoke City	5096 4 Brentford
22049 1 Leicester City	5011 3 Southend United
20124 3 Crystal Palace	4919 3 Chesterfield
19390 2 Bolton Wanderers	4652 3 Shrewsbury Town
19370 1 Coventry City	4609 4 Watford
18957 2 Chelsea	4587 3 Aldershot
18120 1 Burnley	4461 4 AFC Bournemouth
17648 2 Southampton	4159 3 Wrexham
17226 2 West Bromwich Albion	4133 3 Port Vale
16204 2 Bristol City	3880 4 Tranmere Rovers
15343 3 Brighton & Hove Albion	3708 4 Barnsley
14800 2 Plymouth Argyle	3348 3 Colchester United
12805 2 Nottingham Forest	3264 4 Exeter City
12414 2 Notts County	3238 4 Stockport County
11702 3 Cardiff City	3047 4 Scunthorpe United
11629 2 Charlton Athletic	2932 4 Swansea City
11219 3 Sheffield Wednesday	2916 4 Bradford City
10587 2 Luton Town	2640 4 Torquay United
10489 2 Blackburn Rovers	2566 4 Cambridge United
10472 2 Portsmouth	2506 3 Halifax Town
10456 2 Oldham Athletic	2374 4 Crewe Alexandra
10022 2 Bristol Rovers	2227 4 Darlington
9741 2 Fulham	2182 4 Hartlepool
8401 4 Lincoln City	2080 4 Newport County
8307 2 Blackpool	1594 4 Rochdale
8279 2 Carlisle United	1449 4 Southport
8186 3 Hereford United	1276 4 Workington

53710 1	**Manchester United**	7987 3	Preston North End
47221 1	Liverpool	7924 2	Hull City
40058 1	Manchester City	7846 3	Swindon Town
37760 1	Aston Villa	7680 2	Carlisle United
33599 1	Newcastle United	7240 2	Hereford United
32743 1	Sunderland	7145 3	Lincoln City
32671 1	Arsenal	6761 3	Reading
30633 2	**Chelsea**	6682 3	Rotherham United
30530 1	Leeds United	6222 2	Orient
30173 1	Tottenham Hotspur	**6148 4**	**Huddersfield Town**
30046 1	Everton	6035 4	Watford
28338 1	Birmingham City	5996 3	Peterborough United
26672 1	Ipswich Town	5750 3	Northampton Town
26064 1	West Ham United	5630 4	Bradford City
25008 1	Derby County	5529 4	Barnsley
24525 1	West Bromwich Albion	5510 4	Southend United
23522 1	Bristol City	5498 3	Walsall
22305 1	Norwich City	5444 3	Gillingham
21795 2	Bolton Wanderers	5322 3	Chesterfield
21480 1	Middlesbrough	5311 4	Swansea City
21242 1	Coventry City	5299 3	Bury
21227 2	Wolverhampton Wanderers	5152 3	Oxford United
21062 1	Queens Park Rangers	5121 4	Brentford
20197 3	**Brighton & Hove Albion**	4974 3	Shrewsbury Town
19480 2	Southampton	4738 3	Grimsby Town
19027 1	Stoke City	4651 4	Colchester United
18807 1	Leicester City	4631 4	Doncaster Rovers
18064 2	Nottingham Forest	4624 4	Exeter City
16779 2	Sheffield United	4609 3	Chester
16016 3	Crystal Palace	4445 4	Cambridge United
14589 2	Fulham	4357 3	Port Vale
13688 3	Sheffield Wednesday	4035 4	AFC Bournemouth
13329 2	Plymouth Argyle	3851 4	Stockport County
13171 2	Blackpool	3631 4	Aldershot
12790 2	Cardiff City	3483 4	Scunthorpe United
12173 2	Burnley	3251 3	Tranmere Rovers
11564 3	Portsmouth	3005 3	York City
11387 2	Luton Town	2958 4	Torquay United
11057 2	Charlton Athletic	2744 4	Darlington
10943 2	Notts County	2612 4	Newport County
10601 2	Millwall	2379 4	Crewe Alexandra
10130 2	Blackburn Rovers	2340 4	Halifax Town
9944 2	Oldham Athletic	1911 4	Hartlepool
9328 3	Wrexham	1745 4	Rochdale
8439 3	Mansfield Town	1438 4	Southport
8431 2	Bristol Rovers	1338 4	Workington

51860 1	**Manchester United**	8365	2	Cardiff City
45546 1	Liverpool	8197	2	Millwall
41687 1	Manchester City	8108	2	Bristol Rovers
39513 1	Everton	8108	4	Swansea City
35464 1	Aston Villa	7367	3	Swindon Town
35446 1	Arsenal	7287	4	Southend United
33417 2	**Tottenham Hotspur**	7167	3	Gillingham
32501 1	Nottingham Forest	6835	2	Hull City
29186 1	Leeds United	6763	3	Plymouth Argyle
28734 1	Chelsea	5974	3	Peterborough United
25620 1	West Ham United	5659	4	Barnsley
25265 2	Brighton & Hove Albion	5633	3	Cambridge United
24729 1	Newcastle United	5319	3	Carlisle United
24126 1	West Bromwich Albion	5317	3	Walsall
23911 1	Birmingham City	5103	3	Bradford City
23586 1	Ipswich Town	4979	3	Bury
23357 1	Bristol City	4972	3	Oxford United
23353 1	Coventry City	4913	3	Rotherham United
23345 1	Derby County	4900	3	Hereford United
22877 2	Bolton Wanderers	4887	3	Exeter City
22311 1	Wolverhampton Wanderers	4878	3	Lincoln City
22276 2	Sunderland	4866	3	Chesterfield
21167 2	Southampton	4696	4	Grimsby Town
19941 1	Queens Park Rangers	4572	3	Colchester United
19874 1	Middlesbrough	4567	4	Reading
19636 2	Crystal Palace	4508	4	Huddersfield Town
19366 1	Norwich City	4347	4	Aldershot
17768 1	Leicester City	4165	3	Chester
15489 2	Sheffield United	4074	4	Newport County
15038 2	Stoke City	4010	4	Stockport County
12227 2	Blackburn Rovers	3947	3	Port Vale
11651 3	**Wrexham**	3926	3	Tranmere Rovers
11592 3	Sheffield Wednesday	3517	4	Northampton Town
11581 2	Burnley	3378	3	Shrewsbury Town
11352 4	**Watford**	3348	4	AFC Bournemouth
11307 2	Charlton Athletic	3281	4	Scunthorpe United
10550 2	Fulham	3228	4	Doncaster Rovers
10118 2	Blackpool	3135	4	Wimbledon
9678 3	Portsmouth	2878	4	Torquay United
9583 2	Oldham Athletic	2833	4	Hartlepool United
9268 2	Notts County	2290	4	Crewe Alexandra
9252 2	Luton Town	2284	4	York City
8982 2	Mansfield Town	2199	4	Halifax Town
8799 3	Preston North End	1993	4	Darlington
8578 4	Brentford	1873	4	Southport
8400 2	Orient	1275	4	Rochdale

46430 1	**Manchester United**	
46407 1	Liverpool	
36371 1	Arsenal	
36203 1	Manchester City	
35456 1	Everton	
34902 1	Tottenham Hotspur	
32838 1	Aston Villa	
29587 1	Nottingham Forest	
27633 1	Leeds United	
26517 1	West Bromwich Albion	
25778 2	**West Ham United**	
25454 2	Sunderland	
24782 1	Chelsea	
23294 2	Crystal Palace	
23200 1	Bolton Wanderers	
22638 1	Coventry City	
22306 1	Bristol City	
22145 2	Brighton & Hove Albion	
21673 1	Ipswich Town	
21555 1	Derby County	
21330 1	Southampton	
20796 1	Wolverhampton Wanderers	
20494 2	Newcastle United	
20164 1	Birmingham City	
19125 2	Stoke City	
18459 1	Middlesbrough	
17874 1	Norwich City	
16339 2	Sheffield United	
16287 1	Queens Park Rangers	
14435 3	**Watford**	
14187 2	Leicester City	
13746 3	Swansea City	
12117 2	Preston North End	
11519 2	Wrexham	
11048 4	**Barnsley**	
10860 3	Sheffield Wednesday	
10748 2	Burnley	
10135 2	Fulham	
10123 4	Portsmouth	
9563 2	Charlton Athletic	
9281 2	Notts County	
9246 2	Cardiff City	
8792 2	Luton Town	
8640 2	Blackburn Rovers	
7975 3	Swindon Town	
7616 4	Reading	

7593 2	Bristol Rovers
7526 3	Plymouth Argyle
7455 3	Brentford
7323 2	Orient
7143 3	Gillingham
7045 2	Oldham Athletic
7002 2	Millwall
6849 2	Cambridge United
6701 4	Wigan Athletic
6610 3	Southend United
6528 4	Grimsby Town
6099 3	Shrewsbury Town
5647 3	Blackpool
5238 3	Hull City
5204 3	Carlisle United
5151 3	Mansfield Town
4822 3	Chesterfield
4647 3	Oxford United
4640 3	Peterborough United
4466 3	Rotherham United
4408 3	Exeter City
4163 4	Aldershot
4142 4	Stockport County
4052 3	Chester
4047 3	Walsall
3924 4	Bradford City
3782 3	Bury
3759 4	AFC Bournemouth
3731 4	Newport County
3712 4	Wimbledon
3649 4	Huddersfield Town
3419 3	Colchester United
3369 4	Hereford United
3287 4	Port Vale
3168 3	Lincoln City
3000 4	Doncaster Rovers
2997 4	Hartlepool United
2936 4	York City
2895 4	Northampton Town
2721 4	Scunthorpe United
2669 4	Torquay United
2179 3	Tranmere Rovers
1995 4	Crewe Alexandra
1821 4	Halifax Town
1807 4	Darlington
1767 4	Rochdale

51608 1 Manchester United	8118 2 Burnley
44586 1 Liverpool	7918 2 Oldham Athletic
35272 1 Manchester City	7818 3 Brentford
33596 1 Arsenal	7760 3 Chesterfield
32018 1 Tottenham Hotspur	7399 2 Bristol Rovers
29794 1 Crystal Palace	7245 2 Orient
28711 1 Everton	7175 2 Charlton Athletic
27976 1 Aston Villa	6843 3 Reading
27119 2 Sunderland	6131 3 Gillingham
26360 1 Nottingham Forest	6127 2 Cambridge United
25731 1 Wolverhampton Wanderers	5993 3 Rotherham United
24745 1 Brighton & Hove Albion	5986 3 Hull City
23345 2 Newcastle United	5918 3 Millwall
23266 2 Chelsea	5905 4 Wigan Athletic
22872 2 West Ham United	5818 3 Blackpool
22788 1 Leeds United	5776 3 Plymouth Argyle
22418 1 West Bromwich Albion	5774 4 Bradford City
21620 1 Ipswich Town	5549 4 Walsall
21335 1 Southampton	5467 3 Mansfield Town
20427 2 Birmingham City	5139 4 Newport County
20176 1 Stoke City	4832 3 Oxford United
19904 1 Derby County	4758 3 Southend United
19315 1 Coventry City	4574 3 Exeter City
18932 1 Bristol City	4406 3 Carlisle United
18739 1 Middlesbrough	4321 4 Doncaster Rovers
18636 2 Leicester City	4239 3 Bury
18288 3 Sheffield Wednesday	4135 4 Peterborough United
17225 1 Norwich City	3924 4 AFC Bournemouth
16584 3 Sheffield United	3859 4 Aldershot
16353 1 Bolton Wanderers	3816 3 Colchester United
15850 4 Portsmouth	3726 3 Chester
15462 2 Watford	3713 4 Lincoln City
14391 2 Swansea City	3462 4 Port Vale
14087 2 Queens Park Rangers	3426 3 Wimbledon
11890 3 Barnsley	3355 4 Hereford United
11676 2 Luton Town	3184 4 Torquay United
10618 3 Grimsby Town	3024 4 Northampton Town
10311 3 Blackburn Rovers	2915 4 Hartlepool United
10090 2 Wrexham	2911 4 Stockport County
9926 2 Cardiff City	2745 4 Crewe Alexandra
9751 2 Preston North End	2716 4 York City
8902 3 Swindon Town	2582 4 Halifax Town
8818 2 Notts County	2266 4 Scunthorpe United
8782 2 Shrewsbury Town	2246 4 Tranmere Rovers
8714 4 Huddersfield Town	1972 4 Darlington
8419 2 Fulham	1926 4 Rochdale

45071	**1**	**Manchester United**	6766	3	Plymouth Argyle
37547	1	Liverpool	6752	3	Brentford
34117	1	Aston Villa	6510	2	Oldham Athletic
33587	1	Manchester City	6495	2	Wrexham
32480	1	Arsenal	6469	3	Burnley
30724	1	Tottenham Hotspur	**6095**	**4**	**Southend United**
27140	**2**	**West Ham United**	6076	2	Orient
26477	1	Sunderland	5929	2	Bristol Rovers
26105	1	Everton	5863	3	Blackpool
24619	1	Ipswich Town	5796	2	Cambridge United
24483	1	Nottingham Forest	5683	3	Newport County
21551	1	Wolverhampton Wanderers	5616	2	Shrewsbury Town
21482	1	Southampton	5439	3	Reading
21377	1	Leeds United	5412	4	Doncaster Rovers
20331	1	West Bromwich Albion	5060	3	Fulham
19476	1	Leicester City	4715	4	Lincoln City
19280	1	Crystal Palace	4676	3	Gillingham
19248	1	Birmingham City	4559	3	Exeter City
18984	1	Brighton & Hove Albion	4494	3	Millwall
18624	2	Sheffield Wednesday	4434	4	Wigan Athletic
17897	2	Chelsea	4319	3	Hull City
17140	1	Norwich City	4265	3	Walsall
16904	1	Coventry City	4137	4	Peterborough United
16682	2	Derby County	4132	3	Oxford United
16432	1	Middlesbrough	4064	3	Carlisle United
16001	2	Newcastle United	3400	4	Mansfield Town
15580	1	Stoke City	3380	4	AFC Bournemouth
13514	**3**	**Portsmouth**	3115	4	Hartlepool United
13143	2	Swansea City	2989	4	Aldershot
13108	2	Watford	2909	4	Crewe Alexandra
12800	3	Barnsley	2892	3	Chester
12772	3	Sheffield United	2858	4	Bradford City
11684	2	Blackburn Rovers	2748	4	Bury
11548	3	Huddersfield Town	2738	4	Port Vale
10961	2	Grimsby Town	2645	3	Colchester United
10936	2	Queens Park Rangers	2537	4	Darlington
10291	2	Luton Town	2484	4	Wimbledon
9847	2	Bolton Wanderers	2460	4	Rochdale
9765	2	Bristol City	2444	4	Hereford United
9551	2	Notts County	2357	4	Scunthorpe United
7985	3	Rotherham United	2335	4	Stockport County
7631	2	Preston North End	2196	4	Northampton Town
7331	3	Chesterfield	2163	4	York City
7206	3	Charlton Athletic	2050	4	Torquay United
6933	3	Swindon Town	1924	4	Halifax Town
6767	2	Cardiff City	1901	4	Tranmere Rovers

44571 1	**Manchester United**	
35100 1	Tottenham Hotspur	
35061 1	Liverpool	
34063 1	Manchester City	
26780 1	Aston Villa	
26585 1	West Ham United	
25589 1	Arsenal	
24674 1	Everton	
22109 1	Leeds United	
21925 1	Ipswich Town	
21835 1	Southampton	
19937 1	Nottingham Forest	
19608 1	Sunderland	
19170 2	**Sheffield Wednesday**	
18244 1	Brighton & Hove Albion	
18226 1	Swansea City	
17276 2	Newcastle United	
17117 1	Birmingham City	
16786 1	West Bromwich Albion	
15242 1	Wolverhampton Wanderers	
15098 2	Barnsley	
14892 4	**Sheffield United**	
14635 1	Stoke City	
14631 2	Watford	
14183 2	Norwich City	
14182 2	Leicester City	
13413 1	Middlesbrough	
13132 2	Chelsea	
13100 1	Coventry City	
12574 2	Queens Park Rangers	
11881 2	Luton Town	
11828 2	Derby County	
11613 1	Notts County	
10381 2	Crystal Palace	
9857 2	Rotherham United	
8544 3	**Portsmouth**	
8406 2	Grimsby Town	
8405 2	Blackburn Rovers	
7597 2	Bolton Wanderers	
7023 2	Oldham Athletic	
6938 3	Fulham	
6936 3	Burnley	
6746 3	Huddersfield Town	
6649 2	Charlton Athletic	
6511 3	Bristol City	
5933 4	AFC Bournemouth	

5851 3	Oxford United	
5840 4	Wigan Athletic	
5825 3	Swindon Town	
5693 3	Brentford	
5574 2	Cardiff City	
5497 3	Preston North End	
5402 3	Bristol Rovers	
5391 4	Bradford City	
5241 3	Gillingham	
5234 3	Doncaster Rovers	
5083 3	Southend United	
5073 2	Cambridge United	
4792 3	Plymouth Argyle	
4752 3	Chesterfield	
4698 4	Peterborough United	
4626 3	Millwall	
4569 2	Shrewsbury Town	
4459 3	Newport County	
4419 2	Orient	
4409 3	Carlisle United	
4304 2	Wrexham	
4224 4	Blackpool	
4222 3	Lincoln City	
4018 3	Reading	
3993 4	Hull City	
3858 3	Exeter City	
3744 3	Walsall	
3639 4	Port Vale	
3558 4	Bury	
2859 4	Colchester United	
2685 4	Mansfield Town	
2596 3	Wimbledon	
2592 4	Hereford United	
2547 4	Stockport County	
2510 4	Darlington	
2407 4	Halifax Town	
2360 4	York City	
2306 4	Northampton Town	
2248 4	Torquay United	
2232 4	Scunthorpe United	
2196 4	Crewe Alexandra	
2168 4	Aldershot	
2062 3	Chester	
2055 4	Hartlepool United	
1837 4	Rochdale	
1735 4	Tranmere Rovers	

41695 1	**Manchester United**	
34758 1	Liverpool	
30581 1	Tottenham Hotspur	
26789 1	Manchester City	
24166 2	**Newcastle United**	
24153 1	Arsenal	
23748 1	Aston Villa	
22822 1	West Ham United	
20277 1	Everton	
19503 1	Ipswich Town	
19488 1	Watford	
18799 1	Southampton	
17851 1	Nottingham Forest	
17370 1	Sunderland	
16862 1	Norwich City	
16835 2	Sheffield Wednesday	
16622 1	Stoke City	
15994 2	Leeds United	
15667 2	Wolverhampton Wanderers	
15638 1	Birmingham City	
15200 1	West Bromwich Albion	
14662 1	Brighton & Hove Albion	
14095 3	**Portsmouth**	
13601 2	Derby County	
13452 1	Luton Town	
12807 2	Queens Park Rangers	
12672 2	Chelsea	
12380 2	Leicester City	
12341 2	Barnsley	
11764 3	Sheffield United	
11704 1	Swansea City	
10826 2	Fulham	
10552 1	Coventry City	
10265 1	Notts County	
10018 2	Middlesbrough	
9887 2	Crystal Palace	
9261 3	Huddersfield Town	
9086 2	Burnley	
8317 2	Rotherham United	
7741 2	Grimsby Town	
7552 2	Bolton Wanderers	
7213 2	Charlton Athletic	
7103 2	Blackburn Rovers	
7036 3	Cardiff City	
6962 2	Oldham Athletic	
6586 4	**Hull City**	

6221 3	Bristol Rovers
6184 3	Brentford
5944 2	Carlisle United
5732 3	AFC Bournemouth
5419 3	Oxford United
5277 2	Shrewsbury Town
4941 3	Preston North End
4867 3	Bradford City
4806 4	Port Vale
4799 4	Bristol City
4790 3	Lincoln City
4714 3	Newport County
4540 3	Plymouth Argyle
4513 2	Cambridge United
4434 3	Wigan Athletic
4195 4	Swindon Town
4076 3	Gillingham
4013 3	Millwall
3580 4	Scunthorpe United
3541 3	Doncaster Rovers
3529 3	Southend United
3459 3	Reading
3243 4	York City
3243 3	Walsall
3230 3	Exeter City
3226 3	Chesterfield
3097 4	Bury
3002 4	Blackpool
2795 4	Peterborough United
2718 3	Orient
2710 3	Wrexham
2594 4	Northampton Town
2552 4	Colchester United
2347 4	Wimbledon
2336 4	Torquay United
2318 4	Mansfield Town
2309 4	Stockport County
2244 4	Crewe Alexandra
2217 4	Hereford United
2071 4	Chester
1979 4	Halifax Town
1929 4	Aldershot
1921 4	Tranmere Rovers
1688 4	Rochdale
1449 4	Darlington
1368 4	Hartlepool United

42534 1	**Manchester United**	5892 3	Bolton Wanderers
31974 1	Liverpool	5611 2	Carlisle United
29811 2	**Newcastle United**	5550 3	Bristol Rovers
28701 1	Tottenham Hotspur	5336 3	Plymouth Argyle
28116 1	Arsenal	5017 3	Walsall
25604 2	Manchester City	5008 4	York City
22770 2	Sheffield Wednesday	4740 2	Shrewsbury Town
21386 1	West Ham United	4735 3	Brentford
21371 1	Aston Villa	4645 3	Rotherham United
21120 2	Chelsea	4571 3	Preston North End
19343 1	Everton	4471 4	Reading
18089 1	Southampton	4351 3	Millwall
17698 1	Nottingham Forest	4203 3	Bradford City
17464 1	Ipswich Town	4071 2	Cambridge United
16510 1	Watford	4039 3	AFC Bournemouth
16180 1	Sunderland	4023 3	Port Vale
15659 1	Norwich City	3936 4	Blackpool
15493 2	Leeds United	3916 3	Gillingham
15370 1	Queens Park Rangers	3899 3	Wigan Athletic
14923 1	Leicester City	3778 4	Doncaster Rovers
14569 1	West Bromwich Albion	3459 3	Wimbledon
14107 1	Birmingham City	3424 4	Peterborough United
13900 1	Stoke City	3414 4	Chesterfield
13196 2	Portsmouth	3380 3	Exeter City
12881 3	**Sheffield United**	3349 3	Scunthorpe United
12859 2	Derby County	3345 4	Swindon Town
12572 1	Coventry City	3222 3	Orient
12478 1	Wolverhampton Wanderers	3148 3	Lincoln City
12275 2	Brighton & Hove Albion	3142 3	Southend United
11938 1	Luton Town	3135 3	Newport County
11044 2	Huddersfield Town	2984 4	Hereford United
9738 2	Barnsley	2483 4	Aldershot
9463 1	Notts County	2454 4	Crewe Alexandra
8474 2	Middlesbrough	2440 4	Mansfield Town
8199 2	Crystal Palace	2343 4	Northampton Town
8143 2	Fulham	2220 4	Colchester United
8135 3	Hull City	2138 4	Tranmere Rovers
7871 3	Oxford United	2104 4	Bury
7643 2	Grimsby Town	2098 4	Stockport County
7623 2	Blackburn Rovers	2083 4	Wrexham
7287 4	**Bristol City**	1922 4	Torquay United
7067 2	Cardiff City	1764 4	Chester City
6980 2	Swansea City	1507 4	Darlington
6732 2	Charlton Athletic	1505 4	Hartlepool United
6625 3	Burnley	1491 4	Rochdale
6036 2	Oldham Athletic	1412 4	Halifax Town

42881	**1**	**Manchester United**	5054	3	Plymouth Argyle
34444	1	Liverpool	4951	3	Bolton Wanderers
31984	1	Everton	**4907**	**4**	**Blackpool**
31205	1	Arsenal	4812	3	Walsall
28930	1	Tottenham Hotspur	4720	3	Gillingham
27781	1	Sheffield Wednesday	4715	2	Shrewsbury Town
26228	1	Newcastle United	4713	2	Oldham Athletic
24220	**2**	**Manchester City**	4505	3	Rotherham United
23065	1	Chelsea	4421	3	Swansea City
18433	1	West Ham United	4391	2	Wimbledon
18347	1	Sunderland	4363	2	Cardiff City
18318	1	Aston Villa	4177	3	Burnley
18246	1	Watford	4103	3	Doncaster Rovers
18046	1	Southampton	4074	3	Brentford
17219	1	Ipswich Town	4073	4	Chesterfield
16781	1	Nottingham Forest	4016	2	Carlisle United
15185	2	Portsmouth	3889	4	Hereford United
15161	2	Leeds United	3851	3	AFC Bournemouth
15100	1	Norwich City	3793	3	Preston North End
14546	1	Leicester City	3738	4	Darlington
14000	1	Queens Park Rangers	3689	3	Reading
13849	1	West Bromwich Albion	3591	4	Bury
12848	1	Coventry City	3267	4	Port Vale
12733	2	Birmingham City	3265	3	Wigan Athletic
12055	2	Sheffield United	3221	4	Swindon Town
11798	2	Brighton & Hove Albion	3157	4	Peterborough United
10833	3	Derby County	2640	3	Orient
10816	1	Luton Town	2486	3	Lincoln City
10700	1	Stoke City	2412	3	Newport County
10577	2	Oxford United	2352	4	Exeter City
9648	2	Blackburn Rovers	2348	4	Hartlepool United
8507	**3**	**Bristol City**	2314	4	Mansfield Town
8375	2	Wolverhampton Wanderers	2271	4	Crewe Alexandra
7550	3	Hull City	2103	4	Southend United
7238	2	Huddersfield Town	2102	3	Cambridge United
7225	2	Barnsley	2081	4	Colchester United
6639	3	Bradford City	2068	4	Scunthorpe United
6470	3	Millwall	2010	4	Aldershot
6458	2	Grimsby Town	1940	4	Chester City
6446	2	Crystal Palace	1895	4	Stockport County
6211	2	Notts County	1824	4	Northampton Town
6179	2	Fulham	1619	4	Wrexham
5550	3	York City	1595	4	Tranmere Rovers
5258	3	Bristol Rovers	1434	4	Rochdale
5135	2	Middlesbrough	1386	4	Torquay United
5104	2	Charlton Athletic	1378	4	Halifax Town

46321 1	**Manchester United**	
35271 1	Liverpool	
32227 1	Everton	
24229 1	Manchester City	
23824 1	Arsenal	
23434 1	Newcastle United	
23111 1	Sheffield Wednesday	
21985 1	Chelsea	
21179 1	West Ham United	
20859 1	Tottenham Hotspur	
16809 1	Nottingham Forest	
16052 2	**Sunderland**	
15360 1	Watford	
15237 1	Aston Villa	
14877 1	Southampton	
14469 1	Ipswich Town	
13722 2	Norwich City	
13614 2	Portsmouth	
13259 2	Leeds United	
12665 1	Queens Park Rangers	
12386 3	**Derby County**	
12164 1	West Bromwich Albion	
11793 1	Leicester City	
11590 1	Coventry City	
11062 1	Luton Town	
11009 1	Oxford United	
10900 1	Birmingham City	
10798 2	Sheffield United	
9726 2	Brighton & Hove Albion	
8297 3	Plymouth Argyle	
8288 2	Stoke City	
7672 2	Hull City	
6893 3	Reading	
6821 2	Huddersfield Town	
6787 2	Crystal Palace	
6600 3	Bristol City	
6531 4	**Swindon Town**	
6257 2	Middlesbrough	
6067 2	Barnsley	
6028 2	Charlton Athletic	
5826 2	Blackburn Rovers	
5816 2	Bradford City	
5459 2	Millwall	
5157 2	Grimsby Town	
4891 3	Walsall	
4847 3	Bolton Wanderers	

4651 2	Oldham Athletic	
4624 2	Fulham	
4578 2	Wimbledon	
4536 3	Blackpool	
4404 3	Notts County	
4306 3	Swansea City	
4196 3	Bristol Rovers	
4148 3	Wigan Athletic	
4111 3	York City	
4020 3	Wolverhampton Wanderers	
4010 2	Carlisle United	
3957 3	Brentford	
3927 2	Shrewsbury Town	
3764 4	Mansfield Town	
3691 3	Gillingham	
3581 4	Port Vale	
3502 4	Preston North End	
3474 3	Rotherham United	
3424 3	AFC Bournemouth	
3212 3	Chesterfield	
3204 4	Burnley	
3061 3	Cardiff City	
3027 3	Darlington	
2956 4	Chester City	
2889 3	Bury	
2804 3	Doncaster Rovers	
2785 4	Southend United	
2756 4	Hereford United	
2667 4	Stockport County	
2629 4	Orient	
2617 3	Lincoln City	
2593 4	Hartlepool United	
2590 4	Peterborough United	
2494 3	Newport County	
2385 4	Northampton Town	
2328 4	Colchester United	
2089 4	Cambridge United	
1972 4	Exeter City	
1820 4	Wrexham	
1817 4	Crewe Alexandra	
1790 4	Rochdale	
1778 4	Scunthorpe United	
1566 4	Tranmere Rovers	
1480 4	Aldershot	
1406 4	Halifax Town	
1240 4	Torquay United	

40594 1	**Manchester United**		5870 2	Barnsley
36286 1	Liverpool		5754 4	Wolverhampton Wanderers
32935 1	Everton		5313 3	Walsall
29022 1	Arsenal		5169 4	Swansea City
25881 1	Tottenham Hotspur		5050 2	Grimsby Town
24792 1	Newcastle United		4971 3	Gillingham
23148 1	Sheffield Wednesday		4851 3	Bolton Wanderers
21922 1	Manchester City		4729 3	Notts County
20608 1	West Ham United		4304 2	Millwall
19086 1	Nottingham Forest		4097 2	Shrewsbury Town
18172 1	Aston Villa		4085 3	Fulham
17694 1	Chelsea		3918 3	Brentford
17612 2	**Leeds United**		3866 3	Blackpool
17564 1	Norwich City		3715 4	Peterborough United
16120 1	Coventry City		3686 4	Southend United
15800 1	Watford		3432 3	York City
15539 2	Derby County		3398 3	Wigan Athletic
14950 1	Southampton		3342 4	Burnley
13601 2	Sunderland		3312 3	Port Vale
13404 2	Portsmouth		3246 3	Bristol Rovers
12387 2	Plymouth Argyle		3216 3	Mansfield Town
12123 2	Ipswich Town		2983 3	Rotherham United
11754 1	Queens Park Rangers		2857 4	Orient
11697 1	Leicester City		2826 4	Cardiff City
10357 1	Oxford United		2780 4	Cambridge United
10256 1	Luton Town		2740 4	Colchester United
10174 3	**Middlesbrough**		2732 3	Chester City
9992 2	Sheffield United		2644 3	Carlisle United
9987 2	Stoke City		2628 4	Exeter City
9441 3	Bristol City		2584 4	Hereford United
9134 2	West Bromwich Albion		2576 3	Chesterfield
9012 1	Charlton Athletic		2521 4	Wrexham
8293 2	Brighton & Hove Albion		2502 3	Bury
8246 2	Bradford City		2408 3	Doncaster Rovers
8080 4	**Preston North End**		2359 4	Aldershot
7811 1	Wimbledon		2151 4	Rochdale
7709 3	Swindon Town		2126 4	Tranmere Rovers
7583 2	Crystal Palace		2126 4	Scunthorpe United
7427 2	Birmingham City		2113 4	Stockport County
6884 2	Oldham Athletic		2063 3	Newport County
6883 2	Reading		2037 3	Darlington
6773 2	Blackburn Rovers		2023 4	Lincoln City
6674 2	Hull City		1932 4	Crewe Alexandra
6617 2	Huddersfield Town		1777 4	Torquay United
6611 3	AFC Bournemouth		1651 4	Hartlepool United
6316 4	Northampton Town		1327 4	Halifax Town

39582	**1**	**Liverpool**	6841	2	Huddersfield Town
39152	1	Manchester United	6336	3	Notts County
29910	1	Arsenal	6282	4	Burnley
27771	1	Everton	6195	3	Preston North End
25921	1	Tottenham Hotspur	5598	3	Walsall
21059	1	Newcastle United	5514	3	Northampton Town
20272	**2**	**Leeds United**	5018	4	Bolton Wanderers
20118	1	Chelsea	4945	2	Shrewsbury Town
19802	1	West Ham United	4921	3	Fulham
19797	1	Sheffield Wednesday	4596	3	Gillingham
19670	1	Nottingham Forest	4581	3	Brentford
19472	2	Manchester City	4471	4	Swansea City
18342	2	Aston Villa	4390	4	Cardiff City
17509	1	Coventry City	4078	3	Blackpool
17425	**3**	**Sunderland**	3933	4	Leyton Orient
17158	1	Derby County	3847	3	Port Vale
15942	1	Norwich City	3811	3	Mansfield Town
15923	1	Portsmouth	3759	3	Wigan Athletic
14544	1	Southampton	3665	3	Rotherham United
14530	1	Watford	3653	3	Bristol Rovers
14509	2	Middlesbrough	3621	3	Southend United
13268	1	Queens Park Rangers	3416	3	Grimsby Town
12906	2	Bradford City	3322	4	Tranmere Rovers
11807	2	Ipswich Town	3259	3	Aldershot
10280	2	Plymouth Argyle	3233	4	Scunthorpe United
10207	2	Sheffield United	3204	4	Peterborough United
10157	2	Leicester City	3005	4	Torquay United
10126	2	West Bromwich Albion	3003	4	Scarborough
9855	**4**	**Wolverhampton Wanderers**	2760	3	York City
9818	3	Bristol City	2664	3	Chester City
9746	2	Crystal Palace	2662	3	Chesterfield
9607	2	Stoke City	2565	3	Bury
9542	2	Swindon Town	2463	4	Exeter City
9503	2	Blackburn Rovers	2281	4	Crewe Alexandra
8965	3	Brighton & Hove Albion	2272	4	Stockport County
8685	1	Charlton Athletic	2265	4	Cambridge United
8579	2	Birmingham City	2257	4	Hereford United
8417	2	Millwall	2236	4	Carlisle United
8355	1	Oxford United	2195	4	Wrexham
8135	2	Hull City	2191	4	Darlington
8039	1	Luton Town	2129	4	Hartlepool United
7995	1	Wimbledon	1939	4	Rochdale
7873	2	AFC Bournemouth	1913	3	Doncaster Rovers
7683	2	Barnsley	1763	4	Newport County
6945	2	Reading	1754	4	Colchester United
6907	2	Oldham Athletic	1595	4	Halifax Town

38574 1 Liverpool	6352 2 Oxford United
36488 1 Manchester United	6265 2 Birmingham City
35595 1 Arsenal	6108 2 Walsall
27765 1 Everton	5821 3 Huddersfield Town
24467 1 Tottenham Hotspur	5682 3 Brentford
23500 2 Manchester City	5675 3 Notts County
23310 1 Aston Villa	5528 3 Bolton Wanderers
22921 1 Newcastle United	5331 4 Tranmere Rovers
21811 2 Leeds United	5259 3 Bristol Rovers
20785 1 Nottingham Forest	5106 3 Reading
20738 1 West Ham United	5064 4 Rotherham United
20037 1 Sheffield Wednesday	4938 3 Fulham
19999 1 Middlesbrough	4897 3 Swansea City
17535 1 Derby County	4706 2 Shrewsbury Town
16785 1 Norwich City	4547 4 Scunthorpe United
16040 1 Coventry City	4385 3 Cardiff City
15731 2 Chelsea	4302 4 Grimsby Town
15590 1 Southampton	4277 3 Blackpool
15416 1 Millwall	4006 3 Mansfield Town
14878 2 Sunderland	3919 3 Northampton Town
14392 3 Wolverhampton Wanderers	3887 4 Lincoln City
12757 2 West Bromwich Albion	3794 4 Leyton Orient
12666 2 Ipswich Town	3717 3 Chesterfield
12292 2 Watford	3699 3 Southend United
12281 1 Queens Park Rangers	3675 3 Gillingham
12222 3 Sheffield United	3368 3 Bury
10694 2 Leicester City	3296 4 Crewe Alexandra
10655 2 Crystal Palace	3262 4 Peterborough United
10524 2 Bradford City	3176 4 Carlisle United
10201 2 Portsmouth	3151 3 Wigan Athletic
9817 2 Stoke City	3056 3 Chester City
9504 1 Luton Town	2962 4 Scarborough
9398 1 Charlton Athletic	2894 4 Colchester United
9048 2 Brighton & Hove Albion	2792 4 Stockport County
8891 2 Blackburn Rovers	2680 4 Exeter City
8687 2 Swindon Town	2653 4 Cambridge United
8628 2 Plymouth Argyle	2636 4 Wrexham
8121 3 Bristol City	2614 4 York City
8088 2 AFC Bournemouth	2609 3 Aldershot
7824 1 Wimbledon	2350 4 Torquay United
7737 3 Preston North End	2316 4 Darlington
7215 2 Barnsley	2159 4 Doncaster Rovers
7204 2 Oldham Athletic	2132 4 Hereford United
7062 4 Burnley	2048 4 Hartlepool United
6731 3 Port Vale	1968 4 Rochdale
6666 2 Hull City	1947 4 Halifax Town

39077 1	**Manchester United**	6518 2	Hull City
36589 1	Liverpool	6313 3	Preston North End
33713 1	Arsenal	**6222 4**	**Burnley**
28568 2	**Leeds United**	6202 3	Bristol Rovers
27975 1	Manchester City	6151 3	Notts County
26831 1	Tottenham Hotspur	5984 4	Grimsby Town
26280 1	Everton	5820 2	Oxford United
25544 1	Aston Villa	5662 3	Brentford
21590 2	Newcastle United	5630 3	Huddersfield Town
21531 1	Chelsea	5612 3	Rotherham United
20930 1	Sheffield Wednesday	4859 4	Exeter City
20606 1	Nottingham Forest	4804 4	Peterborough United
20311 2	West Ham United	4740 4	Carlisle United
17987 2	Sunderland	4484 3	Fulham
17426 1	Derby County	4365 3	Leyton Orient
17105 1	Crystal Palace	4223 3	Swansea City
17045 2	Wolverhampton Wanderers	4181 4	Chesterfield
16989 2	Sheffield United	4077 3	Walsall
16971 2	Middlesbrough	4075 3	Blackpool
16737 1	Norwich City	4071 4	Lincoln City
16463 1	Southampton	4060 3	Reading
14312 1	Coventry City	4008 3	Crewe Alexandra
13218 1	Queens Park Rangers	3899 4	Stockport County
12913 2	Ipswich Town	3887 4	Gillingham
12449 2	Stoke City	3836 4	Southend United
12413 1	Millwall	3642 3	Cardiff City
11716 2	Leicester City	3524 4	Scunthorpe United
11544 3	**Bristol City**	3521 3	Shrewsbury Town
11308 2	West Bromwich Albion	3450 3	Bury
10748 1	Charlton Athletic	3359 4	Cambridge United
10353 2	Watford	3187 3	Northampton Town
9886 1	Luton Town	3150 4	Colchester United
9727 2	Oldham Athletic	3129 3	Mansfield Town
9624 2	Blackburn Rovers	2758 3	Wigan Athletic
9395 2	Swindon Town	2706 4	Doncaster Rovers
9033 2	Barnsley	2676 4	Hereford United
8978 2	Port Vale	2615 4	York City
8959 2	Portsmouth	2506 3	Chester City
8777 2	Bradford City	2503 4	Hartlepool United
8749 2	Plymouth Argyle	2427 4	Maidstone United
8679 2	Brighton & Hove Albion	2368 4	Wrexham
8558 3	Birmingham City	2325 4	Scarborough
7756 1	Wimbledon	2147 4	Torquay United
7454 2	AFC Bournemouth	2027 4	Rochdale
7449 3	Tranmere Rovers	2022 4	Aldershot
7286 3	Bolton Wanderers	1895 4	Halifax Town

43218 1	**Manchester United**	6644 3	Bradford City
36864 1	Arsenal	6548 2	Charlton Athletic
36038 1	Liverpool	6174 3	Southend United
30632 1	Tottenham Hotspur	6165 2	Hull City
29312 1	Leeds United	6144 3	Brentford
27874 1	Manchester City	6017 3	AFC Bournemouth
26605 2	**Sheffield Wednesday**	5929 2	Bristol Rovers
25663 1	Aston Villa	5780 2	Oxford United
25028 1	Everton	5503 3	Cambridge United
22577 1	Sunderland	5351 3	Huddersfield Town
22551 2	West Ham United	5214 3	Preston North End
22137 1	Nottingham Forest	5211 4	Peterborough United
21461 1	Sheffield United	4600 3	Rotherham United
20738 1	Chelsea	4285 3	Exeter City
19660 1	Crystal Palace	4194 3	Leyton Orient
17023 2	Middlesbrough	4149 4	Walsall
16834 2	Newcastle United	4079 3	Reading
16257 1	Derby County	4059 4	Blackpool
15837 2	Wolverhampton Wanderers	4057 3	Fulham
15468 1	Norwich City	4021 4	Darlington
15413 1	Southampton	3748 3	Crewe Alexandra
13794 1	Coventry City	3712 4	Chesterfield
13524 1	Queens Park Rangers	3710 4	Northampton Town
13495 2	Bristol City	3665 3	Swansea City
13247 2	Oldham Athletic	3572 3	Bury
11993 2	West Bromwich Albion	3562 4	Stockport County
11772 2	Ipswich Town	3523 4	Gillingham
11565 3	**Stoke City**	3442 3	Shrewsbury Town
11546 2	Leicester City	3180 4	Hartlepool United
10846 2	Millwall	3114 4	Scunthorpe United
10325 1	Luton Town	3006 4	Carlisle United
9689 2	Portsmouth	2986 4	Torquay United
9576 2	Watford	2967 4	Lincoln City
9353 2	Swindon Town	2946 4	Cardiff City
8937 2	Barnsley	2889 3	Wigan Athletic
8386 2	Brighton & Hove Albion	2831 4	Doncaster Rovers
8164 2	Notts County	2683 3	Mansfield Town
8126 2	Blackburn Rovers	2599 4	Hereford United
8092 2	Port Vale	2516 4	York City
7882 4	**Burnley**	2238 4	Rochdale
7631 1	Wimbledon	2091 4	Aldershot
7277 3	Bolton Wanderers	1885 4	Wrexham
7237 3	Grimsby Town	1854 4	Maidstone United
7030 3	Birmingham City	1699 4	Halifax Town
6851 2	Plymouth Argyle	1597 4	Scarborough
6740 3	Tranmere Rovers	1564 3	Chester City

44984 1	**Manchester United**		6786 2	Charlton Athletic	
34799 1	Liverpool		6739 2	Plymouth Argyle	
31905 1	Arsenal		6733 2	Southend United	
29560 1	Sheffield Wednesday		6279 3	Peterborough United	
29459 1	Leeds United		6195 4	Cardiff City	
27761 1	Tottenham Hotspur		6115 3	Bradford City	
27691 1	Manchester City		6030 3	Bolton Wanderers	
24818 1	Aston Villa		5850 2	Bristol Rovers	
23721 1	Nottingham Forest		5671 2	Oxford United	
23148 1	Everton		5471 3	AFC Bournemouth	
22097 1	Sheffield United		4896 3	Stockport County	
21342 1	West Ham United		4750 4	Rotherham United	
21148 2	**Newcastle United**		4722 3	Preston North End	
18686 1	Chelsea		4492 3	Fulham	
18390 2	Sunderland		4460 3	Leyton Orient	
17618 1	Crystal Palace		4335 4	Blackpool	
15202 2	Leicester City		4115 3	Hull City	
15087 1	Oldham Athletic		3841 3	Reading	
14703 2	Middlesbrough		3803 4	Mansfield Town	
14664 2	Derby County		3733 4	Crewe Alexandra	
14274 2	Ipswich Town		3643 4	Barnet	
14070 1	Southampton		3627 3	Exeter City	
13876 1	Coventry City		3456 3	Shrewsbury Town	
13858 1	Norwich City		3439 4	Chesterfield	
13743 2	Wolverhampton Wanderers		3367 3	Swansea City	
13592 1	Queens Park Rangers		3367 4	Walsall	
13250 2	Blackburn Rovers		3201 3	Hartlepool United	
13007 3	**Stoke City**		3189 4	Scunthorpe United	
12711 3	West Bromwich Albion		3135 4	Gillingham	
12400 3	Birmingham City		2904 3	Darlington	
11789 2	Portsmouth		2901 3	Bury	
11479 2	Bristol City		2859 3	Wigan Athletic	
10987 1	Notts County		2822 4	Lincoln City	
10521 4	**Burnley**		2789 4	Northampton Town	
10009 2	Swindon Town		2784 4	Rochdale	
9715 1	Luton Town		2735 4	Hereford United	
8845 2	Tranmere Rovers		2734 3	Torquay United	
8511 2	Watford		2608 4	Wrexham	
8002 2	Brighton & Hove Albion		2551 4	Carlisle United	
7921 2	Millwall		2506 4	York City	
7540 3	Huddersfield Town		2142 4	Aldershot	
7508 2	Barnsley		2058 4	Doncaster Rovers	
7382 2	Port Vale		1857 3	Chester City	
7156 3	Brentford		1677 4	Scarborough	
7078 2	Cambridge United		1633 4	Halifax Town	
6920 2	Grimsby Town		1429 4	Maidstone United	
6905 1	Wimbledon				

Home Attendances 1888 – 1992: Divisional Averages

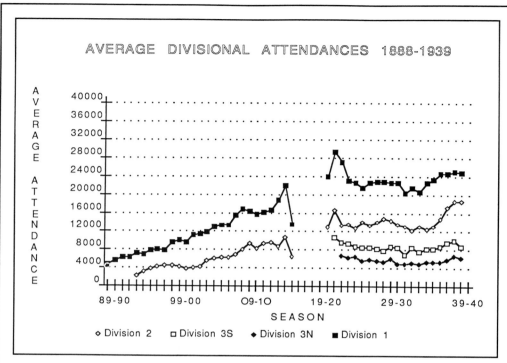

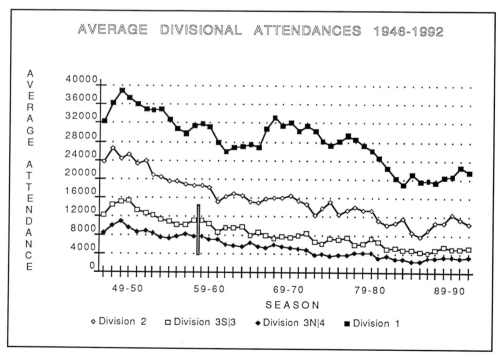

THE TOP SUPPORTED CLUBS AT HOME

Division 1 clubs would be expected to be better supported than clubs from the lower Divisions and to finish top of the average home attendance tables each season. However, Division 2 clubs regularly achieve good average home attendances and in 7 separate seasons a Division 2 club has finished as the top supported League club. The best finish by a Third Division club is 11th by Coventry City (in 1963–64). Hull City (15th in 1948–49) and Fulham (16th in 1931–32) claim the best finishes during the period when the Third Division was regionalised and Sheffield United (22nd in 1981–82) claim the best position achieved by a Fourth Division club.

The most surprising fact to emerge from the average home attendance tables is that only nine different clubs have finished in the top position. Everton, of course, dominated early on finishing top in each of the first ten League seasons. Aston Villa, Newcastle United and Chelsea then began to close the gap. However, Manchester United have dominated in recent seasons. They finished as the best supported home club for the first time in 1956–57 and have since finished top in 18 out of the last 20 seasons. The following list gives the number of seasons each of the nine clubs have finished top of the average home attendance tables:–

26 **Manchester United**
13 **Everton**
12 **Arsenal**
10 **Chelsea**
     Newcastle United
 7 **Aston Villa**
 6 **Liverpool**
     Tottenham Hotspur
 3 **Manchester City**

In order to get an overall impression of the strength of support for all of the League clubs it is helpful to look at the number of seasons that each club has finished within the top ten of the average home attendance tables. This latter list includes a few interesting and, perhaps, surprising names. The same nine clubs dominate the list followed by Sunderland and then by Sheffield Wednesday and Wolverhampton Wanderers. Altogether 38 clubs have finished with a top ten average home attendance in at least one season. However, 21 of the clubs who have competed in Division 1 have failed to finish with a top ten average home attendance in a single season. The most senior of these are Blackpool, Huddersfield Town, Luton Town, Norwich City, Queens Park Rangers, and Southampton.

Remarkably Everton have finished in the top ten of the average home attendance tables in all but 5 seasons. Similarly, neighbours Liverpool have finished in the top ten in 83 out of the 88 seasons they have been League members. The list given below gives the number of seasons the various clubs have finished in the top ten places:–

88	Everton	11	Birmingham City
83	Liverpool		West Bromwich Albion
71	Newcastle United	10	Blackburn Rovers
	Aston Villa	8	Burnley
	Manchester United		Notts County
70	Arsenal	6	Middlesbrough
	Manchester City	5	Preston North End
67	Tottenham Hotspur	4	Cardiff City
61	Chelsea	3	Bradford City
47	Sunderland		Fulham
26	Sheffield Wednesday		Ipswich Town
25	Wolverhampton Wanderers		Leicester City
23	Leeds United		Stoke City
18	Bolton Wanderers	2	Charlton Athletic
13	Sheffield United		Coventry City
	West Ham United		Crystal Palace
	Nottingham Forest	1	Accrington
12	Derby County		Brentford
			Bury
			Portsmouth

The clubs finishing top of the average home attendance tables in their respective Divisions gives some idea of the support for the less glamorous clubs. The Division 1 list consists of the same nine clubs who have finished as the top overall supported clubs each season. In Division 2 twenty different clubs have finished as the top home supported team. This list again includes the same nine clubs together with Sunderland, who have finished the best supported Division 2 team in 6 seasons. Sunderland are, therefore, the most successful team in the Division 2 list never to have finished top in the overall listing. Millwall dominate the Division 3 South list but Division 3 North was much more even. This latter listing shows what a well supported team Bradford once were. The lists for Divisions 3 and 4 include a large number of different clubs. This is a result of the rapid movement of clubs between these Divisions encouraged by the four–up/four–down system. The lists for each Division are given below:–

Division 1

25 Manchester United
14 Arsenal, Everton
8 Chelsea, Liverpool, Newcastle United
7 Aston Villa
6 Tottenham Hotspur
3 Manchester City

Division 2

10 Manchester City
9 Tottenham Hotspur, Newcasle United
8 Chelsea
7 Liverpool
6 Manchester United, Sunderland
5 Aston Villa, West Ham United
4 Arsenal, Birmingham City
3 Leeds United, Sheffield Wednesday
2 Everton, Leicester City, Middlesbrough
1 Coventry City, Darwen, Derby County, Fulham

Division 3 South:–

8 Millwall
3 Bristol City, Coventry City, Fulham, Norwich City, Notts County
2 Crystal Palace
1 Brentford, Brighton & Hove Albion, Bristol Rovers, Cardiff City, Charlton Athletic, Southampton

Division 3 North:–

4 Bradford, Hull City
3 Doncaster Rovers, Oldham Athletic, Stockport County
2 Barnsley, Bradford City, Derby County, Lincoln City
1 Chesterfield, Halifax Town, Port Vale, Tranmere Rovers, Wolverhampton Wanderers

Division 3:–

3 Crystal Palace, Portsmouth
2 Aston Villa, Coventry City, Derby County, Hull City, Middlesbrough, Stoke City, Swindon Town, Watford
1 Bolton Wanderers, Brighton & Hove Albion, Bristol City, Bristol Rovers, Luton Town, Norwich City, Plymouth Argyle, Sheffield United, Sheffield Wednesday, Sunderland, Wolverhampton Wanderers, Wrexham

Division 4:–

4 Burnley
2 Crystal Palace, Southend United
1 Barnsley, Blackpool, Brentford, Brighton & Hove Albion, Bristol City, Coventry City, Doncaster Rovers, Gillingham, Hereford United, Hull City, Huddersfield Town, Lincoln City, Luton Town, Mansfield Town, Millwall, Notts County, Oldham Athletic, Peterborough United, Portsmouth, Preston North End, Sheffield United, Stockport County, Swindon Town, Watford, Wolverhampton Wanderers, Wrexham

Occasionally a team from a lower Division has succeeded in finishing with a higher average home attendance than all of the clubs in the Division above them. The most notable cases are when a Division 2 team has finished top of the overall tables. The following lists also record those seasons in which Division 3 and 4 teams have accomplished the corresponding feat:–

Division 2 teams finishing above all Division 1 teams:

Chelsea	1911–12
Chelsea	1925–26
Manchester City	1927–28
Newcastle United	1946–47
Newcastle United	1947–48
Tottenham Hotspur	1949–50
Manchester United	1974–75

Division 3 teams finishing above all Division 2 teams:

Aston Villa	1970–71

Division 4 teams finishing above all Division 3 teams:

Crystal Palace	1960–61
Oldham Athletic	1960–61
Peterborough United	1960–61
Brighton & Hove Albion	1964–65
Sheffield United	1981–82

No Division 3 South or Division 3 North team finished above all Division 2 teams and no Division 4 team has ever finished above all Division 2 teams.

Eight different League clubs have attracted over 1 million supporters to their home games during the course of a particular season. Newcastle United, then in Division 2, became the first club to achieve this total (in 1946–47). Manchester United were the last club to achieve this total (in 1979–80) but restrictions on present day ground capacities make it unlikely that the total can be achieved again. Altogether Manchester United have attracted over 1 million supporters 13 times, followed by Arsenal (7 times), Spurs (6 times), Newcastle United (4 times), Everton (3 times), Liverpool (twice), and Chelsea and Sunderland (each once). Manchester United also hold the record attendance for a League game when 83,260 spectators watched the game against Manchester City at Maine Road on 12 September 1948. With both Manchester clubs playing their home games at Maine Road between 1946–47 and 1948–49 Maine Road comfortably holds the record for most spectators attending League games in a season (2,049,905 in 1947–48). In complete contrast only 909,918 spectators have watched Wimbledon's home games in the 6 seasons that they have been in Division 1.

The top aggregate attendances are:–

1,208,595	Manchester United	1967–68
1,181,944	Newcastle United	1947–48 *
1,165,697	Totttenham Hotspur	1950–51
1,154,615	Arsenal	1947–48
1,152,689	Manchester United	1947–48
1,149,751	Manchester United	1975–76
1,136,321	Tottenham Hotspur	1949–50 *
1,130,940	Manchester United	1966–67
1,130,029	Newcastle United	1948–49
1,127,980	Manchester United	1976–77

* Achieved whilst a Second Division club.

THE MOST ATTRACTIVE VISITING CLUBS

Average home attendances for clubs in a particular Division can vary widely from the average for the Division. For example, in 1989–90 the average attendance at Division 1 games was 20,757 with the highest home average being 39,077 at Manchester United and the lowest being 7,756 at Wimbledon. In contrast, away from home the range was only from 25,599 (for Liverpool) to 17,428 (for Luton Town). Consequently, although there is considerable overlap between the average home attendance figures for teams from different Divisions, there is little overlap between average away attendances. The average away attendances for a particular club, therefore, reflect those for the Division in which they are competing.

Promotion or relegation results in a corresponding increase or decrease irrespective of how well a particular club may be supported at home.

Spectators are attracted to a game involving the visit of the top clubs in a particular Division more than they are to the visit of the bottom clubs. It is no surprise to find that in the 93 seasons between 1888 and 1992 the Champions of the Football League have finished amongst the top 3 most attractive visiting clubs on no less than 70 occasions and top on 38 occasions. Bearing in mind that the League Champions can often emerge late in the season after a quiet start this is a remarkable statistic. Even in the modern era with its much larger travelling support than used to be the case there appears to be no significant change in this pattern.

Away from home the period between 1888 and 1915 saw Aston Villa dominate as the most attractive visiting team. Villa, though, were the only Midlands team to figure significantly and most of the other "top attraction" teams were from the North. Sunderland, although well behind the Villa, were the most popular Northern visitors with Blackburn Rovers, Newcastle United, and Preston North End not far behind.

Despite their dramatic arrival in terms of home attendances neither Spurs or Chelsea appear as one of the top three most attractive visiting teams and, indeed, there is not a single appearance in the top three by a Southern based club during this period.

The inter–war period sees clubs such as Villa and Sunderland remaining as attractive visitors. However, this period was dominated by Arsenal. A visit by them often doubled an attendance. Apart from Arsenal, however, only two other London clubs (Tottenham Hotspur and Brentford) made any sort of impact and only one other Southern based club, Cardiff City, made an appearance in the top three. Two of the most attractive present day visitors, Liverpool and Manchester United, only managed one top three appearance between them.

From 1946 to the present day four clubs have proved to be the most attractive visitors. Arsenal continue to prove an attraction during this most recent period, but they are joined by Manchester United, Liverpool, and Spurs. There were brief periods when the visit of Blackpool, Leeds United or Wolves proved a great attraction but two of the pre–war favourites, Aston Villa and Sunderland, both fade from the scene.

Over the complete run of 93 seasons Manchester United stand out above the rest. Next come Aston Villa, Liverpool and Arsenal with little between them except that Villa's period was before 1939, Arsenal's since 1919 and Liverpool's since 1946. There is a large gap between these four clubs and the remainder. Perhaps the most remarkable fact to emerge is that apart from Cardiff City, no Southern based club outside London features amongst the top three most attractive visiting clubs over the entire 93 season period.

The complete listing includes 14 Northern, 6 Midland, and 5 London clubs plus Cardiff City. The Football League Champions appear in bold type:–

Season						
1888–89	8400	Preston North End	5540	Aston Villa	5125	Wolverhampton W.
1889–90	10010	Preston North End	8235	Blackburn Rovers	6570	Aston Villa
1890–91	8970	Blackburn Rovers	8595	Everton	8255	Preston North End
1891–92	9660	Sunderland	8540	Preston North End	8335	Blackburn Rovers
1892–93	11635	Sunderland	11180	Preston North End	7740	Blackburn Rovers
1893–94	11015	Sunderland	8790	Blackburn Rovers	8400	Sheffield Wednesday
1894–95	11780	Sunderland	11150	Everton	9880	Aston Villa
1895–96	14095	Aston Villa	10965	Sunderland	10655	Derby County
1896–97	10835	Preston North End	10290	Liverpool	10245	Aston Villa
1897–98	15130	Sheffield United	13845	Aston Villa	11545	Sunderland
1898–99	14745	Liverpool	13810	Aston Villa	12465	Sunderland
1899–00	14840	Sheffield United	14495	Aston Villa	11780	Sunderland
1900–01	14150	Aston Villa	13020	Nottingham Forest	12505	Sunderland
1901–02	14660	Aston Villa	13530	Sunderland	12780	Everton
1902–03	16100	West Bromwich Alb.	14510	Aston Villa	13885	Sheffield Wednesday
1903–04	16910	Aston Villa	15765	Sheffield Wednesday	15290	Manchester City
1904–05	16170	Everton	16040	Newcastle United	15855	Sunderland
1905–06	17270	Newcastle United	17085	Aston Villa	16400	Liverpool
1906–07	22810	Aston Villa	19800	Newcastle United	18320	Liverpool
1907–08	21860	Manchester United	20920	Newcastle United	18940	Aston Villa
1908–09	21630	Manchester United	19965	Newcastle United	18325	Aston Villa
1909–10	19930	Newcastle United	19320	Manchester United	19180	Sheffield United
1910–11	23445	Manchester United	21475	Newcastle United	20165	Aston Villa
1911–12	23200	Blackburn Rovers	21115	Newcastle United	20790	Aston Villa
1912–13	26540	Aston Villa	23990	Sunderland	21750	West Bromwich Albion
1913–14	30785	Blackburn Rovers	28420	Aston Villa	25440	Sunderland
1914–15	17685	Blackburn Rovers	15910	Aston Villa	14895	Sunderland
1919–20	30625	Sunderland	28340	West Bromwich Albion	27590	Newcastle United
1920–21	35145	Burnley	34025	Tottenham Hotspur	33230	Aston Villa
1921–22	31685	Tottenham Hotspur	31665	Burnley	30530	Aston Villa
1922–23	30075	Liverpool	27260	Aston Villa	27030	Sunderland
1923–24	31385	Cardiff City	27070	Aston Villa	26160	Sunderland
1924–25	26570	Huddersfield Town	26065	Sunderland	23880	Newcastle United
1925–26	27035	Huddersfield Town	26376	Aston Villa	24970	Arsenal
1926–27	31731	Newcastle United	28318	Huddersfield Town	25147	Aston Villa
1927–28	29407	Everton	29145	Newcastle United	28208	Huddersfield Town
1928–29	27400	Sheffield Wednesday	26153	Huddersfield Town	26113	Everton
1929–30	26471	Arsenal	26375	Sheffield Wednesday	25083	Manchester City
1930–31	33390	Arsenal	25757	Sheffield Wednesday	25731	Aston Villa
1931–32	30655	Arsenal	30569	Everton	29193	Aston Villa
1932–33	38734	Arsenal	25991	Aston Villa	23738	Everton
1933–34	38222	Arsenal	29074	Tottenham Hotspur	26576	Aston Villa
1934–35	40508	Arsenal	28102	Aston Villa	27630	Sunderland
1935–36	38304	Arsenal	30388	Aston Villa	30330	Sunderland
1936–37	42227	Arsenal	32098	Sunderland	27716	Brentford
1937–38	38219	Arsenal	31519	Wolverhampton W.	28428	Sunderland
1938–39	35733	Arsenal	32615	Everton	31129	Aston Villa

Season	Home		Away
1946–47	37013 Wolverhampton W.	35879 Arsenal	35876 Stoke City
1947–48	46482 **Arsenal**	45224 Blackpool	40982 Manchester United
1948–49	44935 Arsenal	44695 Manchester United	44692 Blackpool
1949–50	46361 Manchester United	44210 Blackpool	42370 Wolverhampton W.
1950–51	47686 Blackpool	43379 Arsenal	**43289 Tottenham Hotspur**
1951–52	43942 Arsenal	**41512 Manchester United**	40206 Tottenham Hotspur
1952–53	44607 **Arsenal**	39560 Blackpool	38469 Newcastle United
1953–54	41983 Arsenal	41568 Blackpool	40521 West Bromwich Albion
1954–55	40604 Blackpool	39054 Wolverhampton W.	37173 West Bromwich Albion
1955–56	42594 Blackpool	36116 Wolverhampton W.	34781 Arsenal
1956–57	39623 **Manchester United**	35385 Arsenal	34861 Tottenham Hotspur
1957–58	45562 Manchester United	**37640 Wolverhampton W.**	36179 Arsenal
1958–59	43552 Manchester United	**37141 Wolverhampton W.**	36099 Arsenal
1959–60	40940 Manchester United	39998 Wolverhampton W.	39583 Tottenham Hotspur
1960–61	43105 **Tottenham Hotspur**	34274 Manchester United	30956 Wolverhampton W.
1961–62	38962 Tottenham Hotspur	33964 Manchester United	31489 Burnley
1962–63	39753 Tottenham Hotspur	35256 Manchester United	**34678 Everton**
1963–64	38840 Manchester United	36105 Tottenham Hotspur	31010 Everton
1964–65	41385 **Manchester United**	34372 Tottenham Hotspur	32274 Leeds United
1965–66	38117 Manchester United	**34508 Liverpool**	31040 Chelsea
1966–67	45718 **Manchester United**	37667 Liverpool	35599 Tottenham Hotspur
1967–68	46015 Manchester United	38114 Tottenham Hotspur	37804 Liverpool
1968–69	44295 Manchester United	**36603 Leeds United**	34943 West Ham United
1969–70	42993 Manchester United	38810 Leeds United	37636 Derby County
1970–71	41325 Manchester United	39375 Leeds United	34942 Chelsea
1971–72	44078 Manchester United	39826 Leeds United	**35469 Derby County**
1972–73	41116 Manchester United	37066 Leeds United	**36935 Liverpool**
1973–74	41853 **Leeds United**	35309 Manchester United	34628 Liverpool
1974–75	34509 Leeds United	34213 Liverpool	29698 West Ham United
1975–76	37205 Manchester United	**34944 Liverpool**	34154 Leeds United
1976–77	36730 **Liverpool**	35084 Manchester United	31551 Arsenal
1977–78	36171 Liverpool	31186 Leeds United	30721 Everton
1978–79	36947 **Liverpool**	33010 Tottenham Hotspur	32064 Nottingham Forest
1979–80	35291 **Liverpool**	34009 Manchester United	30048 Nottingham Forest
1980–81	32785 Liverpool	29789 Manchester United	**29375 Aston Villa**
1981–82	28709 **Liverpool**	27213 Manchester United	26752 Tottenham Hotspur
1982–83	29594 **Liverpool**	25257 Manchester United	24767 Tottenham Hotspur
1983–84	28224 **Liverpool**	24906 Manchester United	22178 Tottenham Hotspur
1984–85	28433 Liverpool	27890 Manchester United	26024 Tottenham Hotspur
1985–86	27899 Manchester United	**26528 Liverpool**	23248 Tottenham Hotspur
1986–87	28845 Liverpool	25177 Manchester United	**23062 Everton**
1987–88	29313 **Liverpool**	23044 Manchester United	22813 Tottenham Hotspur
1988–89	27700 Liverpool	**24251 Arsenal**	24026 Tottenham Hotspur
1989–90	25599 **Liverpool**	25422 Manchester United	24973 Arsenal
1990–91	28082 Liverpool	26898 Tottenham Hotspur	**25345 Arsenal**
1991–92	27798 Manchester United	26580 Liverpool	24918 Tottenham Hotspur

In 33 of the 93 League seasons the same club has finished top of both the home average and away average attendance tables. The feat was first achieved in 1900–01 by Aston Villa. Two clubs, Arsenal and Manchester United, are well ahead of the rest in this respect with United having achieved this "double" 12 times, and Arsenal 11 times. Arsenal had a remarkable run finishing top both home and away each season from 1929–30 to 1937–38. Manchester United first achieved this feat in 1956–57. The other clubs to achieve the feat are Liverpool, Newcastle United and Tottenham Hotspur.

SEASON TICKETS

In amongst the detailed attendance statistics recorded in the ledgers at the Football League headquarters are the number of season ticket holders season by season. These were noted at 10 year intervals starting from 1928–29 more out of curiosity than any intention of including them in this statistical section. However, they proved more interesting than anticipated and are therefore included.

In the 1920's and 1930's the numbers reveal very different season ticket purchasing habits from today. How many readers would have predicted that in 1928–29 Leicester City, albeit a well supported Division 1 team, would have more season ticket holders than any other club? In the 1920's buying season tickets seems a definite habit in Lancashire more so than elsewhere. Blackpool, Blackburn Rovers, Bolton Wanderers, Bury, Manchester City, Oldham Athletic, and Preston North End, three of them Division 2 clubs, all sold over 1300 season tickets. Bury, in fact, claim the second highest total behind Leicester City and Bradford were next with 2399 season ticket sales.

Looking elsewhere where were the London clubs? Several of them barely managed over 100. Everton and Liverpool managed 581 between them only one more than Accrington Stanley and considerably less than Nelson. Buying season tickets seems to have been very much more of a tradition at some clubs more than others.

Why should Walsall, a struggling Division 3 club, sell more season tickets than glamourous neighbours such as Aston Villa, Birmingham City and West Bromwich Albion? Incidentally, several clubs seem to have made a zero return, but it is not clear whether this means that they were unable to sell any season tickets or that they did not offer a service.

By 1938–39 purchasing habits seemed to have changed a little here and there, presumably reflecting changes of fortune of individual clubs. However, the figures are not very different from 10 years earlier. By 1958–59 there was an overall increase with some of the bigger clubs such as Arsenal, Aston Villa and Newcastle United increasing their totals to over 4000. The club with the greatest number of season ticket holders was Blackburn Rovers with Leicester City again at a high level as were Bolton Wanderers and Bury.

There was a significant upwards jump in sales by 1968–69 particularly at some of the big clubs. Everton and Liverpool were well ahead of the rest but Coventry City (11,921) came next. Coventry, of course, were founder members of Division 4 and had climbed the Divisional ladder to Division 1 creating a tremendous interest in football in the city in the process.

Modern day figures (1978–79 and 1988–89) definitely tend to favour the better supported 'popular' clubs such as Arsenal, Aston Villa, the two Liverpool and the two Manchester clubs. However, high figures were achieved at Bolton, Southampton and West Bromwich in 1978–79 and at Newcastle, Tottenham and West Ham in 1988–89. Two less fashionable clubs, Derby County and Nottingham Forest, have high figures in both of these seasons. Overall there has been a decline of nearly 20% in season ticket holders between 1978–79 and 1988–89 but this is less than the decrease in aggregate attendances over the same period.

Combining the totals for all clubs the proportion of supporters purchasing a season ticket has increased in each column since 1928–29, and in 1988–89 represents an average of 14.8% of the total attendance.

	1928–9	1938–9	1948–9	1958–9	1968–9	1978–9	1988–9
Accrington Stanley	580	414	404	577	–	–	–
AFC Bournemouth	280	596	2154	2214	1019	465	1565
Aldershot	–	214	153	220	370	660	387
Arsenal	704	2243	4307	4395	3676	7362	10467
Ashington	49	–	–	–	–	–	–
Aston Villa	190	2561	3215	6044	17953	4955	6267
Barnsley	438	597	647	337	366	412	897
Barrow	230	446	62	154	–	1070	–
Birmingham City	58	335	1683	2818	7899	4947	1995
Blackpool	1429	3595	5240	4024	1050	2788	1084
Blackburn Rovers	1381	1427	1317	7076	2711	3093	3136
Bolton Wanderers	1454	3278	2158	4620	1002	10026	1672
Bradford	2399	907	461	469	187	–	–
Bradford City	1460	530	336	720	588	886	2900
Brentford	168	721	703	613	431	525	1116
Brighton & Hove Albion	914	939	701	1584	3189	1249	2150
Bristol City	956	1283	537	3014	2054	6807	1789
Bristol Rovers	330	490	428	3058	638	1411	660
Burnley	1074	1634	3804	4465	5047	2832	1855
Bury	2573	1289	1825	1196	949	729	1072
Cambridge United	–	–	–	–	–	1364	513
Cardiff City	1077	1065	5511	1998	2596	1394	996
Carlisle United	168	256	930	685	1436	1453	385
Charlton Athletic	57	640	803	434	990	1598	1256
Chelsea	239	782	1377	2212	5686	4859	2970
Chester City	–	207	310	410	418	446	184
Chesterfield	409	1017	1499	908	1045	606	653
Colchester United	–	–	–	963	273	632	497
Coventry City	393	1511	842	7166	586	11921	5709
Crewe Alexandra	225	128	261	254	313	430	477
Crystal Palace	164	206	105	230	1157	3094	1922
Darlington	106	347	494	724	449	284	151
Derby County	1348	2516	4782	3558	12373	6903	9037
Doncaster Rovers	308	613	649	366	267	165	323
Everton	249	1349	1801	3626	12729	13984	17429
Exeter City	408	298	1092	566	683	670	388
Fulham	98	123	374	1094	1643	1232	1067
Gateshead	–	63	0	97	–	–	–
Gillingham	160	–	–	98	144	578	685
Grimsby Town	680	843	1703	1116	478	193	842
Halifax Town	411	247	209	423	176	108	131
Hartlepool United	60	115	42	206	247	161	173
Hereford United	–	–	–	–	–	1084	278
Huddersfield Town	1284	706	1025	1554	520	1152	1889
Hull City	763	410	2946	1693	1480	3362	2117
Ipswich Town	–	633	631	1417	3533	7948	3760
Leeds United	204	136	740	2164	8721	10582	7344
Leicester City	3824	1199	2106	5950	3803	5887	2654
Leyton Orient	0	66	161	828	270	910	499
Lincoln City	495	378	1380	1759	510	341	474
Liverpool	332	689	2019	2995	14343	15877	23431
Luton Town	160	685	1041	1366	855	1206	4434
Manchester City	1522	1708	2966	3508	22663	5792	9663
Manchester United	684	1601	2638	2880	20963	17361	10584
Mansfield Town	–	340	636	519	1364	400	823

149

	1928–9	1938–9	1948–9	1958–9	1968–9	1978–9	1988–9
Merthyr Town	73	–	–	–	–	–	–
Middlesbrough	131	628	1788	1023	5158	2177	7226
Millwall	154	182	128	107	1011	1319	1430
Nelson	1002	–	–	–	–	–	–
New Brighton	156	124	95	–	–	–	–
Newcastle United	166	592	4223	4444	8206	4276	8828
Newport County	70	392	474	421	241	66	–
Northampton Town	411	754	539	829	999	562	552
Norwich City	498	902	934	2108	3391	6566	6636
Nottingham Forest	451	935	1286	3793	6400	13791	10014
Notts County	280	320	2115	704	2739	324	1915
Oldham Athletic	2002	857	1526	355	2006	279	2001
Oxford United	–	–	–	–	1022	823	2318
Peterborough United	–	–	–	–	895	2068	907
Plymouth Argyle	646	1715	1217	2334	1692	1378	2073
Portsmouth	0	250	782	2266	1120	2231	4176
Port Vale	139	238	355	330	174	800	1002
Preston North End	1463	2602	6148	4356	2230	2927	1684
Queens Park Rangers	39	121	1755	348	4602	4087	2627
Reading	960	920	390	656	610	510	931
Rochdale	304	348	350	177	98	118	142
Rotherham United	328	333	130	310	1227	542	723
Scarborough	–	–	–	–	–	–	689
Scunthorpe United	–	–	–	836	192	263	420
Sheffield United	1131	1381	1675	1846	4721	2608	2856
Sheffield Wednesday	1311	1737	1362	1003	3296	7594	6371
Shrewsbury Town	–	–	–	486	368	158	230
South Shields	0	–	–	–	–	–	–
Southampton	294	868	5262	2219	6166	10827	7091
Southend United	392	546	629	1045	542	892	570
Southport	326	421	424	169	404	–	–
Stockport County	325	519	746	979	824	476	393
Stoke City	882	600	728	1304	4591	2372	2384
Sunderland	0	863	2286	3662	5778	6303	2469
Swansea City	531	840	1959	1917	2360	1203	1869
Swindon Town	215	270	634	798	2534	1316	2149
Torquay United	409	237	709	568	913	285	226
Tottenham Hotspur	550	1015	2040	5405	8783	10012	6138
Tranmere Rovers	164	278	180	499	812	153	449
Walsall	634	120	1136	670	1150	527	1615
Watford	491	194	224	287	3592	558	4442
West Bromwich Albion	302	579	1234	7778	10144	4841	4219
West Ham United	128	336	208	1860	5814	2300	8150
Wigan Athletic	–	–	–	–	610	–	678
Wigan Borough	345	–	–	–	–	–	–
Wimbledon	–	–	–	–	–	475	1354
Wolverhampton Wanderers	657	1446	3481	6255	6703	5578	2364
Workington	–	–	–	345	265	–	–
Wrexham	141	119	263	922	2905	466	157
York City	–	589	200	632	155	368	449

❖ ❖

The League Clubs – Aberdare Athletic to York City

The final section of this book surveys the attendances that each club has attracted whilst a member of the Football League. A detailed analysis of the data for each club would, no doubt, be of considerable interest to individual club historians. However, this is not possible in a book of this size and most readers will have an interest in the fortunes of many clubs as well as that of their own. Consequently the entry for each club consists of an overview covering the trends in their average attendances.

In broad terms it is possible to divide the average attendance data into four categories. The first of these categories includes the top clubs; the clubs that attract the largest gates at home (and sometimes away as well!) irrespective of their Division. These are clubs from large population centres (the 'big city' clubs) and include some obvious candidates such as all of those clubs who have, at one time or another, finished top of the attendance tables.

The second category includes those clubs whose attendances struggle to meet the Division 1 average but who, nevertheless, can attract above average gates when in the lower Divisions, particularly during successful playing seasons. Some typical examples, here, include the Lancashire 'town' teams, Huddersfield Town, Ipswich Town, Queens Park Rangers, and Watford.

There are a further group of clubs, who can be placed in the third category, whose average attend– dances would struggle to meet the Division 1 and Division 2 average but who are often above average in Divisions 3 and 4. This group includes clubs from relatively small population centres where there is a keen interest in the game. Typical examples include clubs such as Carlisle United, Leyton Orient, Luton Town, and Rotherham United.

A number of clubs can be placed in the final (4th) category who struggle to achieve the average attendance of either of the lower two Divisions. This category includes clubs who have generally been starved of success and have rarely appeared higher than Division 3. Some typical examples include clubs such as Chester City, Crewe Alexandra, Exeter City, Halifax Town, Rochdale, and Torquay United.

The entry for each club also includes their record home attendance at a League game (Cup games and friendlies are excluded) and their highest average home attendance season. In some cases clubs have played at more than one home venue and the record attendance for each venue has been included where the information is available. The data for all record attendances since 1925 has been taken from that returned by the clubs to the Football League. In most cases these figures agree with those published elsewhere. However, there are occasional differences and these are somewhat puzzling. They may be due to differences reported to the press and the official figures returned to the Football League.

For the period prior to 1925 data is only available from press reports and these are all "rounded" figures except in one or two cases where accurate figures have been well documented. Where a record attendance has been established before 1925 only the rounded figure is quoted and no attempt has been made to associate this figure with a particular game. These figures are intended merely to give a guide to the highest attendance at that venue and, in the case of some clubs near enough the same figure might have been recorded at several games. In a very small number of cases it has not been possible to identify the record attendance, with any degree of accuracy, at a particular venue; such cases are indicated thus: *,***

A change of venue has often resulted in a considerable change in attendance data. The classic example must be Arsenal whose average attendances by 1913 had fallen to the lowest of any of the London based League clubs.

The move to Highbury, however, was an obvious success. Many other clubs have moved to new venues but usually with less spectacular results and sometimes with a decrease in attendance figures.

In addition to moves to a different venue a number of clubs have recently entered into ground sharing schemes. From the attendance point of view, even with a good imagination, none of these can be considered to have been a success. The same may not be true from the financial point of view of course.

The highest average home attendance season of each club is, to some extent, dependent upon their playing fortunes and upon the period of their League membership. Of the eighty eight clubs who were League members in 1946 forty three recorded their highest average home attendance attendances in the first five post–1946 seasons. This was the period, of course, when attendances in all four Divisions reached record levels.

ABERDARE ATHLETIC

Record Home League Attendance :
16,250 v Bristol City 02.04.1923
Highest Average Home Attendance :
9,525   1921–22

Aberdare were elected to the Southern Section from the Southern League in 1921. At first attendances were quite good and in 1921–2 they were the 8th best supported club in their Division with an average attendance of 9,525. However, the recession in the local coal mining industry resulted in a slump in attendances and they finished as the worst supported Southern Section club in 1925–6 and again in 1926–7. The latter of these two seasons was their last as a Football League club when they failed to gain re–election after a tied vote with Torquay United. They returned to the Southern League to survive only one further season before folding.

ACCRINGTON

Record Home League Attendance :
9,000
Highest Average Home Attendance :
3,770   1891–92

The 'Reds' were one of the top Lancashire sides during the 1880s and were founder members of the Football League. However, support was always very poor and at the end of the 1892–93 season they resigned to join the Lancashire League. Financial difficulties continued, however, and they finally folded during the 1895–96 season.

The pavilion at the Cricket Field in 1892

ACCRINGTON STANLEY

Record Home League Attendance :
15,425 v York City 11.04.1955
Highest Average Home Attendance :
9,766   1954–55

Stanley were founder members of Division 3 North. In their first League season they finished as the 5th best supported Northern Section Club. However, in the years up to 1939 they were generally poorly supported, finishing bottom of the attendance table in 1938–39. Attendances were again poor after 1946 although in 1954–55 they finished as the 2nd best supported Northern Section club. Thereafter, however, attendances declined steeply each year until the fateful 1961–62 season when they resigned from the League having completed 33 fixtures (with an average attendance of just over 2,500). That was not quite the end for Stanley, however, as the following season they joined the Lancashire Combination eventually folding at the end of the 1965–66 season.

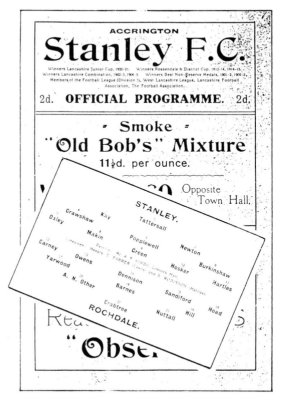

Stanley's first Football League match (Att. 12,000)

AFC BOURNEMOUTH

Record Home League Attendance :
25,495 v Queens Park Rangers 14.04.1948
Highest Average Home Attendance :
16,854   1947–48

Bournemouth were members of the Southern League when elected to the Football League in 1923. Attendances were well below the Southern Section average up to 1939 but since then they have faired somewhat better. There was a good period in the early 1970s (in 1972–73 they were the 2nd best supported Division 3 side) but in a short spell in Division 2 between 1987 and 1990 they were well below the Division 2 average.

A packed Dean Court in 1949

ALDERSHOT

Record Home League Attendance :
15,611 v Reading 22.10.1938
Highest Average Home Attendance :
 7,493   1951–52

Aldershot replaced the ill–fated Thames in the Southern Section in 1932. Average attendances have been very disappointing at Aldershot and it was not until 1961–62 that they first achieved an average attendance above that of their Division. During the intervening seasons they finished as the worst supported Southern Section club ten times.

From the 1960s average attendances were nearer to their Divisional average but still poor. Sadly, financial difficulties at Aldershot increased during the early 1990s. After completing the first 36 fixtures of the 1991–92 season they were formally wound up and so became the first club since Accrington Stanley thirty years earlier, almost to the day, to leave the Football League during the playing season.

A
L
D
E
R
S
H
O
T
F.C.

Fixture List
1991/1992
Season

Barclays League
Division 4

with the compliments of

Ad*line*
■GROUP

The last season.

ARSENAL

Record Home League Attendances :
36,000 at Manor Road
 4,750 at Priestfield Stadium (Gillingham)
 4,000 at Lyttleton Ground, Leyton
73,295 v Sunderland 09.03.1935 at Highbury
Highest Average Home Attendance :
54,982   1947–48

Founded in 1886 Arsenal were the first Southern based club to gain Football League membership (in 1893). At first, with little competition in the locality, attendances were good. They were the best supported Division 2 side in their first season and again in 1894–5. In 1904 they were the 2nd best supported Division 1 club, but increasing competition from the other London clubs soon hit their gates. In 1912–3 they were the worst supported Division 1 club also finishing below Fulham and Clapton Orient then both in Division 2. However, the move to Highbury was a huge success and it was not until 1967–8 that they had another average attendance below that of their Division. They finished as the best supported Division 1 club every season between 1929 and 1938 and altogether they have finished as the top supported club 14 times.

ASHINGTON

Record Home League Attendance :
 8,824 v Wolverhampton Wanderers 05.01.1924
Highest Average Home Attendance :
 5,150   1923–24

Ashington were founder members of the Northern Section in 1921 having previously competed in the North Eastern League. Attendances were really dreadful mainly due to high unemployment in the locality and in their final season (1928–9) they finished as the worst supported club in the League. In 1929 they returned to the North Eastern League and are currently members of Division 2 of the Northern League.

ASTON VILLA

Record Home League Attendances :
20,000 at Perry Barr
69,161 v Arsenal 22.01.1949 at Villa Park
Highest Average Home Attendance :
47,320   1948–49

Founder members of the Football League, Villa are one of only nine clubs to have finished as the top supported club. Their 'heyday' was undoubtedly between 1898 and 1904 when they finished as top supported club in all six seasons. They have finished as the top supported League club only once since then (1938–39) and their best post–war seasons have been 1975–76 and 1980–81 when they finished 3rd in the attendance tables. They have finished as the top supported Division 2 club five times and as the top supported Division 3 club twice. As expected for a 'big city' club they have had some remarkable attendances over the years including an average attendance of 47,320 during the 1948–49 season. In 1970–71 they became the only Division 3 side ever to finish above all Division 2 sides in the attendance tables and one season later they finished as the 13th best supported League club, with an average attendance of almost 32,000, whilst still in Division 3.

ASTON VILLA FOOTBALL GROUND, BIRMINGHAM

A turn of the century postcard

BARNET

Record Home League Attendance :
5,090 v Crewe Alexandra 17.08.1991
Highest Average Home Attendance :
3,643   1991–92

Formed in 1888, the same year as tthe Football League, Barnet gained promotion from the Vauxhall Conference to the League in 1991. They finished their first League season as the 7th best supported Division 4 club.

BARNSLEY

Record Home League Attendance :
35,308 v Sheffield Wednesday 09.10.1948
Highest Average Home Attendance :
21,262   1947–48

Barnsley became members of the Football League in 1898 having previously competed in the Midland League. Early attendances were generally poor and they finished as the worst supported Division 2 club five times before being relegated to Division 3 North at the end of the 1931–2 season. The following season they achieved their first above average attendance for their Division but they have struggled in attendance terms when in Division 2. More recently they have faired better finishing as the best supported Division 4 side in 1978–9, the 2nd best supported Division 3 side in 1980–1 and the 3rd best Division 2 side in 1981–2. Barnsley have spent more seasons in Division 2 than any other club.

BARROW

Record Home League Attendance :
12,759 v Hull City 04.09.1948
Highest Average Home Attendance :
 7,814   1947–48

One of a small number of Lancashire Combination clubs to become founder members of Division 3 North in 1921. Barrow struggled with poor attendances and finished above the Northern Section average in just two seasons before 1939 and in only one post war season. Strangely though, despite their poor attendances, they did not finish bottom of the attendance tables during their post–war seasons. After failing to gain re–election at the end of the 1971–72 season, Barrow joined the Northern Premier League, have also been members of the Vauxhall Conference, and are currently members of the HFS Loans League.

BIRMINGHAM CITY

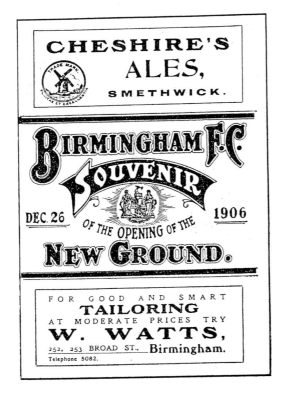

Record Home League Attendances :
32,000 at Muntz Street
59,971 v Aston Villa 23.11.1935 at
St. Andrew's
Highest Average Home Attendance :
38,453   1948–49

Founded in 1875, City were founder members of the Football Alliance in 1889 and of Division 2 of the Football League in 1892. Attendances have generally been good for their Division as might be expected for a 'big city' club. In attendance terms, however, they have always been in the shadow of their city rivals (Villa) and in only 9 seasons (all since 1946) have they finished above them in the attendance tables. Recently attendances have declined from an average of over 36,500 in 1972–73 (when they were 4th overall) to only just over 7,000 in 1990–91.

A crowd of 34,000 attended the match

BLACKBURN ROVERS

Record Home League Attendances :
15,000 at Leamington Street
46,874 v Preston North End 04.10.1947 at Ewood Park
Highest Average Home Attendance :
30,544   1958–59

Founder members of the Football League in 1888, Rovers' attendances up to 1915 were generally below average for their Division although they were the 2nd best supported club in 1890–91. The problems of a town club in the higher divisions show well in the period 1919–1936 when they finished below the Divisional average each season. They finished as the 2nd best supported Division 2 club in 1954–55 and as the 3rd best Division 3 club in 1974–75.

BLACKPOOL

Record Home League Attendances :
 5,000 at Raikes Hall Gardens
 8,000 at Athletic Grounds
38,098 v Wolverhampton Wanderers
17.09.1955 at Bloomfield Road
Highest Average Home Attendance :
26,336   1949-50

Founder members of the Lancashire League, Blackpool were first elected to the Football League in 1896. Attendances were well below the Division 2 average and in 1897-98 and 1900-01 they were the worst supported club in the League. It was not until the 1929-30 season, when they won promotion to Division 1, that they first achieved an attendance above the Division 2 average. When in Division 1, attendances have always been well below the Divisional average although they have only finished as the worst supported Division 1 club twice (1953-54 and 1966-67). Attendances in the lower Divisions have been both above and below the Divisional average; they were the best supported side in Division 4 in 1984-85.

The record (League) attendance at Bloomfield Road

BOLTON WANDERERS

Record Home League Attendances :
14,000 at Pikes Lane
57,989 v Everton 15.10.1938 at Burnden Park
Highest Average Home Attendance :
35,832   1951-52

Another of the Lancashire town teams to be founder members of the Football League. In the period up to 1939 their gates follow the Divisional average closely and it is only in the post 1946 seasons that they really fell below the Division 1 average whilst in that Division. They finished as the 3rd best supported club in 1891-92, 1895-96 and 1905-06. More recently they were well placed in 1951-52 and have finished as the 2nd best supported Division 2 club twice (1975-76 and 1976-77) and as the top Division 3 club in 1972-73. Their gates are typical of a well supported 'town' team.

BOOTLE

Record Home League Attendance :
 3,000
Highest Average Home Attendance :
 2,000   1892–93

Founder members of the Football Alliance, Bootle became founder members of Division 2 in 1892–93. However, they survived only one League season resigning, just before the commencement of the 1893–94 season, due to financial difficulties which led to their almost immediate collapse.

BRADFORD

Record Home League Attendance :
32,421 v Leeds United 25.12.1931
Highest Average Home Attendance :
17,687   1947–48

Formed in 1907, Bradford spent just one season in the Southern League before being elected to the Football League. Attendances were generally good up to 1915 and again between 1919 and 1939 there were some very good seasons (they finished as the best Northern Section club no less than four times). They finished with better average home attendances than their City rivals in 10 out of the first 20 post war seasons. The end for Bradford was, therefore, fairly sudden when they failed to gain re–election at the end of the 1969–70 season. They then moved down to the Northern Premier League but, sadly, folded at the end of the 1973–74 season.

BRADFORD CITY

Record Home League Attendances :
37,059 v Bradford 17.09.1927 at Valley Parade
 7,448 v Sheffield United 26.10.1985 at Elland Road (Leeds)
 8,369 v Sunderland 01.01.1986 at Leeds Road (Huddersfield)
13,831 v Leeds United 20.09.1986 at Odsal Stadium
16,017 v Ipswich Town 07.05.1988 at Valley Parade (Rebuilt)
Highest Average Home Attendance :
22,585   1920–21

Founded in 1903, Bradford City were directly elected to Division 2 in time for the 1903–04 season. Attendances were good, finishing as the 2nd best supported Division 2 side in 1907–08 and the following season (their first in Division 1) they were the 4th best supported English League club. Attendances since then have fluctuated both above and below their Divisional average. They were the best supported Northern Section side in 1928–29 and again nearly thirty years later (1957–58). Their best recent season was 1987–88 when they were the 5th best supported club in Division 2.

BRENTFORD

Record Home League Attendance :
38,535 v Arsenal 08.09.1938
Highest Average Home Attendance :
25,768   1946-47

One of the Southern League clubs to become founder members of the Southern Section in 1920, Brentford have usually been well supported. The short-lived visit to Division 1 saw gates rise to the Division 1 average and in 1936-37 they were the 8th best supported Division 1 club.   Since then gates have fluctuated above and below their Divisional average but, as might be expected for a club from a large population area, there is plenty of support in the locality when the team is successful.

The Bees 4-0 victory (Att. over 12,000) helps to secure the 3rd Div. Championship (1991-92 season)

BRIGHTON & HOVE ALBION

Record Home League Attendance :
36,342 v Fulham 27.12.1958
Highest Average Home Attendance :
25,265   1977-78

Another of the Southern League clubs to become founder members of the Southern Section in 1920. Up to 1946 gates were around the Divisional average with the club spending all of these seasons in the Southern Section. Since 1946 attendances have tended to be above their Divisional average except when in Division 1. They have been the best supported side in the Southern Section (1953-4), Division 4 (1964-5), Division 3 (1976-7), and 2nd best in Division 2 (1977-8). Their best season was in 1979-80 when they were the 11th best supported Division 1 team.

BRISTOL CITY

Record Home League Attendances :
13,000 at St. John's Lane
39,583 v Bristol Rovers 22.10.1955 at Ashton Gate
Highest Average Home Attendance :
26,575   1955-56

City were members of the Southern League when they were elected to the Football League in 1901. Their best early season was 1906–07, their first in Division 1, when they finished with the 12th best average attendance in that Division. By 1922–23 they were in Division 3 South but finished as the best supported club in that Section that season and in the seasons between 1919 and 1939 their attendances were above their Divisional average more often than not. A very good period followed from 1946 to 1959 and the club have been well supported in most post–1946 seasons with attendances only slightly below the Divisional average when in Division 1.

BRISTOL ROVERS

Record Home League Attendances :
35,198 v Bristol City 03.03.1956 at Eastville
 5,171 v Newcastle United 27.09.1980 at Ashton Gate
 9,813 v Bristol City 02.05.1990 at Twerton Park (Bath)
Highest Average Home Attendance :
24,662   1953–54

Founded in 1883 Rovers were founder members of the Southern Section in 1920 (from the Southern League). Gates were generally above the Southern Section average in the seasons up to 1946. The seasons up to the mid 1970s were invariably well supported, their best seasons being between 1952–3 and 1957–8 when they averaged over 20,000 spectators each season. In 1954–5 they finished as the 3rd best supported Division 2 side. They are one of only two sides (Plymouth Argyle being the other) never to have played in either Division 1 or Division 4.

Easville in 1971

BURNLEY

Record Home League Attendance :
52,869 v Blackpool 11.10.1947
Highest Average Home Attendance :
33,621   1947–48

Founder members of the Football League, Burnley's attendances have followed some odd patterns.   Attendances started falling below their Divisional average from about 1893 and in 1902–03 reached an all time low when they finished as the worst supported League club with an average attendance of only 1,500. Thereafter a slow recovery began. More recently they have had some highly successful playing seasons but the relatively low population density in the area makes it difficult to match the Division 1 averages of the big city clubs. Recently residing in Division 4, they finished as the top supported club in that Division from 1988–89 to date and in 1991–92 their average attendance was above that of both Wimbledon and Luton Town of Division 1 and fourteen Division 2 clubs.

BURTON SWIFTS

Record Home League Attendance :
 6,000
Highest Average Home Attendance :
 3,250 ˙ 1894–95

The Swifts were founder members of Division 2 in 1892–93. Support was always below average for a Division 2 club and in 1899–1900 they were the worst supported League team.   In 1901 they amalgamated with Burton Wanderers to form Burton United.

BURTON UNITED

Record Home League Attendance :
10,000
Highest Average Home Attendance :
 4,150   1905–06

Burton United, formed by the amalgamation of the two Burton clubs, the Swifts and the Wanderers, took the former's place in the Football League and remained members until 1907. Attendances were always well below the Division 2 average and when they failed to gain re-election they joined the Birmingham and District League. They folded at the end of the 1909–10 season.

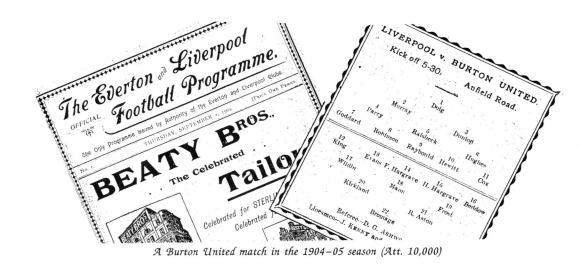

A Burton United match in the 1904–05 season (Att. 10,000)

BURTON WANDERERS

Record Home League Attendance :
5,000
Highest Average Home Attendance :
 2,750   1895–96

Wanderers were elected to the Football League in 1894 from the Midland League. It is difficult to see how a small town such as Burton could sustain one League team let alone two and it was no surprise when they failed to gain re-election in 1897 and returned to the Midland League.   When they amalgamated with the Swifts in 1901 it was claimed that they were the fourth oldest football club in the country.

BURY

Record Home League Attendance :
34,386 v Blackpool 01.01.1937
Highest Average Home Attendance :
19,500   1924–25

Founder members of the Lancashire League, Bury were elected to the Football League in 1894. They won promotion in their first season but by 1897–98 they were the worst supported Division 1 club. They have repeated the 'feat' twice since (1911–12 and 1928–29) and have also finished as the worst supported Division 2 club (1937–38). Attendances have invariably been poor at Bury with very few above average seasons (even when in the lower Divisions).

CAMBRIDGE UNITED

Record Home League Attendance :
11,542 v Mansfield Town 28.04.1973
Highest Average Home Attendance :
 7,078   1991–92

United gained election to the Football League from the Southern Premier League in 1970. Attendances have struggled to reach the Division 3 and Division 4 averages and when in Division 2 they have been well below average. They have finished as the worst supported Division 2 side four times and as the worst supported Division 3 side once.

A crowd of 6,843 was present for the United's entry into the League

CARDIFF CITY

Record Home League Attendance :
60,855 v Swansea Town 27.08.1949
Highest Average Home Attendance :
37,933   1952–53

City were elected directly to Division 2 in 1920 whilst the remaining Southern League clubs formed the new Southern Section. They were the second best supported Division 2 club in their first season (when they won promotion to Division 1) and the 5th best supported Division 1 side in 1921–22 with an average of nearly 33,000. Thereafter gates plummeted but by 1939 had somewhat recovered. The early post–1946 years saw average attendances of nearly 38,000 (in 1947–48 and 1952–53) but a decline in playing fortunes led to a decline in average attendances (to only 2,826 in 1986–87).

165

CARLISLE UNITED

Record Home League Attendance :
20,675 v Liverpool 05.10.1975
Highest Average Home Attendance :
14,530   1974–75

Carlisle were playing in the North Eastern League when elected to the Football League in 1928. Attendances have been good for a small population centre when in the lower Divisions but well below the Divisional average when in Division 1 or Division 2. They finished as the 3rd best supported Northern Section club in their first season and again in 1929–30. In 1963–64 they were the 3rd best supported Division 4 club and 5th best in Division 3 one year later. However, they finished as the worst supported Division 2 club three times and as the worst supported Division 1 club in their only season in that Division (1974–75). Interestingly, when they won promotion to Division 1 only two teams (Hull and Swindon) finished below them in the Division 2 averages.

Near deserted terraces at Brunton Park (Photo: Viv Tabner)
(Match v. Walsall 28.9.91. Att. 2,148)

CHARLTON ATHLETIC

Record Home League Attendances :
10,000 at The Mount
68,160 v Arsenal 17.10.1936 at The Valley
28,095 v Liverpool 23.01.1988 at Selhurst Park
15,357 v Leicester City 25.04.1992 at Upton Park
Highest Average Home Attendance :
40,216   1948–49

Except in recent seasons, Charlton's attendances have responded well to their elevation to Division 1 status. They were the best supported Southern Section club in 1934–35, 4th best in Division 2 one year later, and 5th best in Division 1 in 1936–37. In 1948–49 they averaged over 40,000 (for the only time) but a decline in Divisional status in the following seasons saw average attendances fall as low as 5,306 (in 1973–74). The recent return to Division 1 produced disappointing attendances for which the unavailability of The Valley and the consequent ground–sharing scheme at Selhurst Park are probably largely responsible.

The programme from the record attendance match at Selhurst Park

CHELSEA

Record Home League Attendance :
82,905 v Arsenal 12.10.1935
Highest Average Home Attendance :
48,260   1954–55

72,805 watch the 1921 FA Cup Final at Stamford Bridge

Formed in 1905 and directly elected to the Football League, Chelsea had a most dramatic impact at the turnstiles. By 1906–07 they were the best supported Division 2 side and in their next season the best supported Division 1 side. In 1911–12 they became the first Division 2 club to finish as the best supported League club, a feat they were to repeat in 1925–26, and in 1913–14 they

created a new record average attendance for the Football League of just over 37,000. In 1919–20 they were the first League club to average over 40,000 spectators and between 1919 and 1939 they finished as the best supported club on four occasions. It was not until 1972–73 that their average attendance fell below that of their Division for the first time. Their attendances have been less dramatic since then, but they still remain a well supported club.

CHESTER CITY

Record Home League Attendances :
16,835 v Wrexham 04.02.1933 at Sealand Road
 4,895 v Birmingham City 11.04.1992 at Moss Rose Ground (Macclesfield)
Highest Average Home Attendance :
 8,504   1965–66

Founded in 1884 they were competing in the Cheshire League when elected to the Northern Section in 1931. Attendances were generally above the Northern Section average before 1939 finishing as the 2nd best supported side in that Section in their first season and in 1932–33 and 1936–37. Above average attendances have been rare since 1946. They were the worst supported League club in 1952–53 and the worst supported Division 3 club four times. In 1990–91 they became the first Division 3 club to finish as the worst supported League club since 1958, but there was a bright spot in 1965–66 when they finished as the 2nd best supported Division 4 side.

CHESTERFIELD

Record Home League Attendance :
28,268 v Newcastle United 07.04.1939
Highest Average Home Attendance :
15,372   1947–48

Founded in 1866, Chesterfield are one of the oldest clubs in England. They were first elected to the Football League in 1899 from the Midland League but lost their League status in 1909. This was regained when the Northern Section was formed in 1921. Attendances have been both above and below their Divisional average but they have always struggled at the turnstiles when in Division 2, finishing as the worst supported club in that Division each season between 1947 and 1951.

COLCHESTER UNITED

Record Home League Attendance :
18,559 v Ipswich Town 16.02.1957
Highest Average Home Attendance :
10,573   1950–51

Colchester were elected from the Southern League to the Football League when the League expanded in time for the 1950–51 season. Attendances have tended to be below average for their Division but there were several seasons in which support was quite good. They lost their League status at the end of the 1989–90 season when they finished bottom of Division 4, but this was regained when they finished as Vauxhall Conference Champions at the end of the 1991–92 season.

COVENTRY CITY

Record Home League Attendance :
51,452 v Wolverhampton Wanderers 29.04.1967
Highest Average Home Attendance :
34,705   1967–68

Formed in 1883, City were elected to Division 2 in 1919 along with clubs such as South Shields, Stoke and West Ham United. Gates were below their Divisional average only once before 1939 and they were the best supported Southern Section side twice during this period (1933–34 and 1935–36). There have also been some very good post–1946 seasons when City have finished as the best supported club in the Southern Section (1955–56), Division 4 (1958–59), Division 3 (1962–63 and 1963–64) and Division 2 (1966–67). Since 1967 they have been members of Division 1 but during this period have achieved average attendances above those of Division 1 only twice (in 1967–68 and in 1968–69 when they were the 10th best supported Division 1 club).

CREWE ALEXANDRA

Record Home League Attendances :
 8,000 at Nantwich Road
*,*** at Sandbach St. Mary's
17,883 v Port Vale 28.09.1953 at Gresty Road
Highest Average Home Attendance :
 9,065   1949–50

Founder members of the Football Alliance in 1889 and of Division 2 in 1892, Crewe were later to become founder members of Division 3 North (in 1921) and Division 4 in 1958. Their first period in the League lasted only 4 seasons during which they were the poorest supported club in 1894–95 and after which they joined the Combination. They were one of several Central League teams to join the new Northern Section in 1921. With only a relatively small number of exceptions, their attendances have been below their Divisional average. However, since 1895 they have finished last in the attendance tables only once (1971–72).

CRYSTAL PALACE

Record Home League Attendances :
12,000 at The Dell (Southampton)
20,000 at The Nest
51,482 v Burnley 11.05.1979 at Selhurst Park
Highest Average Home Attendance :
30,167   1972–73

Founder members of the Southern Section in 1920 (from the Southern League) they were promptly its first Champions. Attendances were generally well above their Divisional average and in only one season between 1920 and 1946 did they finish with an average attendance below 10,000. Post-war gates too have been good and have responded well in periods when they have gained Division 1 status. In 1972-3 they averaged over 30,000 for the first, and so far only, time and in 1979-80 finished as the 6th best supported League team.

DARLINGTON

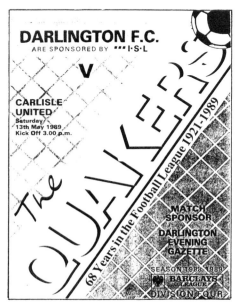

The last Football League programme, (Att. 3,049) before a quick return.

Record Home League Attendance :
18,144 v Middlesbrough 26.12.1967
Highest Average Home Attendance :
10,234   1948-49

Founded in 1883, Darlington were one of several North Eastern League clubs to become founder members of Division 3 North in 1921. Attendances have never been good at Darlington and in 1932-33 they were the worst supported League team and they have been above their Divisional average in only seven seasons since 1921. Relegated to the Vauxhall Conference in 1989 (for one season) they averaged nearly 3,600 as a non-League club; one of their best average attendances since 1968-69.

DARWEN

Record Home League Attendance :
10,000
Highest Average Home Attendance :
 4,920   1891-92

Founded in 1870, Darwen quickly established themselves as one of the top Lancashire sides. In 1879-80 they were the first winners of the Lancashire Cup. Founder members of the Football Alliance in 1889, they were elected to the Football League in 1891. In 1892-93 they were the top supported Division 2 side. Support slowly declined until in 1898-99 they were the worst supported League club. At the end of this latter season they resigned and joined the Lancashire Combination. Darwen currently play in Division 1 of the North West Counties League.

DERBY COUNTY

Record Home League Attendances :
11,000 at CC Ground
41,826 v Tottenham Hotspur 20.09.1969
at Baseball Ground
Highest Average Home Attendance :
35,924   1969-70

Founded in 1884, Derby County became founder members of the Football League four years later. Up to 1915 County's gates were generally poor and their best season was 1895-96 when they finished 6th in the attendance table. There was also a long period from 1926-27 to 1954-55 when they were well below their Divisional average. However, they have fared better since then. In 1955-56 they were the top supported Northern Section club and their best seasons were undoubtedly those between 1969-70 and 1971-72 when their attendances averaged over 30,000.

The record attendance match

DONCASTER ROVERS

Record Home League Attendances :
 8,000 at Intake Ground
37,099 v Hull City 02.10.1948 at Belle Vue
Highest Average Home Attendance :
22,838   1950-51
Formed in 1879, Rovers were members of the Midland League when they were first elected to the Football League in 1901. Attendances have been variable, finishing as the best attended Northern Section club in 1934-35 and 1937-38, but generally well below the Division 2 average when in that Division. They were the top supported Division 4 side in 1965-66 but recent attendances have been poor and it is difficult to imagine a more depressing venue than the Belle Vue ground in recent seasons.

DURHAM CITY

Record Home League Attendances :
 6,000 at Kepier Haughs
 5,000 at Holiday Park
Highest Average Home Attendance :
 3,965   1923-24

City were founder members of the Northern Section in 1921 and, like Ashington, had previously competed in the North Eastern League. They continued as a League club for 7 seasons finishing as the worst supported club in all but one of these seasons. In 1928 they failed to gain re-election and rejoined the North Eastern League but folded 10 years later.

EVERTON

Record Home League Attendances :
18,000 at Anfield
78,299 v Liverpool 18.09.1948 at Goodison Park
Highest Average Home Attendance :
51,603   1962-63

Founded in 1878 Everton were founder members of the Football League and are one of only nine clubs to have finished top of the attendance tables. They are undoubtedly one of the top supported clubs in the country finishing top of the attendance tables in each of the first ten seasons of League football. Strangely, they have only finished top on three occasions since then (1955-56, 1962-63 and 1963-64). Their gates though have been consistently well above average and it was not until 1975-76 that they first had a below average attendance season. In 20 seasons they have averaged above 40,000 spectators and in 1962-63 their home games were watched by an average of over 51,600 spectators.

The new Goodison Road Stand had a capacity of 10,450 in 1970

EXETER CITY

Record Home League Attendance :
19,941 v Plymouth Argyle 03.02.1951
Highest Average Home Attendance :
10,339   1952-53

Another of the Southern League clubs to become founder members of the Southern Section in 1920. Exeter are one of a small number of clubs never to have won promotion to Division 2. In the period between 1920 and 1939 attendances were generally well below average finishing as the worst supported Southern Section club three times. It was not until 1958-9 that they had an average significantly above that of their Division.

FULHAM

Record Home League Attendance :
49,335 v Millwall 08.10.1938
Highest Average Home Attendance :
33,030   1949-50

Formed in 1879 Fulham were elected to the Football League from the Southern League in 1907 and in their first season they finished as the top supported Division 2 side with an average attendance of over 17,000. Attendances remained good, thereafter, finishing as the top supported Southern Section side three times and the second best supported Division 2 side three times before their first below average attendance season in 1937-38. There have also been some good seasons since 1946, such as 1959-60 when they were the 10th best supported Division 1 side, but attendances have fallen away badly since the late sixties.

Craven Cottage c.1914

GAINSBOROUGH TRINITY

Record Home League Attendance :
7,000
Highest Average Home Attendance :
5,380   1908-09

Founded in 1872 Gainsborough Trinity were elected to the Football League from the Midland League in 1896. They remained League members for 16 seasons before failing to gain re-election and rejoining the Midland League. Attendances were invariably poor. They finished as the worst supported club twice (1901-02 and 1909-10) and failed to achieve an above average attendance in any season. They currently play in the Premier Division of the HFS Loans League.

GATESHEAD

Record Home League Attendance :
20,792 v Lincoln City 25.09.1937
Highest Average Home Attendance :
 9,201   1949–50

Formed in 1930 from the South Shields club, attendances were at first quite promising and in 1931–32 they were 3rd best supported Northern Section club. However, five years later they were the worst supported club in that Section, although the remaining post war seasons saw a recovery at the turnstiles. After 1946 they failed to gain a single above average attendance (finishing bottom of the attendance tables three times) and eventually failed to gain re-election at the end of the 1959–60 season (despite finishing above both Oldham Athletic and Hartlepools United in the League table). The club thought of joining the Scottish League but when this was thwarted they settled for the Northern Counties League. Gateshead continued in non-League football until severe financial problems eventually led to their demise just before the start of the 1973–74 season.

GILLINGHAM

Record Home League Attendances :
20,126 v Millwall 02.09.1950 at Priestfield Stadium
 3,934 v Wrexham 25.03.61 at Stonebridge Road (Northfleet)
Highest Average Home Attendance :
12,576   1951–52

Gillingham were founder members (of Division 2) of the Southern League in 1894 and became founder members of the Southern Section in 1920. They are one of only two clubs (Exeter City being the other) who founded the Southern Section never to have gained promotion to Division 2. Gates were below average each season and in 1938 they lost their League status to Ipswich Town. They regained their League status in 1950 (again from the Southern League) but had to wait until 1962–63 to gain their first above average attendance. In 1963–64 they were the top supported Division 4 club and one year later they were the 4th best supported Division 3 club. Gates have only occasionally been above their Divisional average since.

GLOSSOP

Record Home League Attendance :
 9,000
Highest Average Home Attendance :
 4,005   1899–1900

One of the smallest of all the League Clubs, Glossop were elected to the League in 1898 from the Midland League. They maintained continuous membership until failing to gain re-election at the end of the 1914-15 season. They were the worst supported club in the League in all but one of the seasons from 1903-04 to 1914-15. When football resumed in 1919 they joined the Lancashire Combination and currently play in Division 2 of the North West Counties League.

GRIMSBY TOWN

Record Home League Attendances :
 8,000 at Abbey Park
26,605 v Stockport County 11.04.1952 at Blundell Park
Highest Average Home Attendance :
18,056   1949-50

Formed in 1878, Grimsby hold an almost unique position in English League football. Founder members of the Football Alliance, they became founder members of Division 2 in 1892. In 1920 they were founder members of the Southern Section and one year later of the Northern Section. They have played in all six Divisions and have won promotion 11 times. They have also been relegated 11 times. Attendances have been about average except when in the higher Divisions where the small size of the local population puts them at a disadvantage when compared with the big city clubs. They have finished as the poorest supported Division 1 club in no less than 12 seasons including every season between 1935-36 and 1947-48. They were not bottom in 1930-31 however, when Manchester United finished below them! They are, also, the only Division 1 side ever to finish below half way in the attendance tables since the expansion of the League to four Divisions 1921.

HALIFAX TOWN

Record Home League Attendance :
19,935 v Bradford City 10.09.1927
Highest Average Home Attendance :
10,525   1922-23

One of several Midland League sides to become founder members of the Northern Section in 1921. They were the top supported Northern Section club in 1922-23 and attendances up to 1939 were usually above average for the Section. Since 1946, however, support has faded significantly and in only one season (1968-69) have they achieved above average figures. They have finished as the worst supported League club six times, all since 1983, and have always featured in either Division 3 or 4.

HARTLEPOOL UNITED

Record Home League Attendance :
17,118 v Hull City 09.10.1948
Highest Average Home Attendance :
 9,265   1951–52

Another of the North Eastern League sides to become founder members of the Northern Section in 1921. Gates generally have been poor only occasionally reaching the Divisional average. Their best season was 1966–67 when they finished as 7th best supported Division 4 club and their worst was in 1982–83 when they finished as the worst supported League club. United have spent more seasons in Division 4 than any other club.

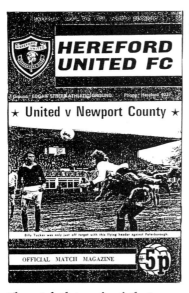

HEREFORD UNITED

Record Home League Attendance :
14,849 v Newport County 07.04.1973
Highest Average Home Attendance :
8,917   1972–73

United were elected to the Football League from the Southern Premier League in 1972 following some sensational results in the FA Cup. In their 1st season they were the top supported Division 4 club and achieved above average attendances in two of the next three seasons. However, since then attendances have slumped and they have usually been below the average of their Division.

The match that produced the League record attendance

HUDDERSFIELD TOWN

Record Home League Attendances :
37,765 v Newcastle United 11.04.1950 at Elland Road (Leeds)
52,479 v Blackpool 07.04.1951 at Leeds Road
Highest Average Home Attendance :
30,820   1953–54

Town were elected to the Football League from the Midland League in 1910. Despite tremendous achievements during the 1920s, when their best placing was as the 14th best supported Division 1 side, they did not achieve an average attendance significantly above that of their Division until 1952–53. They have finished as the worst supported Division 1 side five times, but when in the lower Divisions they have had good seasons in Division 4 (1976–77), Division 3 (1982–83) and Division 2 (1952–53).

HULL CITY

Record Home League Attendances :
24,110 v Middlesbrough 05.02.1927 at Anlaby Road
54,652 v Rotherham United 25.12.1948 at Boothferry Park
Highest Average Home Attendance :
37,319   1949–50

Hull were formed in 1904 and one year later they were elected to the Football League. Up to 1915 attendances were about average for their Division but the period between 1919 and 1939 saw them regularly below their Divisional average. The early post–1946 seasons, however, saw remarkable gates at Boothferry Park. In 1948–49 they averaged 36,763 whilst in Division 3 North and one year later they finished as the 14th best supported club in the country. In 1950–51 they were the 2nd best supported Division 2 side. Attendances declined thereafter, but there were good seasons in 1965–66 (when they again finished as the 14th best supported side in the League, this time whilst in Division 3) and 1970–71.

IPSWICH TOWN

Record Home League Attendance :
35,109 v Liverpool 04.12.1976
Highest Average Home Attendance :
26,672   1976–77

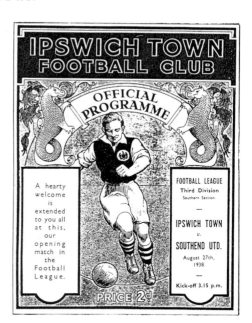

Having turned professional in 1936, Ipswich found a place in the Southern Section of the Football League in 1938. A rapid improvement in League status has led to good average attendances although sometimes struggling to meet the average when in Division 1. Nevertheless, between 1968–69 and 1981–82 average attendances never fell below 20,000. Their best seasons were 1980–81 and 1982–83 when they finished as the 9th best supported side in Division 1.

19,242 attended the first League game

LEEDS CITY

Record Home League Attendance :
25,000
Highest Average Home Attendance :
15,845   1913–14

Originally members of the West Yorkshire League, City were elected to the Football League in 1905 (along with Chelsea). Attendances were generally above average for their Division and in 1912-3 they were the 2nd best supported club in Division 2. City were expelled from the League early during the 1919-20 season (after completing only eight games) as a result of alleged irregularities during the war-time seasons.

LEEDS UNITED

Record Home League Attendances :
56,776 v Arsenal 27.12.1932
20,687 v Wolverhampton W. 21.08.1971 at Leeds Rd. (Huddersfield)
25,099 v Tottenham H. 25.08.1971 at Boothferry Park (Hull)
18,649 v Newcastle United 01.09.1971 at Hillsborough (Sheffield)
Highest Average Home Attendance :
39,204   1970-71

Formed in 1919, United were elected to Division 2 of the Football League in 1920. Up to 1939 attendances were not particularly good, their best season being 1927-28 when they were the 3rd best supported Division 2 club. Post-1946 attendances have been generally above average for their Division. There was a good season in 1956-57 when they averaged over 32,500 but their best period was undoubtedly between 1964-65 and 1976-77 when their average never fell below 30,000. More recently they have finished as the best supported club in Division 2 three times (1986-87, 1987-88 and 1989-90).

Two 'record attendances'

LEICESTER CITY

Record Home League Attendance :
42,486 v Arsenal 02.10.1954
Highest Average Home Attendance :
31,359   1957–58

Founded in 1884, the Fosse were elected to Division 2 from the Midland League in 1894. Attendances at Leicester have been consistently high. They have finished as the best supported Division 2 side in 1899–1900, 2nd best in that Division in 1923–24, and top again in that Division in 1970–71. However, they have struggled to reach the Division 1 average when in that Division and have twice finished as the worst supported Division 1 side (1976–77 and 1977–78). They are one of a select band of eleven sides never to have played outside the top two Divisions.

LEYTON ORIENT

Record Home League Attendances :
37,615 v Tottenham Hotspur 16.03.1929 at Millfields Road
 8,319 v Brentford 22.11.1930 at Wembley Stadium
20,288 v Millwall 13.03.1937 at The Speedway
33,383 v Birmingham City 02.05.1972 at Brisbane Road
Highest Average Home Attendance :
17,254   1956–57

Orient were elected to the Football League along with another London club, Chelsea, in 1905. Gates were generally about average for their Division up to 1939 with a particularly good season in 1923–24 when they finished as the 3rd best supported Division 2 club. Since 1946, however, above average gates have been rare and Orient finished as the worst supported Division 2 club four times during the sixties and seventies.

The record League attendance at Wembley Stadium!

LINCOLN CITY

Record Home League Attendances :
 6,000 at John O'Gaunts Ground
23,146 v Grimsby Town 05.03.1949 at Sincil Bank
Highest Average Home Attendance :
16,775   1952–53

Lincoln joined the Football Alliance in 1891 and became founder members of Division 2 one year later. Attendances were generally below average up until 1915, a period during which they twice failed to gain re-election to the League. They have also lost their League status twice since 1919 only to regain it again. Attendances have been below average when in Division 2, but otherwise they have been reasonable enough. They were the best supported Northern Section club in 1930–31 and Division 4 club in 1975–76.

LIVERPOOL

Record Home League Attendance :
58,757 v Chelsea 27.12.1949
Highest Average Home Attendance :
48,127   1972–73

One of the top supported sides in the country with only one season in which their average attendance has been below that of their Division (1936–37) since they became League members in 1893. They first finished as the best supported League club in 1922–23 and although the next occasion was not until 1965–66 they have finished as the top supported Division 1 club a total of eight times. They have finished below Merseyside rivals Everton in the attendance tables slightly more times than above them.

The famous Championship decider, 1988–89 season
(Att. 41,718 plus an estimated 10.3 million TV viewers)

LOUGHBOROUGH

Record Home League Attendance :
5,000
Highest Average Home Attendance :
3,025   1898–99

Loughborough were elected to the Football League in 1895 (from the Midland League) and maintained League membership until 1900 when they failed to gain re-election. Often in financial difficulties, the club then folded. Attendances were invariably poor with the local Derbys versus Leicester Fosse being the only high spots.

LUTON TOWN

Record Home League Attendances :
5,000 at Bury Park
27,911 v Wolverhampton Wanderers 05.05.1955 at Kenilworth Road
Highest Average Home Attendance :
21,455   1955–56

Founder members of the Southern League, Luton were members of the Football League for three seasons in the 1890s and again from 1920 to date. Attendances at Luton have never been particularly good and although they were the 2nd best supported Southern Section side in 1935–36, they went from 1946–47 to 1965–66 without achieving an above average attendance for their Division. During this period they finished as the worst supported Division 1 team four times and as the worst supported Division 2 team once. However, in 1967–68 they were the best supported Division 4 team and two years later the best supported Division 3 team.

MAIDSTONE UNITED

Record Home League Attendance :
5,006 v Carlisle United 05.05.1990
Highest Average Home Attendance :
2,427   1989–90

Formed in 1891 United had to wait until 1989 before gaining automatic promotion from the Vauxhall Conference to Division 4. In attendance terms, however, they have so far failed to make an impact.

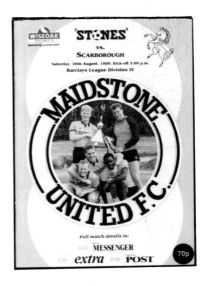

The first home League game
(Att.3,254)

MANCHESTER CITY

Record Home League Attendances :
40,000 at Hyde Road
79,491 v Arsenal 23.02.1935 at Maine Road
Highest Average Home Attendance :
42,725   1947–48

1898–99 season League match versus Darwen (Att. 8,000)

Another of the Football Alliance clubs to become founder members of Division 2 in 1892, City are one of the 9 clubs to have finished top of the attendance tables. Attendances from 1892 to 1915 were excellent. They were the best supported Division 2 club four times during this period and finished top of the attendance table for the first time in 1914–15. They were top again in 1927–28 and 1928–29, the first of these two seasons as a Division 2 club. In attendance terms they dominated Manchester football up until 1939, although since then United have dominated. The best position City have achieved since 1946 is 3rd (three times) and they have averaged above 40,000 spectators three times during this period.

MANCHESTER UNITED

Record Home League Attendances :
10,000 at North Road
20,000 at Bank Street
68,796 v Manchester City 12.09.1936 at Old Trafford
83,260 v Arsenal 17.01.1948 at Maine Road
27,649 v Arsenal 20.08.1971 at Anfield (Liverpool)
23,146 v West Bromwich Albion 23.08.1971 at Victoria Ground (Stoke)
Highest Average Home Attendance :
57,552   1967–68

Founder members of the Football Alliance, United were directly elected to Division 1 in 1892. Attendances were generally good during the early seasons. United finished as the best supported Division 2 club three times between 1903–04 and 1905–06 but in 1930–31 they finished as the worst supported Division 1 club. This was the last season, however, that their gates fell below average and although they were regularly below the gates of their City rivals before 1946 they have completely dominated Manchester attendances since. In 1967–68 they achieved the highest average home attendance ever recorded (57,552) and on a number of occasions since then their average has been more than double the Division 1 average. In the 1974–75 season they became the last club to finish top of the attendance tables whilst still in Division 2 and from 1966–67 they have so dominated English football at the turnstiles that they finished top in twenty two out of the last twenty six seasons.

MANSFIELD TOWN

Record Home League Attendance :
19,500 v Hull City 17.04.1965
Highest Average Home Attendance :
12,128   1949-50

Mansfield Town were elected to the Southern Section of the Football League in 1931, replacing Newport County. Attendances at Mansfield have clung remarkably close to those of their Division. They were the 4th best supported side in the Northern Section in 1932-33, best in Division 4 in 1974-75 and 6th best in Division 3 in 1976-77.

MERTHYR TOWN

Record Home League Attendance :
21,686 v Millwall 27.12.1921
Highest Average Home Attendance :
12,300   1920-21

One of the Southern League clubs to become founder members of the Southern Section in 1920. Attendances were at first good and they finished as the 9th best supported Southern Section club in their first season. However, increasing unemployment in the locality badly affected gates and two years later they were the worst supported club in the Section. They were to repeat this 'feat' on a further four occasions and in their last season (1929-30) they became the first Southern Section club to finish as the worst supported League club. Returning to the Southern League in 1930 they folded four years later.

MIDDLESBROUGH

Record Home League Attendances :
20,000 at Linthorpe Road
53,802 v Newcastle United 27.12.1949 at Ayresome Park
 3,690 v Port Vale 23.08.1986 at Victoria Ground (Hartlepool)
Highest Average Home Attendance :
36,123   1950-51

Formed in 1876 Middlesbrough, founder members of the Northern League, were elected to the Football League in 1899. In 1900-01 and 1901-02 they were the top supported Division 2 side and overall their attendances have followed those of their Division fairly closely. Since then they have finished as the 3rd best supported Division 2 side on five occasions and their best seasons were 1946-47 and 1974-75 when they finished as the 8th best supported side in Division 1.

MIDDLESBROUGH IRONOPOLIS

Record Home League Attendance :
 2,000
Highest Average Home Attendance :
 1,450   1893-94

Members of the Northern League the Ironopolis were invited to join the Football League in 1893. However, they survived just one season before resigning and folding due to financial difficulties.

MILLWALL

Record Home League Attendances :
33,356 v Newcastle United 13.12.1947 at Selhurst Park
44,627 v Notts County 23.10.1948 at The Den
 3,322 v Bristol Rovers 01.04.1978 at Fratton Park (Portsmouth)
Highest Average Home Attendance :
27,387   1938-39

Formed in 1885, Millwall were founder members of the Southern League in 1894 and of the Southern Section in 1920. Attendances up to 1939 were exceptionally good being well above their Divisional average during the whole of this period. They finished as the best supported Southern Section club eight times during this period and 3rd best Division 2 club twice (1928-29 and 1929-30). In 1938-39 they were the 11th best supported League club (with an average of 27,387) whilst still in Division 2. Post war attendances have tended to fluctuate above and below the Divisional average but there have still been some good seasons during this period when they have finished well above the Divisional average.

NELSON
Record Home League Attendance :
14,979 v Bradford City 27.04.1929
Highest Average Home Attendance :
 8,795   1923-24

Formed in 1881 Nelson were one of several Central League clubs to become founder members of the Northern Section in 1921. They were the 3rd best supported club in their Section in their first season and, apart from poor gates in their only season in Division 2, their attendances remained above the Northern Section average up to 1927. They failed to gain re-election at the end of the 1930-1 season, when they were the poorest supported Northern Section club then joining the Lancashire Combination. They currently compete in the West Lancs League.

1928–29 season match versus
Tranmere Rovers (Att. 4,245)

NEW BRIGHTON

Record Home League Attendances :
12,005 v Tranmere Rovers 12.02.1938 at Sandheys Park
14,291 v Tranmere Rovers 21.09.1946 at Tower Athletic Ground
Highest Average Home Attendance :
 6,861   1948-49

New Brighton were members of the Lancashire Combination when they gained election to the Football League in 1923 along with Ashington, Doncaster Rovers, and Durham City. Apart from their first two League seasons gates were always below the Northern Section average. They were the worst supported League club in three of the early post war seasons before eventually being beaten by Workington in the 1951 re-election vote. They then returned to compete in the Lancashire Combination and despite declining fortunes struggled on before eventually folding at the end of the 1982-83 season.

NEW BRIGHTON TOWER

Record Home League Attendance :
10,000
Highest Average Home Attendance :
 3,575   1898-99

The first League match, versus Gainsborough Trinity (Att. 4,000)

The Towerites were formed in 1897 with the sole intention of creating at New Brighton a Division 1 club in order to maintain a winter attraction at this then popular summer resort. They joined the Lancashire League and were elected to the Football League one year later. The strain of trying to mount a serious challenge for promotion on below average gates led to them resigning from the League shortly before the start of the 1901–02 season despite finishing 4th in Division 2 the previous season. They folded without playing another game.

NEWCASTLE UNITED

Record Home League Attendance :
68,089 v Chelsea 03.09.1930
Highest Average Home Attendance :
56,283   1947–48

Formed in 1881, United joined the Football League along with clubs such as Arsenal and Liverpool in 1893. There has always been tremendous support at Newcastle. They were the first Division 2 side to average above 10,000 (in 1897–98), the first League club to average above 30,000 (in 1906–07) and in 1947–48 they averaged 56,283 whilst still in Division 2! Overall they have finished as the top supported League club ten times although the most recent occasion was 1948–49.

NEWPORT COUNTY

Record Home League Attendance :
24,268 v Cardiff City 16.10.1937
Highest Average Home Attendance :
12,505   1946–47

Founder members of the Southern Section in 1920, County had only one above average attendance season (1924–25) in their first few years. Thereafter attendances fell season by season until they eventually lost League status (at the end of the 1930–31 season) for one season.

Upon their return gates improved significantly and when promotion was gained to Division 2 in 1938–39 they averaged nearly 11,500. Post-war seasons were poor, however, and it was not until 1972–73 that their next above average figures arrived. Finishing bottom of Division 4 in 1987–88 they were automatically relegated to the Vauxhall Conference. Loss of League status further increased financial problems and County folded without completing the 1988–89 season.

G.M. VAUXHALL CONFERENCE
SEASON 1988/89
(Saturday K.O. 3.00 p.m.)
(Midweek K.O. 7.30 p.m.)

**With the
Compliments of**

**NEWPORT COUNTY
Football Club**
SOMERTON PARK, NEWPORT, GWENT
Tel. (0633) 277543/277472

Fixture Card for the Club's last season

NORTHAMPTON TOWN

Record Home League Attendance :
24,523 v Fulham 23.04.1966
Highest Average Home Attendance :
18,633   1965–66

Another of the Southern League clubs to become founder members of the Southern Section in 1920. Gates up to 1939 were generally below average although there were a few good seasons such as 1927–28 when they were the 4th best-supported Southern Section club. A good period followed in the early 1960s when they were successively promoted to Division 1, with gates since then fluctuating above and below their Divisional average.

NORTHWICH VICTORIA

Record Home League Attendance :
4,000
Highest Average Home Attendance :
2,500   1892–93

Formed in 1874 the Vics were founder members of Division 2 in 1892 having previously been members of the Combination. However, in 1893–94, their second season, they won only three League games and finished as the worst supported League club. They resigned from the League and rejoined the Combination. At the present time the club competes in the Vauxhall Conference and are, hence, within one promotion of regaining their place in the Football League.

NORWICH CITY

Record Home League Attendances :
22,433 v Newport County 02.04.1934 at The Nest
37,863 v Notts County 28.04.1948 at Carrow Road
Highest Average Home Attendance :
28,420   1972-73

One of the Southern League clubs gaining League status in 1920. Gates started poorly but improved towards 1939. Attendances in the immediate post-war years were often well above average and it was not until 1963-64 that they had their first post-war below average attendance. Norwich is another of those cities where the relatively small population makes it difficult for attendances to compete with the big city clubs when in Division 1 but, curiously, they have finished as the 13th best supported Division 1 club six times.

NOTTINGHAM FOREST

NOTTINGHAM FOREST v MANCHESTER UNITED

The record attendance match

Record Home League Attendances :
15,000 at Town Ground
32,194 v Manchester City 23.11.1946 at Meadow Lane
49,946 v Manchester United 28.10.1968 at City Ground
Highest Average Home Attendance :
32,715   1967-68

Founded in 1865, Forest were founder members of the Football Alliance and were elected directly into Division 1 in 1892. However, gates were well below average in the period up to 1939 as in only three seasons did they finish with an average attendance above that of their Division. More often than not they finished below rivals Notts County in the attendance tables. They were the worst supported Division 1 club in 1923-24 and again in 1924-25. Since 1946 gates have been somewhat closer to their Divisional average with their best seasons being 1977-78 and 1978-79 when they finished as the 8th best supported League club.

NOTTS COUNTY

Record Home League Attendances :
20,000 at Trent Bridge
,* at Castle Ground
46,000 v Nottingham Forest 22.04.1950 at Meadow Lane
,* at City Ground
Highest Average Home Attendance :
35,176   1949-50

Founded in 1862 County are almost, but not quite, the oldest club in the country (Sheffield were formed in 1857). Attendances have always been linked somewhat to the success of their Forest rivals. Although below average as a Division 1 club, attendances have otherwise been about average and in the years up to 1939 they finished with a better average attendance than Forest in 26 out of the 43 seasons. Massive support followed the signing of Tommy Lawton and in 1949-50 they finished as the 17th best supported club in the country despite still being in the Southern Section. Since the mid fifties, Forest tend to have attracted the higher gates. Meadow Lane is a football historians delight and from its two old timbered stands it is almost possible to sense football games of long ago.

OLDHAM ATHLETIC

Record Home League Attendance :
45,304 v Blackpool 21.04.1930
Highest Average Home Attendance :
18,075   1920-21

Joining the Football League in 1907, Athletic have had both very good and very bad average home attendances. In 1914-15 they missed the Football League Championship by the narrowest of margins yet were the worst supported club in the Division. Between 1919 and 1939 they were the worst supported Division 1 club three times and the worst supported Division 2 club twice, yet they had good seasons in Division 2 in 1929-30 and in the Northern Section in 1937-38. The picture since 1946 has been very similar with many ups and downs with 1990-91 being the first above average season since 1973-74.

OXFORD UNITED
Record Home League Attendance :
18,990 v Birmingham City 31.04.1972
Highest Average Home Attendance :
11,637   1968-69

Formed in 1893 Oxford were elected to the Football League from the Southern Premier League in 1962. At first attendances were a little above their Divisional average but, for a long period whilst in Division 2, they were well below the Divisional average and they finished as the worst supported club in this Division twice. The only season they finished above this average was in 1984–85 when they gained promotion to Division 1.

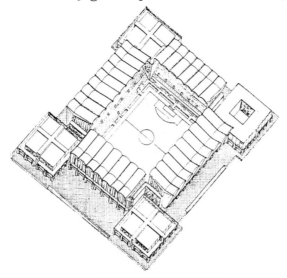

The proposed Ground that was never built

PETERBOROUGH UNITED

Record Home League Attendance :
26,307 v Coventry City 20.04.1964
Highest Average Home Attendance :
14,203   1960–61

United were elected to the Football League from the Midland League (the last side from this League to gain Football League status) in 1960 following some impressive results in the FA Cup. In their first season they were the 2nd best supported Division 4 club and the 35th best supported club in the League. Although average attendances have fallen since then they have oscillated above and below their Divisional average. In 1973–4 they were the top supported Division 4 side and of all of the clubs to gain League status since 1946 Peterborough have been the most impressive at the turnstiles.

PLYMOUTH ARGYLE

Record Home League Attendance :
42,870 v Aston Villa 10.09.1936
Highest Average Home Attendance :
23,375   1946–47

Elected from the Southern League to the Southern Section in 1920 Argyle's gates up to 1939 were usually well above average.

They finished as the 2nd best supported Southern Section club three times and in 1931–2 they finished as the 3rd best supported Division 2 club. Since 1946 their attendances have closely followed the average of their Division with good seasons in the late 50s and also in 1986–7. Along with Bristol Rovers they are one of only two current members of the Football League never to have played in Division 1 or Division 4.

PORTSMOUTH

Record Home League Attendance :
49,831 v Wolverhampton Wanderers 01.10.1949
Highest Average Home Attendance :
37,082   1948–49

Another of the Southern League clubs forming the new Southern Section in 1920. At first gates were above average but from 1927–8, when they won promotion to Division 2, to 1961–2, their first season in Division 3 they failed to achieve a single above average attendance. Since then, however, attendances have tended to be well above average with 1967–8 proving to be a good season when, with an average of nearly 23,000 they finished as the 2nd best supported Division 2 club. They finished as the top supported Division 3 club each season from 1980–1 to 1982–3.

PORT VALE

Record Home League Attendances :
12,000 at Cobridge Athletic Ground
21,089 v Stoke City 06.02.1932 at Hanley Old Recreation Ground
41,674 v Stoke City 25.04.1955 at Vale Park
Highest Average Home Attendance :
20,869   1954–55

An artists impression of the proposed Vale Park

Founded in 1876, Vale were first elected to the Football League from the Midland League in 1892. Attendances were well below average (finishing as the worst supported club in 1892–93 and 1895–96). Port Vale eventually lost their League status in 1907 but regained it when taking over the fixtures of Leeds City early in the 1919–20 season. Between 1919 and 1939 attendances were only twice above their Divisional average but in 1954–55 they averaged over 20,000 for the first time. They have only finished above neighbours Stoke City in the average attendance tables three times.

PRESTON NORTH END

Record Home League Attendance :
42,684 v Arsenal 23.04.1938
Highest Average Home Attendance :
33,226   1948–49

The top English team in the mid 1880s, North End were an obvious choice as a founder member of the Football League. They finished as the 2nd best supported club in their first two seasons but this was by far and away their best placing. From 1908–09 to 1910–11 they were the worst supported Division 1 club. In fact their attendances have been reasonable enough when outside Division 1 and it appears that Preston is one of several towns with a population density below that which can compete with the big city clubs when in Division 1 but are comparatively well supported when in the lower Divisions.

QUEENS PARK RANGERS

Record Home League Attendances :
17,903 v Coventry City 01.03.1930 at Highbury
33,553 v Brentford 02.02.1932 at White City
35,353 v Leeds United 27.04.1974 at Loftus Road
Highest Average Home Attendance :
23,850   1975–76

One of the Southern League clubs to become founder members of the Southern Section Rangers were, on the whole, well supported when in the Southern Section finishing as the 3rd best supported side three times. Their best seasons, however, were in the 70s when they finished four consecutive seasons with an average attendance above 20,000. This, though, was well below the Division 1 average at that time and Rangers have yet to achieve an above average attendance whilst a Division 1 team.

WHITE CITY — 1962/63

READING

Record Home League Attendance :
29,134 v Notts County 24.09.1949
Highest Average Home Attendance :
15,973   1950–51

Reading were founder members of the Southern League and founder members of the Southern Section in 1920. Gates at Reading have closely followed the average of the Division in which they have found themselves.   Good seasons were 1926–7 when they were 32nd in the country and 1985–6 when they finished as the 3rd best supported Division 3 team.

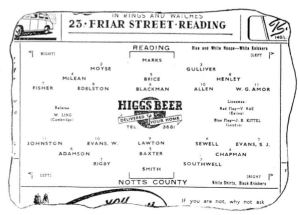

Line–ups for the Club's record attendance game

ROCHDALE

Record Home League Attendance :
20,947 v Bradford City 30.04.1929
Highest Average Home Attendance :
 8,616   1948–49

One of the Central League sides to become founder members of the Northern Section in 1921, Rochdale have always struggled at the turnstiles. In only two seasons since 1921 have they finished with an above average attendance and the most recent of these was way back in 1926–27. They have finished as the worst supported League club five times with their best recent season being 1969–70 when they finished as the 14th best supported Division 3 club. Another of the clubs only ever to have played in Divisions 3 and 4.

ROTHERHAM COUNTY

Record Home League Attendance :
20,000
Highest Average Home Attendance :
12,905   1920–21

County were elected to the Football League in 1919 when Divisions 1 and 2 were expanded to 22 clubs. Attendances were generally below average apart from one season (1923–4) when they were in Division 3 North.   They amalgamated with Rotherham Town to form Rotherham United in 1925.

ROTHERHAM TOWN

Record Home League Attendance :
 5,000
Highest Average Home Attendance :
 2,250   1894–95

Members of the Midland League Rotherham Town were elected to the Football League in 1893. After three poor seasons, both on the field and at the turnstiles, they left the League.

ROTHERHAM UNITED

Record Home League Attendance :
25,170 v Sheffield United 13.12.1952
Highest Average Home Attendance :
18,770   1951–52

Formed in 1925 by the amalgamation of Rotherham County and Rotherham Town, United took over the former's place in the Football League. Average attendances tended to be close to those of the Northern Section before 1939, but in post 1946 seasons a long run in Division 2 led to a long period without an above average attendance. In four of these seasons, they finished as the worst supported Division 2 club, but in contrast they were second best supported side in the Northern Section twice (1947–48 and 1950–51), 3rd in Division 4 three times (1974–75, 1988–89 and 1991–92) and 5th best in Division 3 (1980–81).

SCARBOROUGH

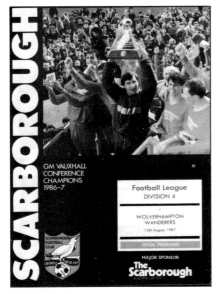

Record Home League Attendance :
 7,314 v Wolverhampton Wanderers 15.08.1987
Highest Average Home Attendance :
 2,962   1988–89

Formed in 1879 Scarborough had to wait until 1987 before becoming the first Vauxhall Conference club to gain automatic promotion to Division 4. They have yet to achieve an above average attendance season and in 1990–1 they were the worst supported club in Division 4.

The first League match

SCUNTHORPE UNITED

Record Home League Attendances :
19,067 v Grimsby Town 02.04.1956 at Old Show Ground
8,775 v Rotherham United 01.05.1989 at Glanford Park
Highest Average Home Attendance :
12,377   1958–59

Scunthorpe are one of the four clubs elected to the Football League in 1950 when its membership expanded from 88 clubs to 92. Attendances have only occasionally been above their Divisional average and they were the worst supported Division 2 club in 1963–4 and Division 3 club in 1967–8. The recent move to their new ground at Glanford Park, however, has resulted in somewhat improved attendances.

The demolition of The Old Showground commences (Photo: David Howgate)

SHEFFIELD UNITED

Record Home League Attendance :
59,555 v Sheffield Wednesday 15.01.1927
Highest Average Home Attendance :
35,094   1947–48

United were founder members of Division 2 in 1892 with attendances closely following that of their Division. From an average of only 2,500 in 1892–93 they had reached an average of nearly 20,000 by 1913–14. Attendances have held good at United despite considerable variations in playing fortunes.

Although they were the worst supported side in Division 1 in 1954–55 they have finished as the best supported Division 4 side (in 1981–82) and Division 3 side (in 1983–84), 2nd best in Division 2 (in 1952–53 and 1970–71) and 9th in Division 1 (in 1971–72).

SHEFFIELD WEDNESDAY

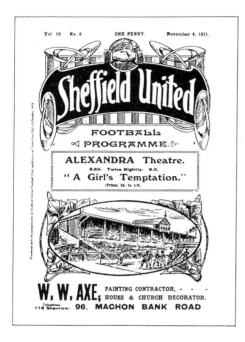

A United v. Wednesday match (Att. 28,000)

Record Home League Attendances :
24,000 at Olive Grove
65,327 v Sheffield United 05.01.1952 at Hillsborough
Highest Average Home Attendance :
42,634   1952–53

Founded in 1867, Wednesday were founder members of the Football Alliance and in 1892 they were elected directly into Division 1 together with Manchester United and Nottingham Forest. Attendances have fluctuated above and below their Divisional average with their best seasons being the immediate post-1946 years between 1949–50 and 1952–53 when they averaged over 40,000. United and Wednesday were fairly evenly matched in attendances up to 1939, but since 1946 Wednesday have tended to dominate.

The record attendance match

SHREWSBURY TOWN

Record Home League Attendance :
18,917 v Walsall 26.04.1961
Highest Average Home Attendance :
9,799   1951–52

Founded in 1886 Town were elected to the Football League in 1950 from the Midland League. Since gaining League status average attendances have been very poor with an average attendance above that of their Division being achieved in only 3 seasons. They have been the poorest supported team in Division 2 five times and in Division 3 once.

SOUTH SHIELDS

Record Home League Attendance :
21,000
Highest Average Home Attendance :
16,450   1920-21

One of the four clubs elected to Division 2 in 1919 when the League was expanded to 44 clubs. At first gates were reasonably good but they were to finish as the poorest attended Division 2 club in 1922-23 and again in each of the seasons between 1925-26 and 1927-28. They were relegated to the Northern Section at the end of the last of these seasons and finished as the worst supported of the Northern Section clubs in 1929-30. Gates had been badly hit by local unemployment and in 1930 the club moved to Gateshead, changing its name in the process, in the hope that better support would be forthcoming there.

SOUTHAMPTON

Record Home League Attendance :
31,044 v Manchester United 08.10.1969
Highest Average Home Attendance :
25,527   1966-67

Southampton were founder members of the Southern League in 1894 and of the Southern Section in 1920. Curiously there were only three seasons before 1939 in which their attendances were above their Divisional average; 1928-9 was their best season during this period when they finished as the 8th best supported club in Division 2. Attendances have been above average when in the lower Divisions but the Saints have yet to achieve an above average attendance when in Division 1 and, indeed, in 1972-3 they were the worst supported club in that Division.

The record attendance match

SOUTHEND UNITED

Record Home League Attendances :
17,313 v Brentford 28.03.1932 at the Kursaal
18,358 v Colchester United 14.10.1950 at Southend Stadium
17,303 v Cambridge United 21.04.1972 at Roots Hall
Highest Average Home Attendance :
12,089   1949-50

Founder members of the Southern Section Southend had to wait until 1957–8 until they achieved their first above average attendance season, up until then their best position had been as the 10th best supported Southern Section club in 1931–2. They have only rarely finished in the top half of the attendance tables although their recent elevation to Division 2 status may shortly correct this situation. They have twice finished as the best supported club in Division 4.

The last League game at Southend Stadium (Att. 8,000)

and the first at Roots Hall (Att. 12,190)

SOUTHPORT

Record Home League Attendance :
14,766 v Rochdale 27.12.1949
Highest Average Home Attendance :
 8,034   1947–48

Southport were one of the Central League clubs to become founder members of the Northern Section in 1921. Gates at Southport were always poor and in only one season (1966–67) during the whole of the time they were a League club did they have an average attendance above that of their Division. They finished as the worst supported League club on nine occasions. At the end of the 1977–78 season they failed to gain re-election and currently compete in the Premier Division of the HFS Loans League.

STALYBRIDGE CELTIC

Record Home League Attendance :
 7,000
Highest Average Home Attendance :
 5,250   1921–22

Celtic were another of the Central League clubs to become founder members of the Northern Section in 1921. With gates well below those they considered necessary to survive as a League club they left the League after only two seasons (both of which were reasonably successful from the playing point of view). The club then joined the Cheshire League and are currently members of the Vauxhall Conference.

STOCKPORT COUNTY

Record Home League Attendances :
 5,000 at Nursery Inn, Green Lane
 *,*** v Leicester City 07.05.1921 at Old Trafford (Manchester),
behind closed doors.
26,135 v Lincoln City 01.05.1937 at Edgley Park
Highest Average Home Attendance :
14,399   1937–38

County first became members of the Football League in 1900 having previously competed in the Lancashire League. Attendances were poor up to 1915 but there were some good seasons between 1919 and 1939, particularly in 1921–22, 1929–30 and 1936–37 when they were the best supported Northern Section side. Since 1946 their attendances have followed closely the average of their Division with a particularly good season in 1966–67 when they topped the Division 4 averages.

STOKE CITY

Record Home League Attendances :
51,480 v Arsenal 29.03.1937 at Victoria Ground
20,049 v Middlesbrough 17.01.1976 at Vale Park
Highest Average Home Attendance :
31,590   1947–48

Another founder member of the Football League, Stoke were always poorly supported in their early seasons, twice finishing as the worst supported club in Division 1. Since 1919 though their gates have followed the average of their Division fairly closely (particularly between 1919 and 1939) and Stoke appear to be another of those clubs who struggle to compete with the big city clubs when in Division 1 but who are comparatively well supported when in the lower Divisions.

SUNDERLAND

Record Home League Attendances :
23,000 at Newcastle Road
26,000 at St. James Park (Newcastle)
 *,*** at Linthorpe Road (Middlesbrough)
68,004 v Newcastle United 04.03.1950 at Roker Park
Highest Average Home Attendance :
47,785   1949–50

Formed in 1879 Sunderland were the first side to be elected to the Football League in the annual re-election votes when in 1890 they gained preference over Stoke. They were the 2nd best supported League side in 1891–92 but, curiously, were the worst supported Division 1 side five years later. The inter-war years saw high averages of around 30,000 and in 1935–36 they were the 5th best supported Division 1 side. Average attendances since 1946 have been very good, particularly in 1962–63 when they were the 4th best supported League club whilst still in Division 2. They finished as the best supported Division 2 side six times between 1962 and 1986.

SWANSEA CITY

Record Home League Attendance :
29,477 v Leeds United 01.10.1955
Highest Average Home Attendance :
22,535   1948–49

Swansea founder members of the Southern Section, started their League career with a series of six consecutive seasons in which their attendances were above the average for their Division. However, for the remainder of the period up to 1939 they were well below average and they finished as the worst supported Division 2 club in 1936–7. Fortunes have fluctuated dramatically since 1946 with the Swans appearing in every Division except Division 3 North. Their best placing was achieved in 1981–2, when they finished as the 15th best supported Division 1 club, with an average attendance of 18,226. Their best average (22,535), however, was recorded in 1948–9.

SWINDON TOWN

Record Home League Attendance :
29,106 v Watford 29.03.1969
Highest Average Home Attendance :
20,075   1969–70

Formed in 1881 Swindon were founder members of the Southern League and of the Southern Section in 1920. Early seasons saw attendances well below the Southern Section average and it was not until the late 1950s that attendances began to climb above average. The period between 1963–4 and 1970–1 was particularly good; they finished as the 5th best supported Division 2 club in 1969–70. There was also a long period of good average attendances from 1974–5 to 1986–7.

THAMES

Record Home League Attendance :
8,275 v Exeter City 29.08.1931
Highest Average Home Attendance :
2,623   1931–32

Thames were founded in 1928 with a view of creating a first class football club to play at the West Ham Stadium. The stadium, then used for Speedway and Greyhound racing, had a capacity of well over 50,000. However, competition was fierce in that part of the city and although they gained League status in 1930 they survived only two seasons. The average attendance of just over 2,000 must have looked meagre at such a large venue. Early in the summer of 1932 they applied for re–election but then withdrew their application and folded.

This match produced a crowd of 4,217

TORQUAY UNITED

Record Home League Attendance :
16,454 v Plymouth Argyle 07.10.1950
Highest Average Home Attendance :
9,096   1967–68

Formed in 1898 Torquay were competing in the Southern League when they were elected to the Southern Section in 1927. Average attendances were very poor and they finished as the worst supported Southern Section club seven times before 1939. It was not until 1965–66, when they were the 7th best supported Division 4 side, that they first achieved an above average attendance, a feat they have repeated only twice since. They were the worst supported club in the League in 1985–86.

TOTTENHAM HOTSPUR

Record Home League Attendance :
70,882 v Manchester United 22.09.1951
Highest Average Home Attendance :
55,509   1950–51

Spurs were founded in 1882 and were prominent members of the Southern League when elected to the Football League in 1908. They were the best supported Division 2 club in their first League season with an average attendance of just over 20,000. By 1911-12 they were the best supported Division 1 side finishing just behind Chelsea who were then in Division 2. Altogether they have finished below the average attendance of their Division only five times since their election. Between 1919 and 1939 they finished as the best supported Division 2 side five times and as the 2nd best supported Division 1 side three times. Curiously they first finished as the best supported club in the country in 1949-50 whilst still in Division 2, and since then they have finished as the best supported Division 1 club five times.

TRANMERE ROVERS

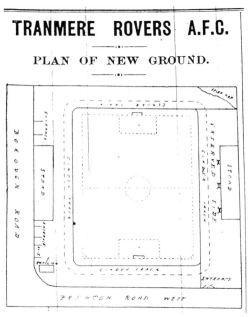

The 'new' (current) Prenton Park in 1912

Record Home League Attendance : 19,615 v Wrexham 30.04.1958
Highest Average Home Attendance : 11,815   1958-59

Rovers joined the Northern Section of the Football League from the Central League in 1921. There were some quite good years before 1939 and in 1935-36 they were the best supported Northern Section club. Post 1946 attendances have fluctuated widely. There were particularly good seasons in 1958-59 and 1964-65 but by 1980-81 they had become the worst supported League club. More recently, however, improved performances have again led to increasing attendances.

WALSALL

Record Home League Attendances :
 2,000 at The Chuckery
 5,000 at The Oval (Wednesbury)
 8,000 at West Bromwich Road
25,453 v Newcastle United 29.08.1961 at Fellows Park
 7,472 v Brighton & Hove Albion 25.02.1970 at The Hawthorns (West Brom.)
 8,051 v Blackpool 11.05.1991 at Bescot Stadium
Highest Average Home Attendance :
15,711   1947-48

Founder members of the Football Alliance in 1889 and of Division 2 in 1892, Walsall were also founder members of Division 3 North in 1921 (from the Birmingham League) and of Division 4 in 1958. They have spent more seasons in Division 3 than any other club. Attendances have tended to fluctuate above and below their Divisional average. They averaged 15,711 in 1947–48 but finished as the worst supported Southern Section club in 1951–52 and 1952–53.

Bescot Stadium begins to take shape (Photo: Brian Tabner)

WATFORD

Record Home League Attendances :
20,395 v Luton Town 20.10.1928 at Cassio Road
27,968 v Queens Park Rangers 20.08.1969 at Vicarage Road
Highest Average Home Attendance :
18,246   1984–85

Watford were one of the Southern League clubs to form the Southern Section in 1920. Starting poorly their gates gradually improved until they closely followed the Southern Section average. Since then gates have been both above and below average although, like several other clubs from small population centres, they have failed to achieve an above average attendance whilst in Division 1. Their best season was 1982–3 when they finished as the 10th best supported side in Division 1.

WATFORD FOOTBALL CLUB
SEASON 1969-70

Wednesday, 20th August, 1969
FOOTBALL LEAGUE DIVISION TWO
QUEENS PARK RANGERS
Kick-off 7.30 p.m.
OFFICIAL PROGRAMME   ONE SHILLING

The record attendance match

203

WEST BROMWICH ALBION

Record Home League Attendances :
18,000 at Stoney Lane
60,945 v Wolverhampton Wanderers 04.03.1950 at The Hawthorns
Highest Average Home Attendance :
38,910   1949–50

Founded in 1879, Albion were founder members of the Football League in 1888. Their attendances have generally followed those of their Division, with good seasons and bad. Their best position in the attendance tables has been 6th (in 1891–92 and 1931–32) but they finished as the worst supported Division 1 club in 1895–96 and 1898–99. They have never achieved an average of 40,000 but they averaged above 30,000 in nine of the early post–war seasons.

WEST HAM UNITED

Record Home League Attendance :
42,322 v Tottenham Hotspur 17.10.1970
Highest Average Home Attendance :
31,125   1968–69

United were elected to Division 2 of the Football League from the Southern League in 1919. Average attendances at West Ham have been remarkably steady irrespective of their Division. Never falling below 16,000, they regularly average somewhere in the 20,000s and only occasionally (three times) have they risen above 30,000. They have been the best supported Division 2 side five times and have a best finish in the attendance tables of 6th (in 1981–82).

WIGAN ATHLETIC

Record Home League Attendance :
10,045 v Bolton Wanderers 26.12.1983
Highest Average Home Attendance :
 6,701   1978–79

Athletic were members of the Northern Premier League when they were elected to the Football League in 1978. Attendances were above their Divisional average in their first 4 seasons but have declined steadily since.

WIGAN BOROUGH

Record Home League Attendance :
15,000
Highest Average Home Attendance :
10,155   1922–23

Borough were elected from the Lancashire Combination as founder members of the Northern Section in 1921. They were generally well supported, finishing as the 2nd best supported side in the Northern Section in 1922-3. In their final season (1931-2) they withdrew from the League after completing only 12 games.

The match versus Ashington (Att. 7,000)

WIMBLEDON

Record Home League Attendances :
15,980 v Liverpool 04.10.1986
at Plough Lane
15,009 v Crystal Palace 26.12.1991
at Selhurst Park
Highest Average Home Attendance :
 7,995   1987–88

Formed in 1889 Wimbledon were elected to the Football League from the Southern League in 1977. Since gaining League status their attendances have always been well below their Divisional average and since gaining Division 1 status in 1986 they have finished as the worst supported Division 1 side each season despite success on the field. It remains to be seen if the ground sharing scheme at Selhurst Park results in any improvement in attendances.

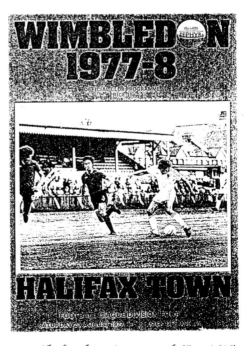

The first home League match (Att. 4,616)

WOLVERHAMPTON WANDERERS

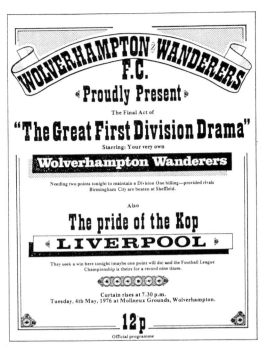

A crowd of 46,097 was present

Record Home League Attendances :
8,000 at Dudley Road
8,000 at The Hawthorns
(West Bromwich)
56,661 v West Bromwich A. 15.10.1949
at Molyneux Grounds
Highest Average Home Attendance :
45,466   1949–50

Wolves were founder members of the Football League in 1888 and at first their attendances were very poor. They were the worst supported Division 1 club in each of the three seasons between 1903 and 1906. Thereafter, though, attendances improved and they have since followed the Divisional averages closely and, indeed, have sometimes been well above. The early post–war seasons were particularly good years and they finished as the 5th best supported Division 1 club in 1946–47 and again in 1949–50. They averaged above 40,000 spectators three times during this same period. More recently Wolves have been the best supported Division 4 side, in 1987–8, and Division 3 side, in 1988–9.

WORKINGTON

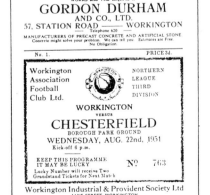

The Reds enter the League (Att. 10,049)

Record Home League Attendance :
18,633 v Carlisle United 26.12.1963
Highest Average Home Attendance :
8,372   1953–54

Workington were elected to the Northern Section in 1951 replacing New Brighton. Prior to their election they were members of the North Eastern League and were one of the more successful non–League clubs in the FA Cup. They twice achieved average attendances above those of their Division but attendances were generally poor. They finished bottom of the attendance tables eleven times and in their last League season (1976–7) they recorded only four victories. After failing to gain re–election they joined the Northern Premier league and currently compete in Division 1 of the HFS Loans League.

WREXHAM

Record Home League Attendance :
29,261 v Chester 26.12.1936
Highest Average Home Attendance :
11,651   1977–78

It is claimed that Wrexham, founded in 1873, are the oldest surviving senior football club in Wales and they were one of only two Birmingham League sides to become founder members of Division 3 North in 1921. Attendances at Wrexham have oscillated above and below the Divisional average throughout their League membership. For example, they were the top supported Division 4 club in 1969–70 and the top supported Division 3 club in 1977–78. By 1981–82 they were the worst supported Division 2 club and one year later the worst supported Division 3 club. Their attendances have been well below average since 1978–79.

YORK CITY

Record Home League Attendances :
 9,439 v Port Vale 21.04.1930 at Fulford Gate
21,010 v Hull City 23.04.1949 at Bootham Crescent
Highest Average Home Attendance :
10,412   1948–49

York were elected to the Football League from the Midland League in 1929. Attendances have made occasional excursions above the Divisional average, but more often than not they have tended to be below. They were the 5th best supported Northern Section side in their first season, and they had two good seasons in the mid fifties. They were the 2nd best supported Division 4 side in 1983–84 but worst supported Division 2 side in 1975–76 and Division 3 side one year later.

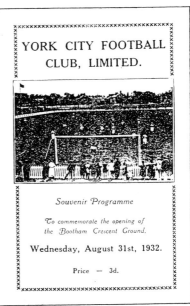

The first match at Bootham Crescent
(Att. 7,629)

THE ALL-TIME ATTENDANCE TABLE 1921-1992

While the object of this book was not to establish which club has been consistently the best supported League club in England it does supply this information season–by season. It is not easy to decide upon a fair way of establishing an "all–time" table and obviously it would be difficult to compare the period after 1921 with earlier seasons when there were only either one, two or three Divisions. Although the data is more compatible since 1921 the best approach is still debatable. In order to obtain some all–time comparisons the position of each club in the attendance tables from 1921 to 1992 has been averaged.

The list below, then, gives all 112 clubs who have competed in the Football League since 1921 in sequence of their average position in the season–by–season attendance tables. It is no surprise to find that the 9 clubs who have finished top of the attendance tables at least once occupy the top nine places. Nor is it a surprise to find that Thames finish last. The clubs in bold type are those whose average position in the attendance tables is better now than it was ten years ago.

1	**Arsenal**	39	Blackpool	76	Stockport County
2	**Liverpool**	40	Millwall	77	Barnet
3	Everton	41	**Queens Park Rangers**	78	Wigan Borough
4	**Manchester United**	42	**Brighton & Hove Alb.**	79	Wrexham
5	**Tottenham Hotspur**	43	**Luton Town**	80	Cambridge United
6	Chelsea	44	**Notts County**	81	**Shrewsbury Town**
7	Newcastle United	45	**Hull City**	82	**Wigan Athletic**
8	**Manchester City**	46	Bristol Rovers	83	Aberdare Athletic
9	Aston Villa	47	Swansea City	84	**Tranmere Rovers**
10	Sunderland	48	Brentford	85	Nelson
11	**Sheffield Wednesday**	49	**Watford**	86	Hereford United
12	**West Ham United**	50	**Oldham Athletic**	87	Exeter City
13	**Leeds United**	51	**Oxford United**	88	**York City**
14	Wolverhampton Wands.	52	**Grimsby Town**	89	Newport County
15	Birmingham City	53	**Swindon Town**	90	Scunthorpe United
16	West Bromwich Albion	54	**Barnsley**	91	Colchester United
17	Leicester City	55	Leyton Orient	92	Chester City
18	Sheffield United	56	**Bradford City**	93	Merthyr Town
19	Middlesbrough	57	Reading	94	Torquay United
20	**Derby County**	58	Bury	95	Aldershot
21	**Portsmouth**	59	Bradford	96	Halifax Town
22	**Nottingham Forest**	60	**Port Vale**	97	**Crewe Alexandra**
23	Stoke City	61	Rotherham County	98	**Darlington**
24	Bolton Wanderers	62	**Rotherham United**	99	Hartlepool United
25	**Coventry City**	63	**Wimbledon**	100	Accrington Stanley
26	**Ipswich Town**	64	Peterborough United	101	Barrow
27	**Southampton**	65	**AFC Bournemouth**	102	New Brighton
28	Blackburn Rovers	66	South Shields	103	Gateshead
29	Burnley	67	Southend United	104	Stalybridge Celtic
30	Fulham	68	Chesterfield	105	Rochdale
31	**Norwich City**	69	Northampton Town	106	Scarborough
32	Preston North End	70	Carlisle United	107	Southport
33	**Crystal Palace**	71	Doncaster Rovers	108	Ashington
34	**Bristol City**	72	**Walsall**	109	Durham City
35	Cardiff City	73	**Gillingham**	110	Workington
36	Charlton Athletic	74	Lincoln City	111	Maidstone United
37	Huddersfield Town	75	Mansfield Town	112	Thames
38	Plymouth Argyle				